James Hider is *The Times* Middle East Bureau Chief, currently based in Jerusalem. This is his first book.

THE SPIDERS OF ALLAH

Travels of an Unbeliever on the Frontline of Holy War

James Hider

BLACK SWAN

TRANSWORLD PUBLISHERS
61–63 Uxbridge Road, London W5 5SA
A Random House Group Company
www.rbooks.co.uk

THE SPIDERS OF ALLAH
A BLACK SWAN BOOK: 9780552775496

First published in Great Britain
in 2009 by Doubleday
an imprint of Transworld Publishers
Black Swan edition published 2010

This book is substantially a work of non-fiction based on the life,
experiences and recollections of the author. In some limited cases names of
people, places, dates, sequences or the detail of events have been changed
solely to protect the privacy of others. The author has stated to the
publishers that, except in such minor respects not affecting the substantial
accuracy of the work, the contents of this book are true.

Extract on page 152, reprinted with the permission of The Free Press, a
division of Simon & Schuster, Inc., from *Gilgamesh: A New English Version*
by Stephen Mitchell. Copyright © 2004 by Stephen Mitchell.
All rights reserved.

Every effort has been made to obtain the necessary permissions with
reference to copyright material, both illustrative and quoted. We apologize
for any omissions in this respect and will be pleased to make the
appropriate acknowledgements in any future edition.

A CIP catalogue record for this book
is available from the British Library.

Addresses for Random House Group Ltd companies outside the UK
can be found at: www.randomhouse.co.uk
The Random House Group Ltd Reg. No. 954009

The Random House Group Limited supports The Forest Stewardship
Council (FSC), the leading international forest certification organisation.
All our titles that are printed on Greenpeace approved FSC certified paper
carry the FSC logo. Our paper procurement policy can be found at
www.rbooks.co.uk/environment

Typeset in 11/14.5pt Giovanni Book by
Falcon Oast Graphic Art Ltd.
Printed in the UK by CPI Cox & Wyman, Reading, RG1 8EX.

2 4 6 8 10 9 7 5 3 1

For Lulu

CONTENTS

ACKNOWLEDGEMENTS

I would like to express my deep gratitude to all my Iraqi friends and colleagues for their great courage and enduring friendship throughout the years of war: I could not have done what I did without them. Special thanks also to Rebecca Strong, my friend and agent, without whose encouragement and guidance this book would probably not have been completed. Thanks also to Doug Young and all the team at Transworld for their instant enthusiasm and continued hard work at each stage.

INTRODUCTION

Al-Qaeda Goes to Hollywood

The two men are chained by the ankle to drainpipes in a squalid bathroom. Each wakes up with a Mickey Finn hangover to find he has a hacksaw at his side. Their faces are pale, full of fear and confusion. Between them is a corpse lying in a pool of blood, a pistol in one hand, a tape recorder in the other. A taped message tells one of them that if he cuts off his foot with the saw, crawls to the pistol in the corpse's hand and shoots his fellow cellmate, he and his family will be spared death.

In an unappetizing hotel room in Baghdad, my makeshift home for the past two and a half years, a bootleg DVD is playing on the television. *Saw* is a gut-churning example of Hollywood psycho-horror, but there's not much else to do in the evenings here, except drink, spout bullshit and watch endless pirated films from Asia, the start of each screening inevitably blurred by silhouettes of Thai cinema-goers slipping late into the theatre. Lying here on my bed, with the antediluvian air-conditioning unit clattering behind me, the question crosses my mind: how did al-Qaeda tap so directly into the Hollywood psyche? Because out there in the city, beyond the blast walls that protect me from the car bombs where human beings explode every morning, waking me before my alarm even has time to count down to eight o'clock, the terrorists are doing this to real people. I've seen the beheading videos, watched the hostages – Americans, Britons, Koreans, Lebanese, countless Iraqi soldiers and officials – forced to endure a similar hell. Told to beg to their governments for their lives, issuing demands on behalf of the masked psychos filming their terror, while all the time knowing, somewhere behind the desperate cooperation, they will never be allowed to go free. Knowing with instinctive certainty that once the orange jumpsuit is on, the slow knife hacking their throat is the only way out. A skinny young Korean translator paces up and down a cell somewhere in the Sunni Triangle, or perhaps in the Triangle of Death (for some bizarre reason, doom is always packaged in triangles in this country). Then, in front of the video camera, a blindfolded Kim Sun-Il, who had been snatched in Fallujah while working for a South Korean supply company, howls and cries like a little kid, screaming: 'I don't want to die, I don't want to die,' begging a government that is completely helpless to deliver him from this evil. The masked men butcher him anyway on film.

Probably all of these victims watched the vast Hollywood blockbuster that al-Qaeda engineered on September 11, 2001, the terrorist ratings spectacular to beat all others. At least one of them, we know now, witnessed it first-hand: watching the planes demolish the New York skyline inspired him to come to Iraq. Now here they are, as a direct result of that day, living out their own nasty little B-movie sequel, the straight-to-video, low-budget gore flicks that followed, and which are peddled for less than a dollar in the sand-blasted shops of the Sunni Triangle. *See Infidel Die A Horrible Death Parts I, II and III.*

Somewhere just out there I could be an extra in this horror movie, I know. Just let my driver take a wrong turn, go out on the wrong story and you're there, man. The star of your very own snuff movie, universally available on the internet, next to the free-porn downloads of girls giving blow-jobs to horses and the voyeuristic footage from college girl spy-cams. For anyone in Baghdad, the horror is just a wrong turn away in a town where no one can be trusted. Just a click away for everyone else sitting out there, bored in front of their computers in suburbia.

In Hollywood, they pay people with grotesque notions about human behaviour to transform their ideas into these movies: a form of therapy, perhaps, externalizing the horror for the director and the audience, indulging their morbid fantasies on celluloid rather than in human flesh. Out here, in Iraq, they do it for real. What do the two have in common? Only this: the limitless but all too predictable human imagination, and the need for a story.

It occurs to me lying here, that's all that religions and movies are: a series of often gory stories, fables told to take the poor, isolated, individual sap out of himself for a little while, let him forget he is all alone in the universe, while sitting there in the flickering lights of the darkened temple or movie theatre. In religion, we're all extras in god's everlasting extravaganza. In Hollywood, we're just the audience. And therein lies the problem, I think: two narratives competing for the same audience. Perhaps that's why the Islamists of Hamas torched all the cinemas in Gaza, why the Shiite militiamen of Basra burn down DVD shops, why the religious right in America rants against Hollywood. Hollywood is considered 'unfair' competition in the market for the human imagination. After all, what religion these days has the razzle-dazzle to compete with Hollywood and its Computer Generated Imaging miracles? Well, now one of them does: only the new epics and the endless snuff movies of this purported faith are audience participation, open to anyone, any time. Not for profit, but for god.

Or perhaps I've just been in Iraq for too long.

Al-Ara Hotel
Baghdad

JAFFA ROAD

The Transmitter of Hopes and Fears

For George W. Bush, the road to Jerusalem led through Baghdad. As a journalist following the latest tide of destruction rising in the Middle East, my road ran in the opposite direction.

In the spring of 2003, I stood on the crumbling sea cliffs of ancient Jaffa, on the outskirts of Tel Aviv, where Jonah was said to have been swallowed by a whale. Behind me, elegant Ottoman storehouses converted into restaurants looked out over the flat waters of the Mediterranean. Next to the swanky fish restaurants I watched American soldiers set up Patriot missile batteries that looked like swivelling garbage trucks pointed at the sky. The batteries were to shoot down the Scud missiles they feared would come from the east, from the deserts and shimmering mirages whence, for so long, danger has emerged with terrifying speed, borne on sweating armies of camel-back riders or Russian-made rockets.

Among the crowd of Israelis watching the strangely

placid scene that morning were two old men chatting in Hebrew. I started talking to them. They both spoke elegant English. They told me they were originally from Baghdad, and proceeded to reminisce about summer afternoons back in the 1940s when they would escape the heat by swimming under the bridges of the Tigris. They could still recall the cool sensation of muddy water on soft boyhood skin. The men smiled, happy and sad at the same time. It was late morning, and the fish restaurants were filling up with businessmen from Tel Aviv. As I departed, I wished them luck if the missiles should come. They smiled and waved, and didn't look at all worried.

When the second Iraq war finally started a few weeks later, I was waiting for those missiles that never came. I used to sleep on a camp bed in my office at the end of Jaffa Road, opposite an empty plot of land that had been a bus station when I had first visited Israel fourteen years before, as a kibbutz volunteer. I lived at the other end of Jaffa Road, in a tiny cave-like apartment tucked behind the vast stone ramparts of the Old City. My rooms were freezing in the winter but pleasantly cool in the summer. The labyrinthine streets were mostly empty, the tourists scared off by suicide bombers. The men selling olivewood figurines of the Baby Jesus sat morosely on the Roman flagstones outside their miniature, cluttered shops. On Fridays, the mosques would crank up their call to prayer, one by one, until the cries from the minarets merged into a howling lament, an air-raid siren announcing the imminent wrath of god.

Every morning, I'd walk through the arch of the Bab

al-Jadid, or New Gate, and head up Jaffa Road, always with the thought in the back of my mind that one of the parked cars might explode at any moment, or that someone would unholster his gun and start shooting. I once saw an old woman with hennaed hair, Sarah Hamburger, carried away from a bus stop on Jaffa Road, dying. As a child in 1929, she'd survived an Arab massacre of the Jews in Hebron, just south of Jerusalem; at that time, an Arab neighbour had saved the five-year-old Sarah. But on this day, she had been shot while shopping on Jaffa Road by a Palestinian man dressed as an Israeli soldier, who had started firing at everyone in the street. Laid on a stretcher, she looked pale and serene, perhaps unaware she was dying. She had been waiting for a bus in order to attend a lecture on mysticism. I wondered if she registered my face leaning down over her, my hand scribbling her death on a notepad, as she was carried away to die.

Such shootings were commonplace in the British colonial streets of new town Jerusalem: a boarded-up Sbarro pizza bar became a candle-smeared shrine to the fast-food customers cut apart inside by a man strapped into an explosives belt; policemen stood at the entrance to the old covered Mahane Yehuda market to stop people blowing themselves to pieces among the fresh cantaloupes, the piles of avocadoes and the dried apricots.

Jerusalem had reverted to what it had once been, thousands of years before, in the rough days of King David, the city whose walls still poked out of holes in the Old City floor – a jittery frontier town on the edge of a wilderness. Bearded settlers carrying pistols on their hips, their bewigged and hatted wives trailing a dozen sullen kids, stalked up Jaffa Road, ready to draw whenever the next Palestinian gunman appeared. In America, a shooting spree can last half an hour: in the English village of Hungerford, a deranged loner called Michael Ryan went on a three-hour gun rampage in 1987. In Israel, with a citizenry armed to the hilt, a berserk gunman could expect to last only a few minutes.

The settlers often had thick Brooklyn or French accents. On the morning of September 11, 2001, I sat in a minibus heading up the highway from Ben Gurion airport, outside Tel Aviv, to Jerusalem. I had just landed on a red-eye from New York, one of the last to leave before nineteen fanatical Muslim men took over the subsequent planes and rammed them into the Pentagon and the World Trade Center, whose towers I had watched twinkling in the dark during its last night on earth. The Tel Aviv minibus was full of American settlers and Yeshiva students with their harsh New York accents, some of them new arrivals talking about the religious schools they would be enrolling in. There were gasps of amazement as news of the attacks filtered over on the vehicle's radio. They asked the driver to turn it up. Some of the men translated for those of us who didn't speak Hebrew.

'Thank Gawd,' crowed one of the Brooklynites who had just heard of the Biblical catastrophe raining down on his native city. 'Thank Gawd, now America will understand what we're up against!'

These religious frontiersmen would stay at the

Crowne Plaza Hotel near our office, where they guzzled herring and matzo at breakfast before returning to their neat little villages on the craggy hilltops of the Wild West Bank. They mingled with the black-garbed *haredim* in thick spectacles and curly side-locks bustling down to Jaffa Road in clusters, bobbing like confused and angry black birds whenever a bomb went off. As the police tried to herd them away from the blood and glass, they'd chant 'Death to the Arabs' before returning to Mea Sherim, a little slice of eighteenth-century Poland just off the main road, one of the last genuine Jewish ghettos left. The *haredim*, or god-fearers, didn't believe the state of Israel should exist before the Messiah's return, and spent their lives in poverty, studying ancient scripture and living on state subsidies in their stony ghetto, refusing to serve in the military or hold down regular jobs. Signs at the entrances to Mea Sherim warned women to cover their arms and legs, and for the now-scarce gaggles of tourists to stay out. On religious holidays, when the traffic stopped and the empty streets fell eerily silent, beautiful chants floated from their synagogues like rollicking sea shanties.

One Saturday morning, a shrunken man who spoke no English emerged from a temple and accosted me as I was walking to work. He beckoned to me to follow him into a darkened synagogue: by gestures, he asked me to turn on the light. When I obliged, I saw a group of men sitting in the room, waiting for the Shabbas goy as patiently as they'd waited for the Messiah. They were forbidden from operating any machinery on the Sabbath, even flicking on a light switch.

* * *

Occasionally one of the *haredim* would show up, dressed in black for the shtetl, in a gay club where a crowd of us used to go after a few drinks to dance, the only place that played halfway decent music in the city centre. Laila's was located, rather incongruously, where Jaffa Road arced alongside Mea Sherim. The black-clad *haredi* would watch in fascination as a lithe Palestinian boy gyrated on the low stage. The Jewish man was married with ten children, and would discuss god and religion and being attracted to other men with Palestinians, both Christian and Muslim, as the crowd of gay and straight dancers pounded the dance floor. Laila's was one of the few places where Jews and Palestinians were still able to come together, the tug of sexual unorthodoxy briefly overriding the pressure of religious conformity.

On the walk to work I would often pass a table manned by two bearded men with tasselled prayer shawls round their waists, who asked me in bad English whether I was Jewish. They were collecting money to rebuild the Temple destroyed by the Romans 2,000 years ago. When they saw I was not Jewish, they would immediately ignore me. Their project faced many obstacles, besides the lack of my goyim contribution: the main one being that two huge mosques were already standing upon the stone-hewn Temple Mount. The day I arrived in Jerusalem to work as a journalist for the French press agency AFP, in July of 2001, a group of extremist rabbis tried to drive a huge foundation stone for a new temple on a flatbed up to the Wailing Wall. The day was called Tisha B'av in Hebrew, the day of the destruction of the temple. According to tradition, the day not only marked the destruction of both temples, the first built by Solomon and destroyed by Babylon in the sixth century BC, and the second razed by the Romans in the first century AD, but also the expulsion of the Jews from Spain in 1492 and the first operation of the gas chambers at Treblinka in 1942. That was a lot of grieving to be packed into one day.

The Palestinians praying above in the mosques rioted at the symbolic return of the temple founding stone, lobbing stones down on Jewish worshippers, who fled holding plastic chairs over their heads for safety. One of the praying *haredim* who had run for the cover of the Dung Gate was British, and explained to me that the rabbis were wasting their time trying to rebuild the Temple. I asked him why.

'Well,' he said in his north London accent, 'according to the scripture there's no point in men trying to build it.'

'Why's that?' I asked.

'Because when the time comes it will simply materialize out of the sky.'

'And squish the Dome of the Rock?' I asked, trying not to laugh at the Monty Python image.

'Yes,' he said. He smiled too, perhaps realizing how odd a flying 2,000-year-old Temple might sound to sceptical ears. But clearly he believed it to be true.

The Jewish historian Josephus, who lived through the first-century revolt against Rome that resulted in the temple's destruction and the Jews' expulsion from the land, wrote that in Biblical times, the Philistines had managed to capture the Israelites' Ark of the Covenant during a battle. But when they took the wooden casket containing the law tablets given by God to Moses back to their city of Ashqelon – nowadays a neat little seaside town just north of Gaza, full of Russian and Ethiopian immigrants – their people started dying off mysteriously. A strange force was emanating from the relic, killing off the victors. The episode is echoed in the film *Raiders of the Lost Ark*, when rats on the Nazi steamer carrying the purloined Ark start curling up and dying.

Sometimes I'd look at the vast mosque domes, ballooning on the high cliffs of the Temple Mount, and imagine them as transmitters of that same strange and dangerous force emanating from the hill, sending out unseen waves into people's minds, the strange radiation of unquestioning faith. Why are the mosques built there? Because in the seventh century a man named Mohammed had a dream that he had flown from Arabia to Jerusalem on a winged horse, before ascending from the huge stone platform to heaven to meet the prophets who had gone before him. This journey on a flying steed, known as al-Isra, is believed by many Muslims to have been not a dream but a literal reality.

According to the rabbinical scholars, there was in fact a simcard at the centre of the baleful transmitter, the buried Ark itself. In 1981, a group of rabbis and students plotted out where the inner sanctum containing the Ark would have stood. Studying their scripture, they decided that Solomon – who had prophesied the fall of Jerusalem – must have buried the covenant tablets directly underneath the shrine housing the holy of the holies. The rabbis had secretly tunnelled to within thirty feet of the spot when word leaked out and the Palestinians started rioting, accusing the Jews of trying to sabotage the mosque compound. Dozens of people were killed before Prime Minister Menachem Begin ordered the tunnel sealed up, and it remains closed to this day.

There were, however, other tunnels leading into the very bowels of this vast global transmitter of hope and woe. Shortly after I arrived in Jerusalem, I was wandering around the streets of East Jerusalem, looking for the remains of that little cow town that King David had conquered 3,000 years ago from the Jebusites, a clan of the Canaanites who were suffering rapid genocide at the hands of the invading Hebrews. The 'city' of David is now largely occupied by a small neighbourhood of sandstone Palestinian houses clustered on an outcrop of rock at the foot of the ancient Temple. The land falls away sharply to the southeast into a ravine, and halfway down the steep slope is the Pool of Siloam. If there had been a metro in Biblical times, it would have looked something like this pool: a cut in the side of a hill, with stone steps leading down to a pool of murky water that disappears into a cavernous hole at one end. There are the stubs of Roman pillars stranded in the grey waters, and a raised stone platform to one side.

As I looked down, wondering what this strange

opening in the ground might be, an overweight Palestinian boy came puffing towards me, shouting something. The sight of him put me on edge: I had recently been stoned by a gang of Palestinian kids while trekking through the hills outside East Jerusalem, forcing me to scuttle away as they lobbed rocks at me and squealed, 'Yehuda, yehuda!' The hue and cry had been taken up by every kid in the village where I had sought refuge, and I was just reflecting on the indignity of being stoned to death by a gang of eleven-year-olds when two young Palestinian men suddenly stopped their car on the road and offered me a free ride back into Jerusalem. It was an unnerving introduction into the abruptly revolving violence and courtesy of the Arab world.

But this kid was beaming as he approached me, and I guessed what he was thinking: a tourist in this godforsaken part of East Jerusalem in the middle of the intifada! *Alhamdulla!* He shouted out to me what turned out to be the only English he knew: 'Pool of Siloam, where Jesus healed the blind man.' Religious education had been dropped at my school halfway through my O-level course, which may have contributed to my lifelong atheism. The various miracles – dead men rising, lepers healing and blind men seeing – all tended to blur in my memory. But I saw the kid was desperate for a customer so I paid him a few shekels, took off my shoes and socks and took the candle and the plastic flip-flops he offered me. Then I plunged alone into the blackness of the tunnel, hewn from solid rock by men using only chisels and crude pickaxes some 3,000 years before.

The murky water rose to my knees and the light of the

entrance was quickly swallowed behind me. The sides of the tunnel were barely wider than my shoulders, the roof forcing me to bend slightly in places. No one knows quite how the well was mapped so accurately by men digging hundreds of feet underground, bringing fresh water into the walls of the city above. Until the beginning of the last century, locals believed the ebb and flow of the water was caused by a dragon that dwelled inside and drank off the surplus. It only filled up again when the beast was asleep. All I knew was that it was a horribly oppressive place for a claustrophobe like me to be, with just the nub of a candle to light the way. As the tunnel curved away into pitch darkness, the candle guttered and went out. Feeling the walls closing in on me, I fumbled for the box of matches the Palestinian boy had given me and relit the wick with a shaking hand. I was inching my way along again when I heard a ghostly howl coming from ahead in the darkness. I stopped and listened for a while, reassuring myself it must be the distorted voices of other visitors further down the tunnel, unseen and perhaps heading back. But my candle flickered again and I desperately put my hand around it to guard it from the draught: it went out, and I turned tail and fled from that dank and suffocating hole.

Much later on, I learned that the tunnel had a key historical significance linked to the transmitter of contagious ideas hunched atop it. It was built around the time of King Hezekiah, ruler of the Biblical kingdom of Judah and heir to the throne of King David. Hezekiah's reign coincided with one of the most significant episodes in the development of mono-theistic faiths, an apparent miracle that secured Judaism, and its Christian and Muslim successors, as the dominant forces in the mind of millions of followers. Much of the world's history spun on this obscure event.

It was the year 701 BC, and the Assyrian king Sennacherib was marching against a rebellious coalition of former vassal states, including Egyptians, Phoenicians, Philistines and Jews. Twenty-two years earlier, another unstoppable Assyrian army had destroyed the northern Kingdom of Israel, laying waste its capital of Samaria and carrying off into exile ten of the twelve tribes of adherents of the still-crystallizing Jewish faith. The exiles lost their religion over centuries of serving Assyria deities in Nineveh, the ruins of which now languish under huge dirt mounds in the centre of the northern Iraqi city of Mosul. Even in my time in Jerusalem, I heard politicians lament the loss of those ten tribes, whose millions of descendants, if they could only be identified, would have helped modern Israel compete with the more robust Palestinian birth rate.

Nineveh's military expansion was part of Assyria's own religious ritual: war was the way in which this empire worshipped its militaristic gods, marking devotions not just in prayer but in feats of arms and territorial conquest. According to the American historian William H. McNeill, the Assyrian religious-military tide was rapidly displacing local gods and introducing the world to its first cosmopolitan, massive empire: a testing time for hick-town deities like Yahweh, whose enduring support rested largely on his ability to deliver his devotees from defeat and slavery. The embryonic empire was dislodging the old ways, creating a religious vacuum in the ancient Near East, as deity after deity failed the test of arms. Had King Sennacherib stormed Hezekiah's Jerusalem in 701, Jehovah would probably be on the museum shelves next to Baal, Ishtar and Osiris, the Jews as forgotten as the Jebusites.

But Hezekiah took precautions, both spiritual and practical: he strengthened his city's walls and ordered the excavation of more wells such as the one I stumbled along 2,702 years later. He also told his people to stop up the wells outside of the city to deprive the invaders of water in the arid hills of Judah. And he also purged the kingdom of false idols and centred its worship on the temple of Solomon in his capital, trusting that his god would live up to his boasts of omnipotence.

There was, according to Biblical scripture, a vigorous amount of psychological warfare between the two foes – what is now known as 'psy-ops'. Rabshakeh, commander of the besieging Assyrian army, warned the Judeans not to trust in their Lord: 'Hath any of the gods of the nations delivered his land out of the hand of the King of Assyria? Where are the gods of Hamath and Arphad? . . . have they delivered Samaria out of my hand?'

To steel the Jewish resolve, the Prophet Isaiah promised that Yahweh would send an angel of death to smite the mighty Assyrians.

'He shall not come into this city, nor shoot an arrow there, nor come before it with shields, nor cast a bank against it . . .' Isaiah promised. The stage was set for a clash of ideas – the one almighty god of the feeble Jewish city-state against the Assyrian war machine and its pantheon of pagan deities.

And then the miracle occurred, the event that secured the devotion of the Jewish people through 3,000 years and two long exiles: the Assyrians mysteriously dropped dead in their thousands outside the walls of Jerusalem. For the Jews, it was the promised deliverance of Yahweh. McNeill argues it was more likely due to the fact that having found the local springs stopped up, the Assyrian army ended up drinking contaminated water. Cholera bacilli were the likely angels of death.

But the psychological impact had been felt in the Jewish people's consciousness – the Lord was all-powerful, the one and only true God. When finally defeat and exile came at the hands of the Babylonians in 586 BC, their faith had become so enduring that, far from being seen as a rout for Yahweh, the Jewish priests interpreted it as their all-powerful God simply using the Babylonian empire as a tool to punish the sins of the Hebrew people. The argument would be used by Muslim clerics following the devastating tsunami in southeast Asia in 2004, which they described as retribution for women not being assiduous enough in their modesty. When bird flu broke out briefly in southern Israel after the forcible eviction of the Jewish settlers in Gaza, fanatical rabbis said it too was divine punishment. And the stroke suffered by Ariel Sharon was seen by the religious right as God's inescapable vengeance, rather than a medical complaint in a heavily overweight, overstressed man in his late seventies.

Exile also adapted the faith into a mobile one, no longer attached to a specific temple or place, laying the roots for its spread around the globe. The time of mere local deities was past: a new strain of ideas had been forged from the pestilence that laid low the Assyrian army before it could storm this dusty little parochial city on the edge of nowhere.

I met my first prophet at Gilad's Farm, an illegal Jewish settlement on the stony hills clustered above the Roman city of Nablus, in the northern West Bank – whence the ten tribes had once been vacuumed up into exile. The prophet was heavily bearded but surprisingly young, in his late twenties. When he explained how things were ordained to be, he would close his eyes and adopt a beatific smile as the ancient Hebrew words flowed, oiled with divine certainty.

All around us, like lithe young beasts ready to pounce, a group of the infamous Hilltop Youth were mustered, rebuilding the farm after a battle with the Israeli police, who had tried to dismantle the settlement and had been repelled by rocks and Old Testament fervour.

The Hilltop Youth were the radical, second-generation settlers, the kids whose parents had reared them in the West Bank and Gaza on tales of Arab atrocities and Jewish virtue. While their parents, who in the 1970s had pioneered the settlement movement that is at the heart of so much woe, had built their townships into pretty little slices of American suburbia surrounded by guns and razor wire in the hills of the West Bank, their offspring were restless and out for their own conquests. They had developed their own fashion, the boys in baggy trousers and large loose-fitting skullcaps, the girls in shawls and with long hair.

The gathering on the rocky hilltop reminded me vaguely of the Glastonbury music festival, but a Glastonbury in a parallel reality. The kids here were celebrating being the Chosen People, on the land God had covenanted to them. Although to an atheist like me that sounds far less rational than something you might hear at a drug-addled hippie love-in in Somerset, they believed it implicitly and they were ready to die or to kill for it.

One of the younger ones wore a T-shirt that said 'No Arabs, no terror' as he sat at the entrance to the 'farm' – in fact, just a few jerry-built huts clinging to a rocky outcrop, with a metal shipping container painted with a Star of David serving as the wildcat settlement's makeshift synagogue. In fact, the farm wasn't a farm at all – it was the seed of what the settler kids hoped would be a new Jewish homestead, if they could just keep out the Arabs, the left-wing Israeli peaceniks and the police. The place was named after Gilad, a settlement security officer who had been shot dead on the nearby road by Palestinian gunmen. His kid brother was the prophet I was interviewing.

'When all of the land of Israel is returned to the Jewish people, then peace will come to the entire world, including the Arabs,' he smiled, eyes closed at the beauty of the vision.

'What about the 120,000 Palestinians who live down there, in Nablus?' I asked through my interpreter, a settler journalist at the moderate end of the movement (he lived in a settlement just outside Jerusalem, and was there as much for the government tax breaks as for the will of God).

'The righteous ones can stay,' the prophet told me.

'How many is that?'

He paused, still with a slight smile creasing his thick brown whiskers towards heaven.

'Maybe . . . four,' he said finally, with great decision. The rest would have to leave the land of Canaan, by bus or car or donkey or on foot. His idea was what they referred to in Biblical days as an exodus, and what the Israeli right-wing these days refer to as 'transfer'. It is normally understood in the rest of the world to be 'ethnic cleansing'.

A beautiful evening embraced us, and the rays of the setting sun crept over the rugged hills where Israelites had battled Canaanites and all comers since, before being themselves booted out for 2,000 years. Now they were back, and for these people around me, the Bible had never stopped. God's time never ends, even if the holy scriptures had petered out some time in the Middle Ages. The people around me were merely writing new chapters.

This was other face of the much-vaunted 'only democracy in the Middle East' that America and Britain were about to go to war to help secure. There was democracy in Israel for sure, far more than in any of the neighbouring countries. But it was a deeply chauvinistic democracy, like Athens in its glory days – great if you were an Athenian male, but not much cop if you were a slave, barbarian or a woman. It was also supported, to the tune of hundreds of millions of dollars every year by American Christian groups. They also believed in the biblical prophecy being fulfilled by the Jews returning to their lands – many believed, however, that such an event would mark the beginning of Armageddon, the return of the Messiah and the final showdown between good and evil. To these Christian fundamentalists, the fate of the Jews was an irrelevance. Many would perish, others would have to convert to survive. It was a profitable, but clearly sometimes tense, alliance.

A fresh-faced girl of about twenty was looking down towards the sea, sparkling in the sunset a dozen miles away. I remarked on what a great view it was, but she was seeing it in purely strategic terms, like some Prussian general.

'You can fire rockets on to Tel Aviv from here. That's why we have to be here, to make sure they don't start hitting our cities,' she said, as resolute as Ariel Sharon with the eternal maps he was famed for carrying every-where in his quest to dominate the land.

I left them to their brittle constructions and cold nights under the stars: my phone was ringing and I didn't want a whole pack of them noticing there was a foreign journalist in the midst, a species that ranked in their eyes only slightly above Palestinians. It was my office telling me a Palestinian suicide bomber had blown up his car full of explosives next to an Israeli bus on the coastal road to Haifa. A dozen passengers were incinerated. The bomber may well have believed he was off to heaven to meet his maker. In fact, he was a lump of burned flesh fused to the steering column of his car. I got in the armoured jeep and drove off. I'd seen all I needed to see in order to get an idea of the funda-mentalists: God and land and fuck the rest of you. It would prove a good grounding for my time in Iraq.

On Jaffa Road there was a bookshop called Steimatzsky's. Browsing there one quiet morning between shootings and bombings, I found a volume entitled *Secrets of the Exodus*, which argued that the original Jews were actually ancient Egyptians. It pointed out that the Egyptians, who meticulously recorded every part of their history, made no mention of the catastrophic plagues catalogued in the Biblical book of Exodus, nor even alluded to a huge slave population of Hebrews.

They did, however, mark the rise of a dangerous monotheistic cult established by the heretic Pharaoh Akhenaton right about the time in history that the Exodus is believed to have occurred: around 1350 BC. The pharaoh threw out the old pantheon of deities and declared there was only one god, Akhen, who would be worshipped in a new capital. Akhenaten and his wife Nefertiti concentrated all their country's wealth on this new capital, plunging the country into crisis – famine broke out, followed by plagues that killed the weakened populace. When Akhenaton died, his cult was erased, his fabulous city razed and his priests and their followers exiled to the Egyptian province of Canaan, where the new pharaoh granted them land so they could act as a buffer state against nomadic tribes raiding the outlands of the empire.

If true, the theory would mean the Jews were descendants of rogue Egyptian heretics, and that the Christian and Muslim faiths were mere spin-offs of a scrambled history. The vast majority of mankind's history may well be based on a misconception. As I paced warily along Jaffa Road, I asked myself what ancient prophecy all these people around me were killing each other for. An ancient game of Chinese whispers, the garbled legacy of a Bronze Age sun-worshipper and the innate violence that seems to be in all of us.

But people apparently need to believe in a higher power guiding them. After the Enlightenment and the rise of science, many people have swapped ancient deities for the more modern alternative of aliens. The Church of Scientology, premised on the imaginings of the science fiction writer L. Ron Hubbard, claims to have ten million followers. Three and a half million Americans believe they have been abducted by extraterrestrials (I imagine these groups must overlap at some point). And even eternal Jerusalem showed signs of moving with the times: the Raelians, who believe that what people understand as 'god' was in fact an alien race come to Earth to tinker with our genes, arrived in the Holy City with an offer to clone victims of suicide bombings, bringing the dead back to life – a speciality of Jerusalem since the days of Jesus Christ.

Raelism is an intriguing sect founded in 1970 by a French UFO enthusiast who believed the Jewish god Yahweh, or Jehovah, was in fact a spaceman who landed on Earth 25,000 years ago and experimented with our primitive Cro-Magnon DNA, turning us into what we are today. To explain this fully to the misguided Jews, the Raelians helpfully wanted to open an embassy in Jerusalem. In 2002, they said they had already started their cloning programme, although they refused to divulge the identity of the lucky recipient of a second shot at life.

So the circle appeared to be about to close: faith would kill and faith would resurrect in the Holy City. But there was a snag: the Israelis, bridling at their deity being misappropriated yet again by yet another upstart sect – and reduced to the status of mere astronaut to boot – sent the Raelians packing. Thus was the future of the Middle East made even more complex, as the Jewish state incurred the wrath not just of its Muslim neighbours but of other planets and species.

THE MICKEY MOUSE DEATH CLUB

The Dirt Lot of the Philistines

At the Israeli army outpost of Nebi Merri overlooking the Gaza Strip, there is a small engraved stone tablet close to the wire fence that encloses 1.4 million Palestinians in what is, effectively, the world's largest prison camp. The inscription says: 'View over the land of the Philistines'.

The Philistines were a mysterious sea people, probably originally from Greece, who drifted into the land of Canaan around the same time as the Hebrew peoples – who may have been the exiled priesthood and aristocracy of the Egyptian Pharaoh Akhenaton. They held five cities on the southern coastal plain, known by later Greek civilizations as the Pentapolis. The principal city was Gaza, where the muscle man Samson was dim-witted enough to divulge to his constantly prying Philistine girlfriend Delilah that the secret of his strength was his long hair, which she promptly snipped off. Shorn of his locks and his strength, he was blinded and enslaved by the Philistines, until God granted him one last burst of energy, which he used to bring down the Gaza temple on himself and his captors. One of the other main Philistine cities was Ashqelon: the towers of its oil refineries can be seen just to the north of the present Gaza Strip, but the city is now Israeli, white-bread suburbs full of Russians who fled the collapsing Soviet Union in the 1990s, many of them merely pretending to be Jews on the basis of a grandparent with a Jewish-sounding name. Israel, in need of fresh manpower, let them in. It used as a guideline the old Nazi Nuremburg laws, which had deemed that one Jewish grandparent was enough to earn execution by the gas chamber or the machine gun. Israel reasoned that if you were Jewish enough to die in the psychotic Reich, you were Jewish enough to live in Israel.

The Philistines survived until around 500 BC, fighting wars with the Hebrews and the Egyptians until they eventually just faded out of history. A few centuries after they had taken their bow from historical records, the Romans arrived and, after the expulsion of the Jews, named the province Palatine to erase memories of their rebellious subjects. From that title comes the name Palestine. If ever you want to see a truly timeworn front line, Nebi Merri is the place to go, especially as it has a viewing tower apparently designed for tourists in the happier days of the 1990s. It gives you the feeling of observing some kind of vast, human safari park. As I stood there with a few other journalists, on the Israeli side looking out over the security fence and a few parched fields of olive trees and cucumbers to the concrete suburbs of Gaza City, a few shots rang out.

Show over: we hurried back to our cars. The place is, after all, called Nebi Merri in memory of a Druze army captain of that name who was shot dead on this spot by a Palestinian sniper.

Inside Gaza during the intifada, you had to watch the skies. That was where the danger came from: Apache helicopters and F16 fighter-bombers. Not that you wouldn't be shot at by soldiers or tanks in the Jewish settlements dotted along the coast or on the borders – but complete obliteration tended to come from above.

I was led, with my translator, through the twisting beehive of Rafah's alleyways by a Palestinian guide sent by men whose whole raison d'être was to kill Israelis. The Gaza Strip had been formed when Palestinian refugees fled behind the lines of the invading Egyptian army in the 1948–49 war of independence, and stayed there after the armistice, building camp cities that became, over the years, squalid squatter towns. By 2002, when I visited, the entire shanty on Gaza's southern border with Egypt was a vast warren, both above ground, where thousands of narrow alleyways intersected and ducked between breezeblock houses leaning up against each other, and below ground, where a network of tunnels fed weapons, drugs and even prostitutes like an intravenous drip under the concrete Israeli fortresses straddling the frontier. The whole town was crumbling and cancerous, the refugee houses nearest the border being eaten away every night by Israeli armoured D9 bulldozers that lumbered out to smash any structure used as a firing position by Palestinian gunmen, or by the ubiquitous smuggling tunnels snaking under their floors.

The street leading up to the border ended in a tangle of wrecked homes, before plunging into a churned-up wasteland. I peered out cautiously across the stretch of smashed cement and knotted rebar, warned by my guide that Israeli sharpshooters were watching us from the high towers staked out along the border. Just to the west, monstrous earthworks and soaring guard towers draped in camouflage netting looked like some fantasy writer's imaginings: in fact, it was the rampart of the Jewish settlements that ran along the coast.

Our guide instructed us to turn off our cellphones so the Israelis couldn't track us. We followed him through the labyrinth. After fifteen minutes of brisk walking, we came to a nondescript house with a concrete wall enfolding a yard where toddlers kicked clumsily at a red ball. We went inside and sat in a typical Palestinian room, devoid of furnishings save a couple of framed Koranic verses on the wall and the brightly upholstered cushions on the floor. There we were greeted, with warmth but a certain reserve, by a bearded, middle-aged man who did not give us his name. He was a leader of the al-Aqsa Martyrs' Brigades, a group that was refusing to stop its suicide attacks on Israel despite orders from the Palestinian leadership it nominally supported. It was popularly described as being part of the 'secular' mainstream Palestinian group Fatah, although, as quickly became clear, it was secular only inasmuch as it did not plan to turn the clock back to the seventh-century heyday of Islam.

The militant leader spouted the usual rhetoric to try and justify suicide attacks – they did not want to kill Israeli children in malls, but the Israelis killed Palestinian children in the streets, the Israelis had stolen their land and were supplied with billions of dollars of US military hardware, whereas the Palestinians had to make their anti-tank mines out of detergent and fertilizer. His talk reminded me of a Palestinian gunman I met once during a gun battle in Beit Jala, a Christian suburb of Bethlehem. The man had been firing a Kalashnikov at an Israeli tank that squatted in a narrow street like a giant, impregnable crustacean. I asked the fighter between bursts of gunfire why he was shooting at a tank with an assault rifle.

'It's all I have,' he said, as though that was logic enough. Then he started shooting again.

The al-Aqsa leader – whose group was named after the shrine built atop the destroyed Jewish temple in Jerusalem, that baleful transmitter of dreams – recited a similar ethos of desperation as his men went off and blew themselves up in crowded streets or died in gunfire in the greenhouses and orchards of the coastal Jewish settlements.

'Our martyrs will be in heaven, *inshallah*, and theirs will be in hell,' he said with a satisfied smile to justify the carnage. A similar sentiment was expressed in a slogan commonly used by US troops in the first Gulf War: 'Kill them all, let God sort them out.' In fact, the phrase dates back to the thirteenth-century papal crusade against the Cathar heretics in southern France, when the Pope, unable to distinguish between true

Catholics and those lying to save their skins, ordered hundreds of prisoners executed with the decree: *'Neca eos omnes. Deus suos agnoscet.'* (Kill them all. God will know his own.) That in turn was a bloodthirsty interpretation of the Biblical scripture, 'The Lord knoweth them that are his' (2 Tim 2:19).

I had no time to contemplate any of this, however. At that moment, there was a blood-freezing roar from outside. An Israeli fighter-bomber was streaking low over the refugee camp, perhaps only a couple of hundred feet above us. There was no time to do anything – the Israelis were regularly bombing militants' houses in the summer of 2002, and here I was sitting inside the home of a wanted and extremely dangerous man. That would easily be justification enough for the Israelis to kill us all. The jet's deafening howl filled the room. Looking back, all I remember doing was bracing for the explosion that would kill us: there was a fleeting notion that I might actually see the nose of the missile come through the window, so accurate was the US-made ordnance.

But it didn't – the plane screeched overhead. As the noise receded, everyone visibly relaxed. There were a few nervous laughs: the al-Aqsa guy, for all his talk of paradise, looked as rattled as I felt. He tried to shrug it off.

Hesitantly, I started to rephrase the question I had been asking, when all of a sudden there was another roar. Everyone froze – the first jet had been scouting the scene, now the killer strike was coming, I thought in the split second before the sound engulfed us. There

41

was no point running, no way to out-run a laser-guided rocket. Then that jet too passed low, right overhead. Once again, I tried to ask a question, thinking to myself: wrap this up right now and get out. But before I could really say anything, the horrific roar of death was bearing down on us once again, blotting out my words. I clutched the cushion I was sitting on, waiting for the impact. As the noise receded a third time, our host said with a tight smile that the Israelis often did this to try the nerves of the Rafah people and freak out anyone with a guilty conscience.

It was working with me: my mind was a total blank. My fixer, who had arranged the meeting, suddenly leapt up, muttered something about having to make a phone call, and fled. I should have gone too – my life was worth far more than the disgrace of running from a killer I'd never met before and would never meet again – but for some reason I didn't. Was it pride? Fear of appearing cowardly? A belief that it couldn't happen to me? Or ridiculously misplaced manners? I really don't know – probably I was looking to my host, far more experienced in such encounters, to tell me how to react. Bad move: this was a man committed to dying a martyr's death.

The jets passed over us a total of six times, each time flash-freezing the conversation, before I had the wit to thank the leader for talking to me and beating a hasty retreat. Walking out of the house and hurrying back into the maze of Rafah's lanes, I had never felt so alive. My translator and I laughed almost hysterically as we half-ran from the scene. That day was my birthday, and I sat on the seafront veranda of the al-Deira hotel in Gaza City, smoking a *narguilah* water pipe and drinking mint tea as I watched the twinkling lights of the fishing boats out at sea, and thanking my lucky stars I was still alive, and not a charred corpse in the Rafah morgue. There was plenty of room in paradise without me.

The Gaza Strip was almost entirely sealed off from the outside world. Even when the Israelis dismantled the coastal settlements in 2005, they kept strict control of the land borders, sea approaches and the air space. It was a bubble the size of the Isle of Wight, rapidly slipping back through time, the sea air slowly decaying the bare brick and concrete buildings, aged asphalt losing its grip on itself in the blistering summer heat. Boys on donkey carts had long since replaced trucks in an economy where money and petrol were constantly in short supply. Although there were different towns stacked on top of each other along the strip, they all blended into one another, an odd blend of twenty-first-century slum conurbation and pre-modern landscape, where fields and orchards and flocks of shaggy sheep formed a patchwork with the higgledy-piggledy buildings. Dusky clots of bougainvillea clung to the colourless walls of apartment blocks, while flaming-orange shade trees lent a dazzling splash of brightness to the sea-salted concrete. On almost every wall, there was a painting or a poster of a martyr killed by the Israelis, which gave Gaza the feel of a giant mausoleum inhabited by souls who often saw themselves as the dead-in-waiting. There is a rare disease of the brain called Cotard's syndrome, in which the patient often believes they are already dead. Gaza often felt as if that syndrome had somehow leapt a physical boundary and become a culture rather than an illness. Most of the dead were shown in military poses, with Islamic bandannas, M16 rifles and ammunition belts criss-crossed with webbing. The various armed factions competed to claim the dead as their own, even when the slain person was just a civilian caught in the endless crossfire. This gave rise to sometimes bizarre posters of children's heads photoshopped on to the bodies of gunmen posing in Rambo stances.

Gaza was not totally isolated from the outside world, however. Basic supplies came in from Israel through a series of crossing points, even when the two sides were at war. When things got really bad, the main crossing point at Karni, where Israeli and Palestinian customs officials worked in proximity, would shut down and all goods move through Kerem Shalom, which means, inappropriately, 'Orchard of Peace' in Hebrew. It had been designed so that goods could transit without either side having a shred of contact with the other. Every morning, from seven till three, Israeli trucks would offload goods in a fenced-in enclosure, watched over by Israeli troops in reinforced concrete positions. They would then close the gate on the Israel side, and the Palestinian merchants would come in from the other and collect their wares until sundown. Then both sides would start shooting at each other again. It was an airlock between two alienated peoples.

Other scraps of the outside world had drifted in

through the high wire border fences that snagged plastic bags and kept modernity at bay. Not all had survived the border crossing in their original forms. Among the most striking of these transformations was what happened to Mickey Mouse when he was teleported through the airlock and entered Gaza's moribund society.

Mickey Mouse first appeared in the Walt Disney cartoon *Steamboat Willie* in 1928. Over the years, he filled out and evolved into the character that now almost every child in the world knows. But his most surreal evolution was at the hands of al-Aqsa television, the Gaza station run by Hamas. As well as kidnapping Israeli soldiers, the hardline Islamist guerrilla organization hijacked several Disney characters and mutated them into icons of the anti-Israeli resistance movement.

Such transformations are not unusual in the long history of the Middle East. Rival gods and idols have been purloined, absorbed and adopted since the first city-states started warring with one another thousands of years ago, often to the dismay of the religious purists of the day. The Hebrew god evolved from the up-close and personal deity who himself dressed Adam and Eve when he expelled them from Eden, through the moody, thundering destroyer of the Flood, until he finally faded from view to become a distant, silent, almost irrelevant Lord in the last books of the Old Testament. All this happened as his migratory worshippers came into contact and conflict with their neighbours and new cultures, incorporating different aspects of each into their own monotheistic but multifaceted Lord. So it is not wholly surprising that the squeaky clean American icon that is Mickey Mouse should be warped into the violent – if still squeaky – voice of anti-American, anti-Israeli Islamic resistance and martyrdom, a spokesman for the battle to take back Jerusalem for the Muslim world.

Gaza is a long way from the innocent slapstick humour of *Steamboat Willie*. And in his new incarnation, Mickey – now renamed Farfour, and played by an actor in a Mickey Mouse suit – appeared on the children's show *Pioneers of Tomorrow*, where he extolled the virtues of memorizing the Koran, implementing Allah's will and dying for the cause.

The show, meant for children aged up to thirteen years who aspired to die for Palestine – and there are a shocking number in Gaza who fit that profile – was one of the strangest of television experiences, a place where Sesame Street met al-Qaeda. Sara, the eleven-year-old headscarfed presenter, would lecture children on the need to drink milk, say their prayers and bide by Allah's rules. Farfour was her sidekick, an adult actor affecting an irritatingly whiny voice in which he would shape the minds of Gaza's already traumatized youth with visions of paradise and victory. It was his last appearance on the show that caused international outcry. It was not quite the death of Bambi, beloved of western cinema audiences.

The final episode starts out with Farfour and his grandfather in an olive grove in Gaza. The grandfather (who by some unexplained genetic anomaly is not a mouse but a human) announces he is dying, prompting distressed squealing from his rodent grandchild. Before he croaks, he makes a speech urging Farfour to do all he can to safeguard the ancestral family property, for which he pulls out the deeds and the key from under his gown.

'The land, which was occupied in 1948, is the land I inherited from my fathers and forefathers. I want you to protect it. It is a beautiful land, all covered in flowers and olive and palm trees. I want you to protect it, Farfour . . . The land is called Tel al-Rabi. But, unfortunately, the Jews called it Tel Aviv after they occupied it.'

After passing Farfour the key and deeds, and amid much high-pitched piping from the giant mouse, grandfather flops back on his rug and dies. His distressed grand-mouse starts wailing, then contemplates the task at hand. 'Grandfather entrusted me with this great trust but I don't know how to liberate this land from the filth of the criminal plundering Jews who killed my grandfather and everybody.'

But Farfour tries, and is arrested trying to cross the Gaza border fence. The scene switches to a room where a man who is supposed to be an Israeli interrogator tells Farfour he wants to buy the documents off him. Farfour rather foolishly spills the beans on what he is up to.

'These are the land documents which my grandpa entrusted to me, so that I would safeguard them and use them to liberate Jerusalem. When the lands are liberated we will go and live there. Give them to you? My grandfather didn't tell me to give them to you.'

The interrogator offers him great amounts of money, to which Farfour pipes defiantly, 'We are not the kind of people who sell land to terrorists.' The interrogator, in suit and shades, starts shouting angrily, then walks round his desk and starts pummelling and kicking the giant mouse. Farfour, screaming in his ridiculous squeaky voice, continues to call the Israelis 'terrorists'. The camera eventually pans back to eleven-year-old Sara in the studio, who is watching the shouting and squealing and nodding sagely. 'Yes, my dear children,' she says to the camera, 'we have lost our dearest friend Farfour. Farfour was martyred while defending his land, the land of his fathers and forefathers. He was martyred at the hands of the criminals, the murderers of innocent children.'

It was hardly surprising the show caused such a hullabaloo, with Israel accusing it of helping raise a new generation of terrorists in Gaza. But the director of al-Aqsa television, Fatih Hamid, was unrepentant when I met him in his offices in Gaza City. I had trouble trying not to laugh when I asked him about a giant Mickey Mouse figure being beaten to death by a secret policeman in his show. He smiled back, and explained that in Gaza, kids grow up faster than anywhere else, exposed to Israeli tank raids, helicopters firing rockets in the streets and the inevitable proximity of death.

'We want to teach our children how to defend themselves to take back their rights stolen by the Israelis,' he told me. 'They are kids, but they are the young men of tomorrow. They were sad when Farfour was killed but every day they witness the killing of men, women and children. Just yesterday two children were killed by the Israelis here in Gaza, and the kids weren't surprised.'

Mr Hamid said that in light of the criticism his show received, he had tried to tone it down a bit. He put a tape in to show me a new style of broadcast for *Pioneers of Tomorrow*. In it, a boy of about twelve sang in front of pictures of the al-Aqsa mosque, built on the Temple Mount in Jerusalem. He promised the mosque the children of Palestine would 'redeem you with our blood'. As he sang, various other images flashed by, including a bearded man strapping on a suicide bomber's explosive belt and kissing his little daughter goodbye. I looked at Mr Hamid as the film finished.

'I didn't know the explosive belt sequence was in it,' he said, rather lamely. 'I wouldn't have allowed it. But it's too late now, it's already aired.'

I went out into Gaza to see if kids were really watching this atrocious fare. In Khan Younis, in the south of the territory, we came across a crowded funeral tent off the main road. The streets of Gaza are full of funeral cortèges parading the flag-swaddled corpses of fighters freshly killed in a mission or blown up in an airborne assassination. This one was of a 23-year-old Islamic Jihad militant. We stopped and introduced ourselves and were invited to sit with the mourners. Serving soft drinks were boys in Islamic Jihad T-shirts, kids barely in their teens. I asked if they were members of the fanatical group and was told they were supporters, a sort of jihad social club. The would-be martyrs poured garish orange squash for the older men who were already in the suicide club. Afterwards, they staged a little parade with flags, where they stood in disciplined military ranks. I started talking to one of them, a twelve-year-old who said he wanted to die fighting Israel. But within minutes, I had to call the interview off – we were being mobbed by the wild, terminally bored gangs of little boys who hang out all across Gaza, and who fell upon me and the solemn kid from Jihad who was respectfully trying to answer my questions as the feral children climbed all over, screaming and shouting and eventually lobbing handfuls of stones. Eventually there were so many pebbles flying in the streets that the little flag parade was forced to break up, despite the threats and calls to order from the young men who had organized it. Surrounded by a crazed mob of kids tugging at my clothes, slapping and pushing, I climbed back into the car as they tried like locusts to swarm inside, shouting for money, attention, anything to alleviate the tedium of their thwarted young lives.

Driving back into Gaza City, we stopped by one of the beaches. Two young boys led a black stallion by its halter through the low surf, while two men in deckchairs sat by the waterline smoking a *narguilah*. Across the coastal road, behind a concrete wall, a group of youths were learning to march in file, standing to attention and dressing off in parade-ground fashion. My translator and I went over to talk to them. They too were affiliated to the fanatical Islamic Jihad, a group so bent on martyrdom that it was rumoured to barely even bother planning many of its attacks, just giving young men guns and bombs and sending them off into the fray against some of the best-trained soldiers in the world.

Marching awkwardly through the sandy lot, the

over-sixteen lads group looked almost like any other junior cadet force in the world. And that is how their drill instructor, a snaggle-toothed, bearded 21-year-old called Abu Abdullah, described them.

'We only give them scout training,' he told me. 'We want them to have a sense of purpose, to be better able to face the future. Fighting Israelis is not a condition, this training will help them in any field of work.' I asked him what kind of sports they did: he told me they played football, martial arts and crawling on their bellies. What practical use did crawling on your belly have, I asked, thinking of the wire fences just a few miles away. Abu Abdullah shrugged and thought for a long while. He couldn't think of anything. By now, the lads were sitting round listening to a young bearded preacher lecture them on the need to heed Allah's laws and be ready for jihad. I spotted one short child clearly younger than all the others and went and talked to him. His name was Mohammed Mena. He was fourteen, with a sweet chubby face and an earnest, respectful demeanour.

'I want to join Islamic Jihad's armed wing, god willing, but I have to be eighteen,' said the boy.

'Aren't you afraid of being killed by the Israelis?' I asked. He didn't hesitate before answering.

'I'm not afraid. That is my ambition.'

The boys were told to fall in again, given another quick pep talk on the need to hold themselves ready for the fray, then dismissed. After they fell out, almost the entire group headed straight for the mosque. I felt fairly confident young Mohammed wasn't long for this world. But he didn't care. His young eye was already on the next.

God wasn't something that really occurred to me as I was growing up. The school I attended taught the basic stories of the New Testament, but at the same time the teachers read us stories about Olga da Polga, a talking guinea pig, Paddington Bear and the tales of Beatrix Potter. Somehow, they all got mixed up, and I grew up regarding the Bible as just another children's story, only a bit duller (we never made it to the bloodthirsty Old Testament, which I'm sure would have appealed far more. I remember thinking how boring it was that the gospels all told exactly the same story).

At the same time, my junior-school class would take school trips from my small market town in rural West Sussex up to London, to the grandiose Victorian halls of the Natural History Museum. There I would gaze in awe at the life-size dioramas of ape-men looking out across a vast, painted backdrop of the African Rift Valley, a back-lit cobalt sky drifting away to infinity, herds of wildebeest roaming the plains beyond. What wonder and wanderlust those displays inspired: into my nine-year-old mind, so far exposed to nothing more than the neat fields of southern England that were being eaten away by drab suburban sprawl, were injected endless vistas of space and time. The idea that there had been people around for so long, slowly evolving over millions of years and roaming huge empty continents populated by exotic, extinct beasts, filled me with a tingling excitement, a thirst to travel out into that world and see what these shaggy predecessors of mine had seen. Compared to that, the idea of Jesus curing a bunch of lepers seemed, to a child growing up in the cosseted age of penicillin and modern healthcare, positively prosaic, barely even mythical.

FALLEN IDOLS, RISEN ANGELS

Into Iraq

When I first arrived in Baghdad, the crowds were still felling statues like trees. It was a sticky evening at the end of May 2003, and I headed out on the streets as soon as I had checked into the Hamra Hotel, near the university.

The mobs had already run out of Saddam Hussein effigies. It was, after all, a whole month since the giant figure on Paradise Square had been ripped from its leaden feet by an American tank repair truck in front of the world's assembled news cameras. Since then, Baghdad had witnessed a frenzy of sculpture toppling. At the Jordanian border, I had passed a surreal tangle of metallic horse's legs, dictator's riding boots and mini Scud missiles stranded on a roundabout, lurking like a giant insect in the tall, dry grass. Saddam had wilfully indulged in the tyrant's cult of personality, littering the country with his own image. He had, however, allowed a few other fallen figures from the regime the honour of being immortalized in metal, although almost all of them were comrades rumoured to have died at his own hands.

It was a measure of the popular hatred of the megalo-maniac that the anger of the mobs could outstrip the vast number of his monuments in just a month. The frenzied mobs had even broken into a workshop where new statues were being cast and smashed a King Kong-sized model of the dictator: only a severed arm still dangled from a brace in the ceiling, like a gnawed coyote paw discarded in a trap. Outside, a crowd of anonymous, leaden generals huddled impassively in the empty yard, waiting to be melted down and cast in the image of the country's new rulers.

With no more Saddam effigies to hack to pieces, the frustrated mobs had started attacking any figure sus-pected of association with the old regime. Driving through the city centre on that first evening in the capital, past bombed telecommunications buildings, shut-up shops and flame-grilled ministries, we came across a squad of statue lumberjacks happily beheading a larger-than-life figure in dark bronze.

I was probably Iraq's first post-war tourist. I had not come out to work, but to see my girlfriend Lulu, who was working as an Associated Press radio reporter. Therefore, all of my research into Iraq consisted of having read one rather lurid Saddam biography during the fourteen-hour drive across the desert from Jordan. I hadn't the faintest idea who the disgraced patriarch now being dismantled before me might be: to me, he looked like just another moustachioed Baath Party flunky in a bad suit, some faceless Levantine Lenin. I asked Lulu, who had been there since before the war, who he was. She hemmed and hawed, then admitted she had no idea. Neither did her translator Omar, who sheepishly asked one of the jeering members of the throng. The man shrugged, and in turn asked a fellow crowd member who was watching as a chain was fixed round the statue's neck.

'I think it's . . . what's-his-name? The one before Saddam?'

'Ahmed Hassan al-Bakr?' chipped in Omar, a recent graduate of biochemistry now earning his living as a translator. The general had led the Baathist coup of 1968, before being slowly isolated and then, according to popular belief, murdered by Saddam in one of his own luxury palaces.

'Yeah, that's the one,' said the man, as a looted crane dragged the ex-leader crashing to the ground. A flurry of howling Iraqis scampered off down the street with the head, an ominous augur of bad times still to come.

The scene was played out in a street in Mansour, often described as Baghdad's equivalent of Mayfair, and home to some of the city's most exclusive restaurants and shops. Needless to say, after twelve years of sanctions and regular cloudbursts of high explosives, the shops and eateries weren't quite up to Mayfair's standards. It wasn't ruined by any stretch of the imagination – Baghdad was no Grozny or Kabul – just depressingly shabby. 'Classy' restaurants, like the famed as-Saah, or the Clock, looked more like KFC diners than high-end bistros. And unlike most cafés I'd been to before, as-Saah boasted a huge crater out the back where a cruise missile had killed a dozen Iraqi civilians, in a failed American 'decapitation' strike against Saddam, who had apparently risked his life for one of the restaurant's famed kebabs. Almost every storefront in the street was shuttered, the owners terrified of the armed looters who were marauding across the city in packs. The looters could still be seen, wandering like zombies, picking over the charred skeletons of government buildings and hospitals, brazenly using oxyacetylene torches to cut down street lamps for scrap, or wobbling on ladders as they unhurriedly chopped up telephone cables to resell the valuable copper wiring, severing the very sinews that hold society together.

I didn't realize at the time, but that encounter at the fallen statue was a salutary introduction to Iraq. Nobody really knew anything any more. After decades of being kept in the dark by a vicious, paranoid regime, there was suddenly no government, no media, the first US administrator had already fallen foul of an internal squabble back in Washington and been booted out, and the indigenous security forces had simply evaporated. There was no telephone contact with the outside world unless you had a 750-dollar satellite phone. All the threads that kept people in contact with each other and with reality – even the reality of a brutal dictatorship – had been severed. Baghdad was floating on a cloud of fear and hope, hallucinating its past and future.

From the pulpits of Shia mosques, imams blared demands for Saddam and his cronies to be hunted down and hanged, even as shady Iranian-backed militias like the Badr Brigades shot dead mid-ranking

Baathist functionaries – the people who once made the country function – on their doorsteps. The same mosques often demanded an immediate departure of the US troops who had just overthrown the Shias' oppressor. 'No to Saddam, no to US occupation,' I heard blaring from the loudspeakers of the golden-domed Qaddumiyah shrine one blistering June lunchtime. Similar angry messages were being broadcast in Sunni mosques, planting the seeds of future violence.

The only visible signs of authority were the US tanks and Humvees, manned by alien-looking soldiers in full battle gear and sunglasses, most of whom had only the sketchiest idea about where they were, beyond a few grid coordinates on a military map. All news was served up as gossip, outrageous rumour, colourful distortions of Islamic theology and the poisonous dregs of Saddam's ingrained anti-western rhetoric. Conspiracy theories abounded, strange ideologies were evolving in the feverish vacuum: people swore the looting was the handiwork of vengeful Kuwaitis getting their own back for the 1990 invasion; that America was allowing it as part of a plot to gut their old enemy; Mossad agents were said to be stalking the cities with bags of cash to recruit would-be Zionist agents; American soldiers were allegedly deserting in droves and being smuggled to the Gulf via an underground organization based in Fallujah. An overweight, sweaty man who claimed to be a member of a fledgling resistance group told me one day, as we sat talking by the hotel swimming pool, that the American army was secretly burying scores of its dead in a mass grave out in the western desert, in the hopes of keeping the real casualty figures from the folks back home.

I had quickly become used to such credulity in my first weeks in Iraq, but forced myself to argue with the lardy guerrilla just for sanity's sake.

'I think the parents of the dead soldiers might notice if their kids never came home,' I told him. He smiled and held up a cautionary index finger, as though about to make some profound point.

'But what if they were *black* soldiers?' he asked, with all the assuredness of a barrister delivering a courtroom coup de grace.

'They have parents too,' I said. He looked confused, as though he thought black people came from orphan farms somewhere in Alabama. I wrapped up the conversation as soon as I could. But as I spoke to more and more people, I realized that a vast number held such bizarre and outlandish beliefs, as if they had just emerged from – or I had just entered – a strange world through the looking glass, where people were the mere playthings of angry deities and vast conspiracies.

It called to mind a friend of mine in Jerusalem. Let's call her Shiri, since she never wanted her name mentioned in print. Shiri was an elderly estate agent who found apartments for foreign journalists and other visitors to the eternal city. She would tell me about all the Christian zealots moving to the city, looking to rent places on the Mount of Olives or the Sea of Galilee in order to be in the right place when the Messiah returned. When she asked them what their price range was for this one-stop resurrection, they said they would pray to God to tell them. If she laughed, or expressed exasperation, they accused her of subverting God's will.

Shiri's family originally came from Germany. Her father won two Iron Crosses fighting for Germany in the First World War. But because he was Jewish, he was thrown into the concentration camp of Buchenwald in 1939, and only escaped because his brother had already fled the country for the Caribbean and promised to pay the passage for her father to leave the Reich on a steamer. I asked her why her father had stayed so long, and she said, 'He was a very sane man, he just couldn't foresee what his own country would do to him.'

And it struck me that a large part of human history has been the total inability of a sane, rational person to foresee the advent of total insanity, and how quickly it can so engulf their world. Given that sanity is such an ill-defined commodity – after all, most people believe in gods and demons that patently don't exist, and yet are not considered to be off their heads – then it is unlikely that this state of affairs is about to change any time soon. It seems the rational world, that thin mirage of enlightenment shimmering in a heat haze of illusions, will continue to be blindsided in a bloody fashion by the madness within us.

Mokhalid was convinced he had seen an angel of God out on Paradise Square. The day had been April 9, when Baghdad fell to the American blitzkrieg. A mob of Iraqis, aided by the first American armoured vehicle to reach the square in central Baghdad, dragged the tyrant's statue to the ground. It was a triumphant moment, but Mokhalid, a rather surly car salesman, was not impressed.

'When they pulled down Saddam's statue, lots of men were jumping on it like monkeys,' he said, sitting in a small café decorated with rugs and cushions to look like a Bedouin tent. 'Then a child came up and kissed the head. Why?'

I shrugged.

'I think the child was an angel,' he announced solemnly. No one in the 'Tent' café laughed: if anyone found his comments strange, they kept it to themselves. I looked at Ali, my translator, to query if he was speaking allegorically. Apparently not. He really thought he had seen an angel kiss the mass murderer's metal noggin.

Mokhalid was in his mid-twenties, a Sunni and a fervent supporter of the now fugitive president. The Ace of Spades, as Saddam was dubbed in the deck of playing cards issued to US grunts to help them spot fleeing regime leaders, had done a spectacular vanishing act in the dying days of the invasion. One day he was standing in a crowd of chanting loyalists outside the Abu Khanifa mosque in the Sunni district of Addumiyah, thrilling one last time to the old chant of '*B'roh, b'dam, navdiq ya Saddam*' – 'With my soul, with my blood, I sacrifice for you, Saddam'. The next day he was gone, as puffs of smoke from US missiles rose in the sky behind him. The man who had carefully controlled every aspect of Iraqis' lives for three decades, even lecturing them for hours at a time on television as to how they should bathe and brush their teeth, was no longer there.

But had the bogeyman really been banished? Mokhalid, like many others, believed Saddam could never be killed. Sitting in the narrow coffee shop on Arasat Street, puffing away on his *narguilah* and sipping tea, he revealed Saddam's secret – he had a magic stone.

In fact, it wasn't much of a secret: I stopped randomly in a street later that day and asked people about it. A crowd of men quickly gathered around the foreigner – still a novelty so soon after the war – to swear that the dictator wore a necklace with a protective stone. It had been specially prepared by magicians imported from China, India and Japan. This was the reason he had survived so many assassination attempts, from being shot in the leg as a young putschist in the 1950s to dodging the cruise missile fired at his hideaway behind the Clock restaurant. People told tales of killers' bullets fired at close range that magically swerved around the laughing tyrant, who would slowly draw his own pistol and gun his thwarted assailant down.

Urban myths, I thought at first. But as I talked to more people, I realized many actually believed them implicitly. People believe all sorts of wild stories around the world, but usually with a smirk, or a knowing wink. In Iraq, there was something different going on: there was an earnestness, an insistence in these wild stories that went beyond anything I'd seen before. By some strange alchemy, the myths were being transformed into a truth that people subscribed to in large numbers.

There were a number of reasons why. Like most dictatorships, Saddam had tried to keep his people living in the dark, feeding them a version of reality calculated to perpetuate his rule. In the decades of darkness, bizarre notions and superstitions had sprouted like weeds of insanity in the dank cellars of Iraqis' souls, slowly choking off any sense of reality. The dictatorship had created a Fertile Crescent of credulity. In this atmosphere, anything seemed believable to ordinary Iraqis. Myths have traditionally been used by people to process and filter the bewildering reality around them. In Iraq, the myths needed to be huge and wild to match the horrors that the nation had recently endured (and would soon be facing again). There was no spirit level to tell them what was normal, and what was merely a figment of their traumatized imaginations.

T. E. Lawrence, that great British champion of the Arab cause, had commented ninety years earlier on how his Bedouin companions and comrades in arms in the desert – themselves cut off from any contact with the outside world – had viewed their world.

'They were a limited, narrow-minded people, whose inert intellects lay fallow in incurious resignation. Their imaginations were vivid, not creative,' he wrote in *The Seven Pillars of Wisdom*. He lamented that their belief was clear and hard, 'almost mathematical in its limitations and repellent in its unsympathetic form'.

And this from someone who loved them.

Mokhalid too spoke with the absolute conviction of someone living in a place where, with no objective point of reference, nothing can be either proved or dismissed. It was enough to merely voice an idea for it to have a life of its own. No doubt Saddam's all-pervasive system of spies, the bugging devices, snitches and two-way mirrors in hotel bedrooms, coupled with his own paranoid practices (he was constantly on the move, and dinner had to be prepared every night in each of his dozens of palaces scattered around the country, just in case he happened to drop in) added to the widespread myth of his supernatural powers.

Like the Nazi leadership which back in the 1940s had so inspired his favourite uncle Kheirallah – and who provided much of the future dictator's early inspiration – he and his entourage liberally indulged their passion for the paranormal, with all the gusto of peasants who have overrun palaces. While many senior Nazis were linked to the Thule Society, reviving ancient beliefs of German destiny and dabbling in the occult, Saddam's own beliefs may have been bolstered at an early age by the reputation his mother had enjoyed as a village soothsayer in his birthplace of Ouja, able to read the future in the casting of seashells.

'It's all true about the magic stone,' insisted Mokhalid, stretching back against the red and blue weave of a Bedouin carpet hanging on the wall. 'First of all, he put the stone on a string and hung it on a chicken and tried to shoot it. Then he put it on a cow, and the bullets went around it too.' I looked around again: this time, I was relieved to see at least one of the younger patrons of the café was smiling slightly. Mokhalid ignored him, with all the superiority of the insider brushing aside the uninitiated. Most of the patrons nodded in solemn agreement.

Another story on the streets suggested that some of Saddam's magic gems actually needed to be fed. A hungry, supernatural rock would be left overnight with a bowl of rice, and come morning, the dish would be half empty. I was surprised by how many people shared Saddam's belief in the occult: even Mohanned, one of the translators working with me, who was a well-educated, bilingual anaesthetist working the hospitals of Saddam Medical City, believed in genies. This took me aback, but the reason was simple: the djinn, or genie, is mentioned in the Koran. Not to believe would be blasphemy. End of story. Mohanned's only scepticism was confined to whether mere mortals could summon or manipulate the spirits, some of them good, some evil. The door to the supernatural was propped open by Islam's official documents of faith.

And why not? About six in ten Americans also believe in the devil and hell, according to a 2005 Harris poll. Another seven in ten share Mokhalid's belief in angels, heaven and the existence of miracles and of life after death. Another poll carried out by Baylor University showed that 92 per cent of respondents believe in a personal god. This is a society that prides itself on its openness and rationality, a nation born of the Enlightenment. Little wonder then that Iraqis, battered and persecuted and cut off from the outside world, believed just about anything.

Ancient creeds had a strong grip on every aspect of Iraqi life, even as the American occupation tried to force-feed the country a diet of democracy and the rights of the individual. For millions, Islam provided the only model for social order, and if democracy fitted in with that, they could accept it. People now had the right to 'one man, one vote', but millions voted according to the word of a septuagenarian, Iranian-born Grand Ayatollah, Ali al-Sistani in Najaf. When he issued a fatwa to the faithful ordering them to vote in the first post-war elections in January 2005, the choice for the conservative Shia millions was simple: risk the terrorist bombs to cast your ballot, or face eternal damnation.

The problem was, the reclusive ayatollah would never appear in public (there was even a conspiracy theory that he had been arrested during a trip to London for heart surgery, and that a more pliable, pro-western geriatric lookalike had been sent back in his place). The ayatollah's opinions on any given subject were divulged by whichever politician or aide happened to have visited him last. Each gave his own spin to the venerable cleric's views. Thus it was that the most influential leader in Iraq at the time had the communications policy of Sooty the glove puppet. It was not difficult, therefore, in the run-up to the 2005 elections, for the main Shia coalition, made up of religious parties that had spent decades in Iran, to manipulate the religious decree for its own gains. Leaflets were distributed and imams told their flocks at Friday prayers that the fatwa actually told them to vote for the conservative Shia list, not for the godless secular parties that the Americans were backing. The result was a landslide for the Iranian-backed theocrats. The US administration hailed the polls as a victory for democracy.

While I was researching the myths that were shaping Iraqi minds, Mohanned described to me how his cousin, upon finding that a thief had stolen his pistol while he was out of the house, had gone not to the police but to a magician in touch with a djinn. The magician had called on the cousin's twelve-year-old brother to act as medium to reach the spirit he usually consulted. The boy was hypnotized and, while in a trance, described to the magic man how a neighbour had taken the weapon and put it in a box under his wardrobe. Mohanned's cousin went to the neighbour's house. He was out, but had left the door open, so he went in and looked under the wardrobe: there, in a box, was his pistol, he said. The neighbour, upon hearing that he had been exposed as a thief by a man who now had his gun back, fled to Kurdistan.

Mohanned swore the story was true. There appeared to be no rational explanation for it. I asked to see this master of the djinn.

Abu Ali was a tiny bearded gnome of a man with a ready grin. He earned his living by summoning up the djinn for those seeking to regain stolen property, or to lift and inflict curses. I went to see him at his small house in Shurta Arba in southern Baghdad. Abu Ali was polite and hospitable, and appeared not to even countenance the idea that someone coming to him might not believe in his magical prowess. The story he told sounded like a tale recounted by Scheherazade to the murderous, sleepless Caliph in the *Thousand and One Nights*.

One day, a few years before, Saddam's psychotic son Uday had sent one of his bodyguards to summon Abu Ali to his domed palace. The magician was informed that a thief had taken the opportunity to go through the pockets of Uday's party crew when they had fallen asleep at dawn, dead drunk, after one of his habitual all-night debauches. Uday was well known for such parties – he would typically have his cronies dance in front of his wheelchair and then fire his Kalashnikov into the ceiling, sending the terrified revellers scattering for cover. Abu Ali, employing his otherworldly abilities, unmasked the thief, who turned out to be one of Uday's own hangers-on. The seer never found out what punishment was meted out, though it was likely to have been highly unpleasant: a few hours with Uday's crowd, and people tended to confess to anything.

Word of Abu Ali's supernatural prowess spread through the regime. He soon found himself being called upon by Saddam's cousins and aides to lift curses and cure ills. He always found such trips to the palaces unnerving, however lucrative – if you fell foul of these people, you were likely to disappear into a hell no genie could save you from.

One day, he almost did become a victim of the same rampant superstition he was tapping into. Saddam's security agents turned up at his house and accused him of plotting to use his juju against the president. After much pleading and invoking of his powerful patrons, he managed to convince them he was doing no such thing, and was eventually released unharmed. Using his psychic powers, he divined that a female neighbour had betrayed him to the police, most likely out of jealousy over his gift. His response was swift – he laid a curse on her, and proudly boasted to me that the woman had become paralysed after a blood vessel burst in her brain.

I received a brief glimpse of how he worked. Yassir, my devout and rather credulous driver, had been sitting in on the interview, riveted by what the diminutive shaman was saying. He asked Abu Ali if he could help him find his father's silver Mercedes that had been stolen a few weeks earlier in a desert hold-up near Kirkuk. Abu Ali dutifully took 25,000 dinars off Yassir, a sum of around eighteen dollars, and wrote several of the ninety-nine names of god on Yassir's right hand in black felt-tip. Yassir was instructed to hold the hand up in front of him while the magus recited five minutes of prayers and then started barking instructions at his little finger.

'Tell me if he will get the car back. Move to the right, move to the right, if he'll get the car back!' After several minutes of exhortations, Yassir's little finger – numb from being held upright for so long – twitched to the right. He was impressed, and gratefully handed over the money. He never saw the car again, though, and his father scolded him for throwing away good money.

It is worth noting the more pernicious side of these 'magic men'. An Iraqi psychoanalyst told me how distraught parents with children suffering mental illness would often bring their son or daughter to a seer, who would pronounce them possessed by a demon or evil djinn. The shaman would proceed to torment the child with beatings, hypnotic trances and fear of the devil and damnation. Men whose wives wanted to leave them would also take advantage of a shaman's services, accusing the disgruntled spouse of being possessed by a demon. It was a brutal but effective ruse: the magician would beat the devil out with the help of prayer and a length of rubber hose. Many tortured women were pronounced 'cured' when they recanted their desire to leave their husband, and the beating ceased. Abu Ali himself solemnly informed me that the post-war chaos and looting was not the result of a breakdown in law and order, but the presence in Baghdad of Jewish djinns sent by Zionist cabalists in Israel to wreak havoc. The war in the Middle East was being fought, it seemed, in all dimensions, both the physical and the spiritual.

CUT ADRIFT

Freedom's City

A shocked pause hung over Baghdad in those days of early summer 2003, as the whole world began to suspect that no one, from the gloating US president on his aircraft carrier to the stunned nay-sayers who had confidently predicted a bloody five-month siege of Umm Qasr, knew what the hell to do next. After so many years of waiting for Saddam to go, he was suddenly gone. Behind the Clock restaurant, US soldiers sifted through the bomb crater to see if they could find any scraps of Saddam DNA.

Operation Iraqi Freedom I – the technical title of the invasion of Iraq, which has since run into the un-scheduled sequels of OIF II, OIF III and counting – had been a blinding success. Too blinding, in fact. In a matter of weeks it had delivered to an enslaved, brutal-ized people more freedom than any other society on the planet enjoyed, more than any could rightly swallow. It was like watching people who had been dying of thirst in the desert suddenly fall into a deep blue swimming pool. Society was convulsing, gulping down its freedom and then vomiting it right back up, unable to cope with such a surplus of the one thing it had been craving for so long. Iraq had gone from one of the most repressive dictatorships to a Hobbesian state of nature in the time it takes an armoured column to blast its way up the Euphrates river valley.

A month before, possession of a satellite phone would have merited a death sentence. Satellite television dishes were not only unavailable but strictly forbidden, and carried the same hefty price tag. Now, not only were the shops suddenly full of both, but you could also buy one of Uday's lion cubs in Baghdad's animal market or watch one of Saddam's sleek Arab studs pulling a rickety cart piled high with propane gas cylinders through the slums of Sadr City. Looters scuttled around the city with ancient Assyrian idols from the National Museum and outdated Panasonics from government offices on their backs, washed their clothes in stolen oil drums that once contained radioactive yellowcake, or fought each other in corpse-reeking palaces over air-conditioning units for houses that had no electrical power.

And all the while, American soldiers in armoured vehicles looked on, giving the thumbs-up, indifferent Vikings outsourcing their pillaging franchise. Their commander could only muster a terse, dismissive comment when informed of the locust-stripping of the land. 'Stuff happens,' Rumsfeld announced. 'Democracy is messy.' So is chaos.

In the abandoned palaces, journalist trophy-hunters

jostled with wild-eyed Iraqis for some of the spoils, although for themselves they called it souvenir-hunting rather than looting. An embedded American photographer who had not changed his underwear in a month of fighting across southern Iraq stole two pairs of Saddam's silk boxer shorts. A naive Japanese journalist packed up a yellow cluster bomb as a souvenir in his luggage. It exploded at the Jordanian border, killing a customs officer.

But many of these 'souvenirs' also had historical importance. In Taha Yassin Ramadan's house, Lulu wrestled with an armed Iraqi man for the vice-president's photo album, a damning collection of nostalgia from the 1980s, when Saddam was the West's handy bastion against the Iranian mullahs. Lulu, who is a small but very feisty woman of Cuban descent, proved more than a match for the Iraqi looter. After a brief tug-of-war over the large, leather-bound volume, she scampered off with snapshots of the soon-to-be hanged war criminal smiling with Margaret Thatcher back in the day. A western photographer offered her 15,000 dollars in cash, on the spot, for the album, but she hung on to it. The pictures were later published in the British press, a small reminder of how the West had once cosied up to these murderous thugs they now so vociferously condemned.

There was even more explicit evidence of the luxury and sleaze in which the old regime had lived. In Uday's palace, Lulu turned on a computer that was still standing on his desk. Uday was famous for pulling girls off the streets and raping them: she was not surprised to find the laptop was bookmarked to a host of porn sites around the world.

The day after my arrival, Lulu and I visited a TB clinic set in green fields on the edge of Baghdad. Marauders had pillaged all the drugs, including those needed to prevent the disease from becoming infectious in the patients. The doctors, however, were keen to take us on a tour and introduce us to their long-suffering patients. In one room, the doctor presented us to a gaunt, dignified old gentleman with a drooping moustache and deeply sunken cheeks. He was a distant cousin of Ahmed Chalabi, the dissident who had provided so much of the fake evidence of Saddam's terrifying arsenal of weapons of mass destruction. The man had lived in London for many years, and was desperately keen to speak to the newly arrived westerners in his husky English. Not knowing how contagious he might be, we were wary about getting too close, yet afraid we might embarrass our courteous host. Strategically taking cover behind my back, Lulu prodded me into the small cubicle and lurked at my shoulder. But as the kindly old gent spoke of the terrors of the looting, pointing to the crushed pill husks still littering the floor, a large fleck of spittle flew out of his dried lips. We both watched in horror as the gob of spit arced, as though in slow motion, past my face, over my shoulder and straight into Lulu's eye. The old man didn't seem to notice Lulu's muted squawk of disgust, but the minute we got out of the hospital we cranked up the satellite phone and made a paranoid call to my mother, a retired nurse, to see if Lulu was at risk. My mum, with the unnerving matter-of-factness that comes with forty years on National Health wards, pointed out that Lulu could well be infected. Apparently those painful injections you get at school don't last. But there was not much to be done about it then: Lulu fretted a while, picturing herself in some pale sanatorium, hacking her lungs out, but then life went on at its crazy pace again. At least the looters had not found the locked fridge where the doctor said vials of Ebola were stored for some less-than-clear experimental purposes.

The same doctor told us, as we left the overgrown grounds of his clinic, that the smouldering wreck of a building across the meadow had been a clinic where HIV-infected prostitutes had been kept under strict guard to prevent the spread of AIDS. As the regime fell, the hookers had taken advantage of the mayhem and fled.

'They are probably working again,' said the doctor, adding with some satisfaction: 'They are probably selling themselves to the Americans soldiers now.'

Seeing a city, a whole country, cut adrift is a spectacular, unsettling experience. Absorbed by the events unfolding before me, I spent long days travelling around in a state of constant fascination, often forgetting that the lawlessness meant that anyone might shoot, carjack or kidnap us at any time. Somehow it didn't really occur to me back then, although Yassir my driver was constantly reminding me, with a hint of perverse pride, 'These are very bad people, Mr James, you don't know Iraqis. Very bad. Crazy people.' The last comment was usually followed by a wicked cackle. Yassir knew first-hand how bad things could get: immediately after the war, a few weeks before my arrival, he had been stuck in one of the interminable traffic jams that inevitably accompany civil collapse. A man walked up to his car, stuck a pistol through the open window and told Yassir to get out. Yassir was unimpressed: he reached down beside his seat and pulled his own gun on the carjacker. There was a brief *Reservoir Dogs* moment as they pointed their weapons at each other, then the attacker turned and fled.

'I don't think he had any bullets in his gun,' Yassir told me, cracking up in his maniacal laugh. A few days after recounting this hair-raising tale, he suddenly executed a U-turn as we drove down Saddoun Street in central Baghdad. Two cars ahead of us, a group of four men armed with knives were pulling people from the vehicles stuck in the traffic jam ahead, stabbing them and making off with their cars. A crowd was watching, but no one was lifting a finger to prevent this. Yassir swung a sharp turn before they fell on us and we sped off round the corner, where we found an American patrol idling by the side of the road. The soldier in charge looked put upon when we told him what was going on just a block away, like a tired and bored parent being told the kids were misbehaving. God knows what he had been through in recent months – he was clearly dreaming of just getting the hell out of there. But we were insistent, and he realized we weren't budging until he did something. By the time his Humvees rolled up, however, the crowd had coalesced into an angry mob and set about the attackers, beating them to the ground. The patrol arrived just in time to save the men they had wanted to arrest.

Driving through Baghdad called to mind the model dioramas I would make out of plastic kits when I was a war-obsessed kid, painting and assembling random scenes from lost conflicts out of Airfix boxes I bought in a local toy shop: a bombed street in Stalingrad, a bamboo jungle outpost in Burma, a trench scene from the Somme. On the central reservations and the dirt banks of the highways of the Iraqi capital, abandoned tanks and burned Iraqi army trucks cooked in the dry heat, while under palm groves anti-aircraft guns and vast Soviet missiles of Vietnam vintage pointed harmlessly at empty blue skies. There were so many charred military vehicles lying around that the conquering armies used them to reinforce the defensive perimeters around their new bases, stacking trucks and amphibious assault vehicles atop armoured personnel carriers. What had once been the fourth largest military in the world was now just so much American fencing.

The decomposition of the military hardware was hastened by the desperately poor stripping them for usable parts or junk metal. The hulks were towed from the roads where their crews had died or fled, many of them still full of live munitions, to a scrapyard on the southern fringe of Baghdad. Here an entire eco-system developed around the stripping of parts. Down boulevards of upturned Russian APCs and de-turreted battle tanks, grubby men toiled with spanners and wrenches in the most spontaneous swords-into-ploughshares project in history. The pickings were so good for those who worked the tank graveyard that the contractors dragging the wrecks in were soon auctioning off their hauls each time they arrived. A decent T55 tank that once cost hundreds of thousands of dollars could go for a hundred bucks, a fortune for these threadbare metal merchants.

The site had grown up on a piece of wasteland next to the southern highway. A middle-aged man whose house was right next to it fretted that his children would contract cancer from the depleted uranium he suspected had been used to turn so much battlefield hardware into spare parts.

'Nobody cares, my backyard is full of bombs. Who knows what might come off these tanks, they are full of radiation,' he lamented, though no one was listening except us. There was no one for him to turn to, and most of the recyclers appeared to have little concern about safety, working next to rockets whose wire innards spilled out, and whose warheads were still intact.

To prove to us that an evil-looking, eight-foot rocket was safe, one foolhardy old man sat down next to it, a cigarette dangling from his chapped lips, and started banging a wrench around in its spilled guts.

'Jesus, look at this guy, he's going to blow the whole place apart,' I said. Ali tried to reason with him, but he kept up his assault, metal clanging on metal. We decided it was wiser to make a hasty exit, and trotted off through the coral reef of faded military might, expecting the whole yard to be engulfed in a fireball at any minute.

Not only was Baghdad cut loose from its moorings, it was awash with unexploded ordnance. One morning, our car was stopped by a squad of American soldiers scouring a flyover for a suspected booby trap. I noticed a westerner sitting in the truck behind me, and got out to talk with him. His name was Ollie Allerhand, a man so blonde and sunburned that his expression seemed to have been leached from his face by the unrelenting Mesopotamian sun. He was a former British Army bomb-disposal expert, now working for a demining charity, risking his life every day to clear the vast litter of bombs lying everywhere in Baghdad. In the back of his truck were stacked hundreds of unexploded shells, like turnips headed for market. He had picked them up that morning, working with a team of cheerful Iraqi bomb experts who were trailing him in a minivan. Ollie collected around eight hundred shells a day from abandoned Iraqi army positions and the weapons dumps that Saddam's forces had littered across the city in anticipation of the final showdown. They had nick-named one weapons dump on the road north to Mosul the 'House of Hell' after they found a homeless family living shin-deep in shells and highly explosive rocket propellant, with their cattle roaming freely through this cordite swamp. One stray cigarette butt could have blown the whole place sky high. It took five days to remove the bombs. All the while, one of the last functioning fire engines in Baghdad hosed down the scene to prevent an explosion. It was difficult to find fire engines that still worked, not because of the bombing but because the fire crews had realized they could make more money by selling off their water to households whose supplies had been cut by the lack of pumping facilities. For a few dollars, they were happy to ignore fires and fill up homeowners' storage tanks instead.

All across the city, there was a massive movement, mostly of the poor, migrating across town on foot or in rusted cars held together only by wire and prayer. Saddam's government had long imposed strict limits on where people could live, afraid that Shia migrants from the dirt-farming south would flood the capital and cause unrest. Already there were an estimated two million Shia living in Baghdad's huge northeastern slum of Saddam City, which had been so named under the dictator, although the people who lived there hated him for his bloody suppression of their sect.

During the invasion, the residents of Saddam City were the only ones to actually take up arms against the government irregulars, squads of thugs known as the Fedayeen Saddam. The fighters comprising this nascent Shia militia, the germ of what would grow into the Mahdi Army with its terrifying death squads, set up makeshift checkpoints on street corners and netted around two hundred Fedayeen, most of them Syrians who had come to Iraq to fight against the Americans. The Shia gunmen, less a militia than an armed neighbourhood watch, were a tough bunch. Saddam City, before its renaming, had been called Thawra, or

Revolution; it had been built back in the 1960s to accommodate the poor Shia drifting from the southern deserts and marshes, attracted by the growth of the capital and the job opportunities it afforded. By the start of the war in 2003, it was a two-million-strong city within a city, with all the tribal loyalties and traditions of the Shia south. When the local Shia militia caught the Syrians – all of them Sunni fighters, would-be jihadists, mercenaries or nationalists hoping to attack the Americans before the Americans attacked Damascus – the Saddam City gunmen deported them to Ramadi, the capital of the western desert province of Anbar, soon to be dubbed the Sunni Triangle. There the Syrians stayed, in turn to form the core of the *muqawama*, or Sunni resistance. The triumphant citizens' militias declared that Saddam City would now be known as Sadr City after the revered cleric Mohammed Sadiq al-Sadr, a vociferous opponent to Saddam who had been murdered in 1999. He was also the father of Moqtada al-Sadr, the permanently scowling young leader who hated the Americans above all else, and who was to found the Mahdi Army. The name Sadr stuck, and when the capital's bullet-riddled road signs were finally restored, it was Sadr City – synonymous among Baghdad's middle classes with Ali Baba's lair of thieves and looters – that was signposted.

To escape the squalor and overcrowding of the slums, Baghdad's underclass – most of them from the over-crowded slums of Sadr City – started spilling out across town. Makeshift homes were carved out of abandoned government offices, recently emptied jails and gutted barracks. Outside the looted air force headquarters, a ten-year-old kid selling cigarettes had fashioned his kiosk out of the tailfins of an RAF Tornado shot down in the previous Gulf War. Squatters even set up home in the bowels of Saddam's massive nuclear bunker, passing through eighteen inches of ripped metal doorway that had been blasted open by US Rangers looking for the missing tyrant. When the homeless Iraqis arrived, the basement of the bunker was flooded, but most of the facilities were intact, from the map displays in the control room and the huge table in the planning office to the satin-sheeted beds in Saddam's own suite.

Sitting on top of the bunker was an empty palace, an elaborate subterfuge meant to disguise the subterranean system below. The palace had only one functioning ceremonial hall, which had witnessed some of the more terrifying rites of the old regime. Here it was that Saddam would hold dinner parties for his generals and senior party officials. Halfway through the meal, he would announce that one of his guests was a traitor whose food had been poisoned. As a hush descended over the assembled diners, the dictator would scan the worried faces and see who hesitated to lift his fork to his mouth. Anyone who refused to eat was quickly whisked away to the dungeons and torture chambers on which the regime was built. Or perhaps, knowing what awaited them there, they chose the option of eating poison.

Their last moments were swept away in the destruction of so much of the city's past, in looting and arson. Now, in that same room, two round holes in the arching cupola, side-by-side and a couple of feet wide, showed the entry point for the American missiles that had gutted this luxury decoy. The bunker below had been turned into a festering cavern by its ragged new occupants.

In places, the migration of the poor dovetailed with an exodus of the rich. In the posh three-storey houses of Abu Nuwas street, once the Chelsea of Baghdad stretching along the Tigris waterfront, decorated generals and their heavily lipsticked and bejewelled wives were hastily packing all their valuables into BMWs and SUVs and fleeing for Jordan, even as squatter families from Sadr City moved in. Sometimes the migrants overlapped: there would be awkward stand-offs in doorways as Sunni officers in snappy suits found ragged Shia families, the men in tribal *dishdasheh* and the women in cover-all black *abbaya*, waiting at their gates as they were leaving. One man, pleased as punch with his new riverside residence, told me how a Baathist general who owned the house had handed him the keys when he found him moving in as the officer moved out.

'He asked me to protect the house against looters, as I have a Kalashnikov,' the man said, smiling as the river breeze cooled him and his half-dozen undernourished children. No doubt the presence of the gun had helped in the acting out of this charade. Maybe the general really did think he'd be back one day. Maybe he will. But already, the whole street was full of contented squatters hanging out their washing in the gardens of the rich. It was as if Londoners bombed out of the East End in the Blitz had suddenly found themselves living on Cheyne Walk as their rich brethren fled for France. No one knew how long it would last, and nobody seemed to care either.

On the city dump at Tajji, on the northern edge of Baghdad, there were families living in houses made of discarded vegetable oil cans and scraps of trash. They had not even known the war had started until the first missiles crashed down on the nearby military base, and didn't seem too bothered either way: when you're that low in the social scale, living in shacks made of old olive oil cans held together by twine, a change of leadership – even invasion by a foreign power – sweeps past the daily grind of survival. The families had to pay the garbage collectors to offload the rubbish at their dump and not another. All they cared about was having enough garbage for their goats to graze on, even though the locals didn't want to buy the animals' milk because they had been fed on trash. Liberty and democracy were not something to get fired up about here: scurvy and dysentery were their principal concerns. All around them were piles of reeking trash, a foul harvest upon which their scrawny animals grazed as though they were green English pastures.

Not everyone had a garbage heap or an abandoned general's condo to move into. Not sure if the future would bring a gold rush or a famine, landlords took advantage of the power vacuum and feathered their nests by pushing up rents, hitherto strictly controlled by the regime. In their despair, hundreds of families were moving into barracks abandoned by the security forces that had evaporated into thin air. Behind the Interior

Ministry, a training complex for police recruits became a Dickensian slum, with families living in the toilet blocks and shower rooms and having to navigate rickety wooden gangways over huge pools of mud and sewage during the winter rains. There was no electricity, heating or running water, and many of the new residents were sick or undernourished. The kids played in an abandoned training plane that had been stripped of all its working parts.

The most striking paradox of this destitution was that former torture victims had moved into the very same jails where they had been beaten, electrocuted and strung up. Hatem Abed was one of them, a man who combined the expediency of housing himself and his five kids with a mission to preserve all the incriminating documents contained within his ex-prison, just behind the old air force headquarters.

It was a task that put his life at risk from those who had once tortured him within the walls of his Spartan new home. He still woke up most nights imagining he was in jail – which of course he was, but at least now his tormentors were on the run and he was armed with an AK47. Despite having no money, he had declined bribes of up to 10,000 dollars from former jailers who would come sniffing round, trying to secure the files that would incriminate them. In two rooms upstairs, he jealously guarded loose-sheaf yellowed files on thousands of people sent away to the labyrinthine jails of the Baathist regime over the decades. He led me through the knee-high piles of paper with their minutiae of destroyed lives, written in dry bureaucratese by bored functionaries decades before. It was over-whelming, and this was only one of hundreds, perhaps thousands, of such places. Flicking through a pile of papers the colour of weak tea, I saw that some of the victims had been sent into this hell just because a distant relative had been a member of the outlawed Communist Party, or because they had made some inappropriate joke about a member of the dictator's family in front of the omnipresent spies and snitches who were now trying to deny their pasts. Peering at the faces in the faded black-and-white pictures, I couldn't help but wonder what these people had endured in the tiny concrete cells with the sinister hooks poking out of the ceilings. Some had scrawled their names on the walls, next to dates, a last trace for relatives seeking them should the hated regime ever collapse. Hatem allowed these people in, but kept the gun handy against those who might try to destroy his treasure trove.

Hatem's history was a perfect example of the Kafkaesque world Iraq was only just emerging from. His case should have been resolved in a divorce court, not a torture chamber. A car salesman, he had wanted to end a marriage that was not working out. What he didn't know was that his mother-in-law was one of the hundreds of thousands of people on the payroll for the Mukhabarat, Iraq's all-seeing secret police force, which retained a huge network of casual informers. Fearing for her daughter's reputation, his mother-in-law trumped up charges against Hatem that he had played a part in the 1996 assassination attempt against Saddam's mad son Uday. Such denunciations were commonplace in Saddam's Iraq, and continued well after the Americans arrived: people would simply settle old scores by denouncing a rival as a Baathist or guerrilla loyalist. With no police force, the undermanned Americans would arrest the person, who could disappear for months into the brutal, chaotic prison system because the American warders could not spell their names correctly, or confused their tribal name with their father's name, making them impossible to track down.

What made Hatem's case particularly surreal was that, between fingernail-extraction sessions, he was dragged off to one of Saddam's palaces. There, the dictator took time out to deliver Hatem a long speech on the value of marriage. The dictator seemed unconcerned about the allegations of Hatem having tried to kill his son – presumably he knew they were groundless – and tried to persuade him not to leave his wife. I never met Hatem's wife but I imagine she must have been a pretty terrible spouse, since Hatem still refused to revoke his decision and was led back to his cell. He eventually escaped by selling everything he had to bribe the police into releasing him. Penniless, he now burned with an avenger's zeal.

'This is part of the evidence that will send Saddam to hell. I want to rip out his fingernails, like he did to me,' he told me as I flicked through the endless files full of vanished faces. In fact, Saddam was hanged long before Hatem's case – one of hundreds of thousands – ever made it to court.

* * *

Even the dead were on the move in those wild days of summer, and the living were chasing after them. Saddam's executioners had tortured and murdered hundreds of thousands of people in order to cling on to power, and thousands more had been killed during the recent war. Now the bodies were emerging from the ground, a nightmare resurrection at the end of days for the old regime. Some rose again as desiccated skeletons of decades-old purges, others as moist, reeking cadavers murdered on the eve of liberation, even as American fighters scoured the skies overhead, so close but still too far for deliverance. In Salman Pak, a village on the southeastern outskirts of Baghdad, I met a man whose predicament I could only describe as being a mass-grave tourist. His name was Nassir Taleb Nassir, a rangy, short Shiite man in his mid-forties, with grey in his beard and dirt under his fingernails. He was filthy and he had a wild stare in his eyes, borne of years of suffering and uncertainty.

Nassir was looking for his younger brother. Once upon a time, he had had two, both of whom were arrested in the 1990s. One had been executed and his broken body returned to the family for burial. But the other, a youth named Hafeth, had disappeared without trace. As the fighting of this past war subsided, thousands of Shiites started digging in the mass graves, their way guided by locals who recalled seeing trucks full of prisoners arriving, hearing gunfire, and then watching as the same trucks departed, empty.

Every time Nassir's family heard of a yet another mass grave being uncovered, he would head to the scene by whatever means he could: by foot, hitching, bus if he had the money. He reeled off a list of burial pits he had been to around the city, and others he had visited in the south. Each time he arrived, he would help dig through the horrors emerging from the sandy soil. He didn't have a spade, so he dug with his hands, like a terrier looking for a lost bone. That scorching day in May, he stood in his tattered, mud-streaked black shirt in the vast grounds of what had once been a Republican Guard training ground, into whose scrubby woods the special forces had led more than a hundred prisoners during the US bombing.

Unlike the dried husks pulled out of the mass graves left over from the 1991 Shia uprising, or the Kurds killed in the 1980s, these recently executed bodies were foul, shiny lumps of yellowing meat that ejected a stench so strong it induced a mild sense of panic, the true horror of death and decomposition. It was difficult to believe that a few weeks ago these hanks of rotten flesh had been people, terrified and uttering their last prayers, knowing they were beyond all earthly help. The stench alone made it all the more remarkable that Nassir could dive into the grave and excavate with his bare hands: there was a hint of insanity in his despair. The faces that emerged seemed unrecognizable, but grieving relatives checked each corpse for clues: an item of clothing, a familiar sandal or shirt, perhaps a tattoo like the scimitar on Nassir's own grime-covered hand. Even a packet of cigarettes, a missing relative's favourite brand, might offer some allure of closure.

There was another slit trench dug alongside the grave

he was helping excavate. It was empty, indicating that the soldiers had either been interrupted during their labour or had overestimated the number of prisoners they would take charge of. One of the Islamic charity workers overseeing the exhumation said he believed the dead were common criminals or suspected enemies of the state who had been rounded up for interrogation. Under pressure from the advancing US forces, their guards had simply executed them before fleeing. Deliverance had in fact spelled damnation.

The remains, in their tens of thousands, were being moved every day, some to identification and forensic centres where there was a hit-or-miss attempt at putting a name to a bag of bones, others taken to the Shiite holy city of Najaf, around two hours' drive to the south. There the small sacks of assorted bones, most of them unidentified, were laid to rest in tiny holes in the Wadi as-Salaam cemetery, the largest graveyard in the world. An estimated million Shiites were already interred within sight of the golden dome of the Imam Ali mosque. It was a good business for the gravediggers, local Shiite men who took a commission on the burials. Being buried so close to the tomb of Imam Ali, the son-in-law and cousin of the Prophet, was seen as a way of currying favour with the Almighty. A veritable metropolis of graves and subterranean tombs had sprung up. In some of the sunken family mausoleums wild dogs, lured by the smell of decay, snarled as funeral processions passed, looking as forbidding as Cerberus, the three-headed hound that guarded the gates of Hades.

But the killing was far from over. Although we didn't know it then, it had scarcely begun. Every night, in the blacked-out city, the sound of gunfire echoed for hours as gangs raided houses, distraught relatives sought revenge or nervous housekeepers fired off warning shots at shadows flitting in the streets or palm groves. Occasionally you would also hear an explosion followed by an exchange of gunfire, as some desperate Fedayeen fighter or opportunistic young man launched a rocket at an American patrol.

It was becoming increasingly clear that I was no longer a tourist, offering the occasional freelance article to *The Times*. My editor had envisioned a brief tenure for me to cover post-war reconstruction – now I was their Baghdad war correspondent. I had drifted into a job that would dominate my life for years to come.

To try to gauge the extent of the killings, I decided to spend an entire day at the main Baghdad morgue. I showed up before eight, before the mortuary opened for business. As I arrived, there was already a queue of grieving families huddled in the street, the men taut-faced, the women keening. At eight a.m., the blue metal gates opened for the day's grisly business.

First through the gates was the family of Mohammed Abed al-Hussein, a seventeen-year-old who had died overnight in hospital. He had just arrived home from work the week before and had been washing his hands under the garden tap when a bullet hit him in the head. The bullet had been fired by an Iraqi who had mistaken a defiant television broadcast by Saddam Hussein as news of his arrest and let off volleys of celebratory fire. The boy's father Abed was distraught, not just at the loss but how he was going to pay for the autopsy (under Iraqi law, no one could be buried without a death certificate – in the case of killings, those could only be issued by the mortuary authorities for the princely sum of ten dollars, a large sum to Iraq's poor), as well as for the three-day mourning tent, the food and refreshments the mourners would have to be supplied with, and the gravedigger's fees in Najaf.

'Every day you can hear the guns – why doesn't the US take away all the weapons that are killing us, that killed my son?' asked the father, his effort not to cry gradually fading in a welter of tears. In fact, the Americans had recently ruled that every household could keep a gun for self-protection, an explicit admission that it could not protect the people. They were on their own.

As the Hussein family left, another group of men came in. This time, the victim was a 21-year-old man who had only just gained his MSc in biology the year before. During his studies, Omar al-Najjar had picked up good English, a skill that would prove to be both lucrative and fatal. Wanting to help the Americans bring freedom to his country, he had signed up as a translator for the army at ten dollars a day. The Humvee he had been riding with on a lush, reed-fringed road on the southern edge of the city had been hit with an RPG a couple of days before. The unit's captain had been killed. Omar, who had been provided with neither flak jacket nor helmet, was hit in the head.

'He enjoyed his job very much,' his brother Ahmed

said in English, desperately trying not to cry. 'They loved him. Now we are picking up his corpse. What can we do, it's destiny.'

Despite his profession of fatalism, Ahmed's face suddenly crumpled. I put my arms around him and hugged him in the yard of the morgue, trying not to cry myself. I didn't tell Ahmed that an hour earlier, before the morgue opened its gates, I had watched as Doctor Tariq al-Ibrahimi, the chief pathologist, had performed an autopsy on his kid brother. His head was so badly split open that the doctor had been able, with a few scalpel cuts, to remove the skull almost entirely from the skin, leaving Omar's face and scalp hanging from his neck like an empty hood. I watched in grim fascination, more amazed that such a thing was possible than sickened by the sight. Across the room, another pathologist was sawing through somebody's sternum with a hacksaw. The place was a veritable factory of corpses.

By nine-thirty a.m., there was a large throng of relatives inside the mortuary courtyard, angry and eager to use me as a sounding board for their impotent fury. They jostled around coffins that were already blood-stained from previous occupants – Iraqis are buried only in white shrouds, and the coffins serve as reusable boxes to transport them to the cemetery. Some were threatening the tired, overworked mortuary staff with tribal retaliation if they did not release the bodies without an autopsy, seen by the less educated as a violation of the dead. The air was so thick with the odour of putrefaction and formaldehyde that it was difficult to breathe. Inside, the fridges – which only worked inter-mittently because of the unreliable electricity supply – were already full, and some of the unclaimed bodies had been left outside, oozing oxidized fluids. Mohanned, my translator, despite being an experienced anaesthetist, gagged into his handkerchief as we passed a woman's blackened husk that was melting in the summer heat. The morticians seemed not to notice. I concentrated on my notebook and tried to block out the unholy stench.

As Omar's mangled cadaver was hoisted on to the roof rack of a hired minibus, another family shuffled in, this time with a ten-year-old boy killed in a hit-and-run accident on Baghdad's chaotic streets. He was quickly replaced by the body of a young man shot in the street for no apparent reason, the killer unknown and still on the loose.

'Iraqis are monsters. We are supposed to be Muslims. What happened to us?' the man's uncle moaned. 'Beg the US to help us!'

But his was one of the rare cases of introspection. As the debate developed in the morgue yard, most were blaming the Americans who had unleashed this whirl-wind of murder and who seemed unwilling to do anything about it.

'Is this freedom? It's freedom to die!' one man spat. Another added, in English, for my benefit: 'It's the people who make the freedom. Why blame the Americans always?'

Unfortunately, at that moment the Americans' own direct contribution to the body count arrived. An elderly hospital driver pulled a stiff body from his van, saying that he had been shot dead by US troops the night before.

'Fuck Bush, fuck America,' he muttered as he slammed the door and pulled away. 'We're not afraid of them.' However, others in the yard did not share his rage: several men pointed at the blanket-draped corpse and laughed.

'Ali Baba,' one man chuckled. 'He was caught stealing power cables to sell for a good price.' He had been shot dead for doing what others were doing with impunity across the country. But the men at the morgue were happy to see looters shot like vermin before they stripped the city bare. Many wanted to see them strung in the hundreds from lampposts. The man's body lay unclaimed in the yard for a long time before a morgue attendant came and hefted it unceremoniously on to a soiled canvas stretcher.

A silver Toyota pulled up, windscreen smeared in coagulating streaks of blood that had leaked from the coffin tied to the roof. Angry men got out and informed us that the body inside was that of nineteen-year-old Nasser Salim Rahim, killed by a single sniper bullet the evening before as he was riding in a car with four other men.

'It was the Americans,' an uncle snapped. 'They just shot him in the back of the head.' The young men had been passing an American unit in the city centre when the bullet struck, spraying the other passengers with gore.

As the hot morning swelled into boiling noon, the

bodies kept rolling in: a young man shot dead in the street by thieves; a father of three who was playing football for his local team when three men in the crowd pulled out pistols and shot him.

'If his family knows who killed him, there will be revenge killings,' said a friend waiting for the body to be released.

Still the corpses came: a taxi driver shot twice in the head by a thief, who took his car and dumped his body by the roadside. Such crimes were common in the city in those days, with scores of drivers hijacked, murdered and left by the roadside. Often the killers were criminals that Saddam had released from Abu Ghraib jail the previous autumn in an amnesty to celebrate his unanimous re-election. An estimated hundred thousand hardened jailbirds had been unleashed on the capital, a time bomb waiting to explode in the invaders' faces. Now, with no police or security, they had turned Baghdad into a jungle. Among the carousel of corpses, we would bump into distraught men and women looking for missing relatives, who had visited all the city hospitals and were now scouring the morgues. A woman was looking for her son, a 21-year-old conscript she had not seen since the war began. She had been told by his comrades he'd been wounded, but there was no record of where he had been transferred to. Three months later, she was trying the morgues, having already made the long journey to Basra and Hilla to check the hospitals there.

A white pick-up truck, the type of government vehicle looted in the thousands, pulled into the courtyard. In the back, covered by blankets, were two bodies, only their gnarly, yellowed feet sticking out from under woollen covers. The driver told me they belonged to an elderly mother and her adult son, shot dead an hour before in a tribal dispute dating back thirty-five years.

Next was the body of a man killed at a wedding, when the groom's family had taken offence at a request from the bride's side that no guns be allowed in for celebratory fire. The offended guests pulled out their guns, killing three people; the wedding was cancelled. Then came an elderly woman, blown up when someone threw a grenade into her house, another seemingly random act that could happen only in a lawless metropolis emerging from decades of war and repression, overlaid on centuries of tribal rifts. A police officer brought in the body of a middle-aged man shot by his brother in an inheritance dispute. 'We have fifty policemen in our station, but only two cars and no guns. We can't keep control,' Sergeant Esam Numer said.

Finally, another policeman pulled up at the wheel of a smart grey BMW, two bullet holes in the hood. Slumped across the back seat was the owner, a bullet hole forming a black hole where his right eye had been. He had fallen victim to a well-known gangster released by Saddam from Abu Ghraib. The policeman said the criminal had been shot in the leg during his arrest. The police had handed him to the Americans, but the officer complained that the occupiers, without any evidence against the criminal, would soon release him back on to the streets.

At eight p.m. the morgue closed. Tariq al-Ibrahimi,

the chief pathologist, swabbed down the floors and locked up for another night.

'This was a quiet day, for these times,' he said with a faded smile. Out in the city, gunfire crackled in the twilight.

A friend once asked me how an unbeliever like myself could deal with so much death, so close. It wasn't hard. Despite my easy upbringing in suburban England, I never really thought that man was anything more than a fleshy animal, an extraordinary one to be sure, but one that would die soon enough. I never managed to subscribe to the illusion of an after-life. If anything, that day at the morgue, among the corroding matter of human existence, the blood hosed across the concrete yard and the screamed fury and grief at its wanton squandering, only made me more convinced I was right. One minute you are driving your BMW through the streets of Baghdad, the next some foreign journalist is examining the bloody mess of your eye socket as you lie on the leatherette back seat of your car at the morgue gates. We are here, then we are gone. It's not good or bad. Just fleeting.

BRING 'EM ON

The Birth of an Insurgency

A ribbon of pitted blacktop evaporated into a horizon of sun-bleached palm trees. To the east of the road, a dilapidated car repair shop, tyre vulcanizer and an over-grown picnic spot with bare concrete seats provided the only signs of human habitation. Yassir stopped the car to ask if this was where the bomb went off.

A mechanic ambled out, wiping grease on his trousers, more to see the foreigner up close than to offer any help. A few other men loitering around the cluster of stifling tin-roof shacks stopped whatever it was they were doing and looked on. The mechanic squinted at us, baring tobacco-tanned teeth. He nodded. 'Na'am.' This was where the blast hit the Americans.

He led us up the road towards the trees. It was late afternoon, with a heat haze rising off the concrete picnic table. I wondered if anyone had ever stopped to eat here: wayward diners sentenced to this fossilized, picnic purgatory? To the north, the empty road snaked on for hundreds of miles towards Mosul and, beyond it, Syria;

Baghdad lay a few dozen miles behind us to the south. The wizened mechanic pointed to a spot where the tarmac had been ripped off like a scab, leaving a shallow dent in the surface of the road. It wasn't a particularly impressive hole, but it had been enough to kill an American soldier riding convoy duty north.

'I don't know who did it,' muttered the mechanic. The other men had come out now to see who the foreigner was, poking around in this neck of the backwoods. Emboldened by their presence, the mechanic stuck his neck out, exercising free speech for perhaps the first time in his life. Given the fact that just a couple of months before he could have vanished into a prison for expressing his views, it was a rather brave act.

'But they were right to do it, whoever they were!' he blurted out, suddenly angry at the world. 'There's no electricity, no water, no security, they are right to attack the Americans. What else can they do?'

The response shot from my mouth before I realized how pointless it was. 'Couldn't you demonstrate, show how you feel peacefully? How will killing people help?'

The men looked at me, suspicious and confused. Who the hell demonstrated in Iraq? The last time there had been anything even vaguely resembling a democracy, Teddy Boys had been the latest fashion craze upsetting middle-class London. The only demonstrations in the memory of most Iraqis were those whipped up by the authorities, when hand-picked lackeys were ordered to punch the air in front of news cameras and chant their support for Saddam. As a rule in Iraq, you didn't demonstrate: you formed a secret society with similarly angry members of your tribe or sect and then went out and blew something up.

Not that Iraqis hadn't tentatively tried out the concept of public assembly, after the US occupation authorities officially disbanded the army, making more than 250,000 soldiers unemployed in one fell swoop. It was true that many of the Shia conscripts were ecstatic to be free of a corrupt and badly run military, but the officer class, both Sunni and Shia, saw their entire careers and incomes vanish with a payout of a few hundred dollars. Outside the Muthana army base in Baghdad, I had seen thousands of them lined up to collect their final salary: a pathetic parade of generals, staff officers, special forces veterans, all dressed in civvies and corralled behind razor wire to wait for hours in the sun for a handout from the army they had been fighting just a month before. Everyone seemed to know some general who was now driving taxis to survive, or a lieutenant colonel who spent his days sitting in his house, curtains drawn, waiting for a Shia hit-squad from the Badr Brigades to come and settle old scores. They were angry, humiliated and afraid.

'We will turn ourselves into human bombs!' one sweating, heavyset ex-officer yelled in my face during the first small protest outside the looted air force headquarters. Only a handful of soldiers were there, milling around on a roundabout besieged by gridlocked traffic. No one took them particularly seriously.

But a week later, they managed to muster a couple of hundred ex-military men to demonstrate outside the Assassin's Gate, where US troops guarded the grandiose archway leading into the Green Zone. They chanted demands for money and jobs as the American soldiers stood impassively with their guns raised, keeping them from entering the palace compound. But then firing erupted, killing at least one of the protestors and wounding several others. The crowd was furious, and threw wild accusations as we moved among them.

'It was Kuwaitis,' howled one man. 'I saw them get out of a BMW. I am Iraqi, I know what Kuwaitis look like!' I very much doubted that a group of rich Kuwaitis would drive through hundreds of miles of lawless Ali Baba territory to spray random Iraqis with gunfire. I noted it down anyway.

Another group was convinced that a blonde woman soldier in the ranks of guards had opened fire. The US soldiers were now standing with fixed bayonets facing the baying mob.

'It was the woman. She hates Arab men!' they shouted. This time, I thought I had better ask, although I knew the accusations stemmed from their macho shame that a woman should be serving as a soldier, and one who was fully armed while they, professional soldiers themselves, were sacked, defenceless and unable to provide for their families. I stepped up to the woman, who looked tense and harassed.

'Er . . . excuse me, I'm a reporter from the London *Times*,' I said. She stared at me like I was the carrier of some contagion. 'These men here said that you opened fire on the demonstration. Is that true?'

'Step away from me, sir!' she barked. She was carrying a very sharp bayonet attached to an assault rifle, so I quickly obliged. A military investigation later revealed that the shooting had begun when an American supply convoy had tried to enter the Green Zone through an adjacent checkpoint, and the soldiers riding shotgun had become spooked by the angry mob. A soldier on the convoy had fired a warning shot, which the troops on sentry duty had mistakenly thought came from the crowd. They opened fire, and the soldiers' experiment with street democracy was effectively over.

It was often said that the Americans who came to Iraq knew very little of the country's history. But that day, it was their own history they seemed to have forgotten: only five people were killed in the Boston Massacre of 1770, yet that bungled bit of policing by British soldiers trying to contain an angry crowd triggered the American Revolution.

Washington, DC, July 13, 2003. Two months and twelve days since President Bush's triumphant appearance on the *USS Abraham Lincoln*. Now he was back in front of the cameras, more soberly posing in front of the White House and offering his response to the alarming number of attacks on the troops he had sent into Iraq.

'There are some who feel like the conditions are such they can attack us there. My answer is, "Bring 'em on," ' the president said. It appeared as ill-judged a remark as his earlier declaration of victory.

Listening to the speech on television back in Iraq, my translator, Ali, laughed when he heard the American president's comment. 'Oh, they will,' he said. 'They will.'

And they did. Within a few days, we pulled up outside

a depot where cooking gas canisters were being handed out, part of the subsistence rations the Iraqis depended on. In the midst of all the hubbub and pushing and shoving, someone had shot dead an American soldier. By the time we arrived, much of the crowd had cleared, but we spotted an old man sitting across the road in a grimy shop selling engine lubricants, his clothes black-streaked with oil. He looked genuinely distraught by the death of the American soldier.

'There was a big crowd of people outside the depot, waiting to get their gas canisters,' he said, rubbing his calloused hands in anxiety. 'There were hundreds of them waiting there, pushing and shouting.'

Business was slow that morning, and he had been staring absently out across the broad highway at the fenced-off depot in southern Baghdad. What happened next was horribly simple, he recalled. Two men worked their way through the throng of people. When they were close to the two Americans guarding the depot, they pulled pistols out of their pockets and shot the soldiers. One was shot through the head and died instantly. The other, perhaps hearing the first shot, raised his arm, and was shot through the hand. The panicked crowd fled. The killers simply pocketed their guns and ran with them. No one was caught.

All across Baghdad, such unhindered attacks were spreading, putting the Americans on the defensive. The attacks were mostly unsophisticated at first. An Iraqi man, sometimes just a bored or angry kid, would stand on a highway overpass and drop a hand grenade into a Humvee passing below. The attacker then simply ran away to merge with the crowds. Hand grenades cost a few dollars in the gun markets that had sprung up across the capital, flogging off all the munitions that had been stolen from the deserted army barracks. Otherwise, they could be picked up by anyone daring enough to venture into the weapons depots, which were so poorly guarded that the only real danger came from other looters. Soon, all of Baghdad's bridges and over-passes were fenced with chain-link to curb such casual grenade attacks. But still, there was sense of permissive-ness: if a few bored, angry teenagers could get away with such casual killings, what did that say about the invincible Americans? There were massive round-ups and house searches, but these only served to anger even more frustrated Iraqis into chancing their own hand at attacking the Americans.

And despite their armour and sophisticated weapons, the Americans were vulnerable, if only because they believed the war to have finished, while their foes knew it was only just beginning. In Baghdad, US military spokesmen briefed the press in the sweltering, un-ventilated Green Zone convention centre that the sporadic attacks on the military were the work of Baathist 'dead-enders' who couldn't accept the bright new future America was offering. What we were witness-ing, we were assured, was merely the twitching of the 'tail of the snake', whose head had already been cut off.

But the numbers of dead American soldiers con-tinued to rise every week. There were headlines declaring 'pressure mounts on Bush as the US death toll passes 100'. It seemed that nobody, least of all the White

House or Downing Street, understood what was going on or why the violence was rapidly reaching its tipping point into insurgency. In Baghdad, just around the corner from where I lived, a gun battle broke out on the bustling shopping street of Karada Harej: an Iraqi man had fired a rocket-propelled grenade at an American patrol, according to the official account were we given. What witnesses told us was the Americans hadn't been patrolling at all, but doing what Americans do best: shopping. With the borders now open, Baghdad's shops were filling up with cheap DVD players, televisions and air-conditioning units; the Americans, based in bombed-out palaces with no AC or entertainments, had been out buying cheap consumer goodies when they were ambushed. In the newly set up internet cafés, American platoons took time out from patrolling to contact distant wives and girlfriends, while one of their men stood watch at the door. I once saw an American soldier chatting to his girlfriend on the internet, asking her to mail him candles because his base outside a power plant did not have electricity.

Some attacks were clearly planned, others were more spontaneous. A Humvee crashes on the outskirts of Baghdad on a routine mail run to Kuwait. The Hummer behind it stops and the crew jumps out to help their injured comrades. A crowd forms around them, some offering to help. While the soldiers are evacuating the wounded driver from the stricken vehicle, someone in the crowd sets fire to the empty Humvee. The act of casual arson could not have been planned round a random road accident, but it showed both a smouldering resentment of the Americans and a crazy level of bravado, torching the vehicle of well-armed men who had spent weeks killing your fellow countrymen, and who are still authorized to shoot at will.

But who were these shadowy guerrillas out there, attacking the American convoys? By luck, it turned out that Mohanned the translator had another cousin who knew a cell that was willing to talk. It was based in Rutba, way out west. One cold winter's day, late in 2003, we headed out to meet the resistance.

Rutba was, is and always will be a forlorn little smuggling town straddling the middle of nowhere. Jittery convoys of four-wheel-drive jeeps streak past on the desert highway, headed west for Amman and civilization, dodging the gaping cruise missile crater on the motorway bridge. You barely notice the little town huddled off in the desert, its buildings camouflaged against the open expanse by dust and drab design. The tribesmen are obsessively private, and you rarely see anyone out in the streets. The squat adobe houses clustered along empty, muddy tracks called to mind the towns that must have once made up the far-flung outposts of ancient Sumer. Only the ziggurats were missing.

We drove for hours to get there, then almost missed the turning. The only landmark was the semi-destroyed highway bridge spanning a wadi. We turned off the thin band of surviving tarmac, the only trace of modernity for hundreds of miles around, and trundled off south, into a previous century.

Mohanned's cousin was living in Rutba, and knew some members of the resistance cell. After a certain amount of wrangling, the guerrillas had agreed to meet us. We arrived in a late wintry afternoon, just as the sun was going down.

Mohanned's cousin told us the guerrillas were nervous and would only meet us after dark, so we spent the rest of the day lounging around in a guest room, or *diwan*, on worn rugs and cushions covering a bare concrete floor. It was bitterly cold: we huddled close to a three-bar electric heater, or an oil lamp whenever the electricity cut out. Mohanned's cousin fed us meat stew but wouldn't allow us to go outside, fearing his neighbours might spot us and suspect him of being in league with the hated foreigners. Any kind of visible collusion was enough to earn a grenade through the window, or a burning jerry can under your car.

Some of the cousin's friends, whom he trusted enough to introduce to us, visited and recounted tales of how they used to go off into the desert for weeks at a stretch to hunt for hawks and eagles before the war. They would sell the birds to Emirati princes for up to 20,000 dollars a time. They showed me the clever little slipknot snares they would attach to a live chicken acting as bait: when the eagle swooped, its legs became entangled in the strings and the hunters would move in, chasing the bird of prey as it struggled to fly with a live chicken attached to its feet. Eventually it would tire and they would bag their prize. But the hunters we met had recently been rounded up during one of their desert forays by the American army, who suspected them of being gun-runners. They showed me the red welts where they had been bound in over-tight flexi-cuffs, forced to sit on bare concrete for days at a time. Some had been beaten senseless before being released more than a hundred miles from Rutba, with no money to return home.

Around eleven p.m., Mohanned's cousin slipped outside to contact the guerrillas. After an hour, he returned to tell us we could drive off to meet them. Our photographer Jason would have five minutes to duck into their stone house in a back alley and take pictures of them with their weapons and *yeshmaks* wrapped round their heads, then we would conduct the interview driving around in our car to make sure no one was following us. The guerrillas were jittery that night: the day before, seven of their comrades had been killed fighting the Americans in Fallujah.

We set out through the unlit, windy lanes of Rutba, driving for at least a quarter of an hour. I noticed we were driving in circles and asked our host if he was shaking off potential spies. He laughed and said in a way, yes: he was trying to make sure his kid brother had not followed us, as he would then tell his mother, who in turn would be furious at our man for getting involved with the resistance.

In the distance, we spotted another car inching its way down a rutted alleyway: I wondered if every guerrilla operation started off with an elaborate procession of gunmen trying to throw off their over-protective mothers.

Eventually we pulled up outside a hovel with a couple

of stone steps leading inside. Jason jumped out and we sat idling in the car while he took his shots: guerrillas in heavy winter greatcoats, their heads wrapped snugly in red and white scarves, only their boyish brown eyes peering out, betraying no emotion. In their hands they held grenades, Kalashnikovs and a Koran, the basic ammunition of the jihad that was brewing in these remote towns and villages. No fancy chemical weapons, just a cheap Soviet grenade made a decade before in some Communist country that had long since shed its ideology, and bought for a couple of dollars at the local market. The standard-issue AK47 was probably looted from an abandoned weapons dump, or had been filched from the disintegrating army months before.

As for the guiding prophecy, that was provided by a caravanserai manager who claimed to have met the Archangel Gabriel in the Hejaz desert some 1,400 years ago.

Conducting an interview in a dark car on a bumpy road with a masked guerrilla holding a grenade in his pocket was not easy. I could barely read my scrawled notes afterwards. We also worried about what would happen if we came across any American patrols in the middle of the freezing desert night: would our companions decide to sell their lives dearly, and would the jumpy American soldiers even bother asking what we were doing out there before opening fire? I tried to concentrate on the interview at hand.

What the cell leader – he called himself Mohammed, though it was not his real name – told us was remark-able. The insurgency was still in its early stages – it would not really erupt into its full force for another few months, in April 2004 – and the American military insisted they were fighting a last-stand group of a few hundred former Baathists bitter about losing power. Very few westerners had actually met any of the shadowy guerrillas by this time. What Mohammed said proved how completely out of touch the Americans were, and why they were fighting in the dark.

There was a simple reason he had chosen to fight: it said so in the Koran.

'It says if the infidels invade an Islamic country, you must fight,' Mohammed explained to me. Simple. An open and shut case for the village boy with the looted rifle. Mohammed had been a soldier during the invasion, and survived heavy fighting in Hilla, a mainly Shiite town sixty miles south of Baghdad. As his army started to unravel about him, and as his capital suddenly fell overnight, he took his gun and headed home to this forgotten backwater. Slowly, he had met up with other young Sunni men nursing their wounded national pride, and who were enraged by the presence of outsiders in their country. Their cell of five ex-soldiers gradually expanded, coalescing with other groups, until they had almost a hundred fighters, shuttling down the Euphrates valley in open-back pick-ups, posing as unemployed day labourers looking for work.

'It's all lies that the resistance is led by Baathists,' Mohammed said. 'The resistance is Islamic, we are ordered by God, we have no relation to that party,' he said in a steady voice, squeezed into the back of the car between me and Jason.

'Saddam oppressed us and persecuted us,' he said, adding that he would be willing to work with Baathists if they fought in an 'Islamic way'. He quoted a number of Hadiths, or sayings of the Prophet, calling for resistance against any and all occupiers, but forbidding attacks on civilians. 'But we don't know of any Baathists fighting. They are all at home,' he said with disdain.

Saddam had, however, become a belated, if unintentional, inspiration. His public humiliation by the Americans – filmed looking like a homeless wino pulled into custody from the dirt hole where he had been hiding, almost within sight of one of his former palaces, an American military doctor swabbing his mouth for DNA samples – had infuriated even those who hated him. His humiliation was theirs too: for better or worse, he had ruled them for three decades. His humiliation was the Iraqi people's shame.

'We want the Americans to get out of Iraq, they came here against Islam and they stole all of Iraq's fortune,' Mohammed insisted. 'The Americans persecuted us and humiliated us and treated us very badly. Even Saddam Hussein was not this bad.'

I nodded and noted his words, though I was thinking of the hundreds of thousands of people still being shovelled out of mass graves, the legacy of Saddam's regime. Did these Sunni kids really not know about them, about the mass executions in the desert? Were they in some kind of denial, like Germans after the Second World War? Or did Iraqi pride outweigh that mass of desert carrion that had once been their fellow citizens?

An explosives expert, Mohammed claimed to have already killed twenty-five Americans with remote-controlled bombs, the notorious IEDs, or Improvised Explosive Devices, that were proving to be the bane of the occupation forces. His cell had carried out thirty attacks in recent months, using looted TNT hooked up to 155mm artillery shells to blow Humvees off the roads. Other units were already specializing in mortar attacks on US bases and the use of RPGs on patrols. Soon there would be sniper brigades using sharpshooter manuals written by American Vietnam veterans and freely available on the internet as the source of their training.

The guerrillas would bury their explosives in caches in the desert. Others would scout out targets and give them their missions. Then Mohammed and his team would dig up their arms and plant them by the roadside, triggering them with stereo remote controls or washing-machine timers. His preferred tactic was to lie in wait around two hundred metres from the road, selecting the vehicle with the most soldiers in it and then destroying it. Lawrence of Arabia, eat your heart out, I thought.

Escape was rarely a problem, Mohammed said, especially with smaller convoys: the accompanying vehicles would speed off to make sure they were not also caught in the ambush. For Mohammed, the greatest danger was informants: their tip-offs had led to the deaths of fifteen of his comrades. Even those caught doing commercial business with the Americans were dealt with roughly, beaten or their houses burned.

But most worrying for the Americans was

Mohammed's source of inspiration: Osama bin Laden. The guerrillas had not yet made contact with al-Qaeda, but Mohammed said they would love to work with them. The opportunity would soon present itself, as the American military had made no effort to secure Iraq's borders and militants were flooding in with money, contacts and know-how.

'Al-Qaeda is an Islamic group and we've learned from them, and we learned much from Osama bin Laden. He is our sheikh also,' said Mohammed. I could see no end to this fight. Six months before Paul Bremer hastily handed sovereignty to a US-picked Iraqi government, Mohammed swore that he would fight any Iraqi proxies the Americans put in their place.

'We don't accept that the US should put any government in place, even one made up of Iraqis. They will be ruled by the devil Bush. We will fight until we are martyrs,' he said, before stepping out of the car.

After we had dropped them off at the same featureless hovel whence they had emerged, we went back to our host's freezing *diwan* to bed down for what remained of the night. Lying there in my sleeping bag, I started to suspect this war was a complex knot of misshapen beliefs, a clash of ideologies already bent out of shape, and knew it was hardly going to be the straightforward mopping-up operation the Americans in their newly occupied palaces had thought it was.

Despite the undercurrent of violence that was growing every day, people still went about their normal business. Most had no choice – you either went to work, opened your shop or visited the market, or you ran out of money. The best place to test the mood in the restless city was to drop by the Mutanabi book market on a Friday morning before prayers, where people from all walks of life took a break from the trials of Baghdad life.

There was a joke going around the book market, where sellers displayed their second-hand volumes: an eclectic mix of lurid English and French paperbacks from the 1970s; dog-eared *National Geographics* reporting volcanoes that erupted decades ago; the occasional first edition of Wilfred Thesiger's works on the Empty Quarter; religious tracts; posters of Shiite imams and dusty school textbooks. You could still pick up the odd volume by the elusive Saddam himself, though nobody seemed to be interested. The street was dead-ended on the Tigris, in the long-since purged Jewish quarter around Rashid Street, a shade-cooled Ottoman avenue of shuttered balconies sagging over ornate, rusted iron-cast pillars. If you half closed your eyes, you could almost imagine you were in New Orleans after a particularly bad hurricane. The book market was always crowded on Fridays, and Baghdad's ageing intellectual elite would gather at the Shahbander café, sitting under faded photos of vanished Ottoman Baghdad, sipping endless glasses of lemon tea and smoking perfumed *narguilah* as they discussed the history swirling on the dangerous, bustling streets outside.

The joke ran like this: a man complains to his neighbour that his rooster's crowing keeps him awake at night, and asks him would he kindly kill the damn bird. The neighbour complies, and the man thinks he will rest easy at last. But that night he is awoken by a cacophony of crowing, so he goes to his neighbour the next morning to complain yet again.

The neighbour hears him out, then shrugs and explains, 'The problem is, the rooster I killed was keeping all the others under control.'

The men would laugh heartily when they heard it. They knew that already dozens of would-be leaders were marshalling their forces to launch into the huge power vacuum. There were legions of exiles returning from Iran, the United States, Britain and the Gulf, many with their own private armies; there were jittery neighbours sending agents across the unwatched borders, terrorist cells and on-the-run Baathist bigwigs setting up shop in rented safehouses in the western desert; there were homegrown demagogues like Moqtada al-Sadr setting up their own quasi-autonomous fiefdoms, all of them frantically plotting their next move. There were also battalions of profiteers, private security guards, hired guns from South Africa, Britain, America and Serbia, a host of Wild West entrepreneurs queuing up to get rich or die trying. It was little wonder, then, that there was a nervous edge to the laughter in the Shahbander café in those days after the invasion, because they already saw the shadows of bloody mayhem in their little henhouse joke.

TRANSLATOR WARS

Learning to Pity the US Proconsul

During the high summer of 2003, I held a very dim view of Paul Bremer. Every day Baghdad was sliding deeper into bedlam, but the US proconsul, lord of all he surveyed in his snappy dark suits and unfailingly glossy bouffant hair, was living in one of Saddam's palaces, cut off from the harsh reality around him. He seemed as obsessed with jogging round the Green Zone, with his sweating bodyguards in tow, as his boss was about pounding the treadmill back at the White House. As the country started to smoulder, he was a distant figure, aloof and imperious.

It was only after we moved into our own mini palace, and my modest crew of Iraqi staff began to grow, that I started to appreciate just how gargantuan was the task he faced. Trying to persuade Iraqis to get along and work together after decades of divisive dictatorship and mutual mistrust, and with an uncertain future looming, was a huge undertaking, even on the small scale of a newspaper's offices.

The Times had decided to move out of the hotel rooms we were living in and rent a house. Finding a house is rarely easy, but in a collapsed economy in a rudderless city, it proved an expensive and dicey business. Like almost every other foreign organization in Iraq, we had no idea just how bad things could get, both inside our offices and out. Within a few months, warring factions had developed among my staff, even though when dealing with me they always tried to come across as one big, happy family. There were almost unbelievable rumours of kidnap, but never anything you could prove, or necessarily even believe for that matter, yet neither something you could afford to ignore. And in less than a year we were forced, like the hapless Mr Bremer, to abruptly flee our mansion, leaving our staff to their own devices in a town growing more lethal by the day.

The place we rented was a merchant's mansion, built in the palatial, over-the-top style dubbed by some wag as neo-Babylonian for its combination of sandstone pillars, marble floors and fleeting resemblance to the halls of Belshazzar. After months of living in noisy, dingy hotels, it seemed to promise a haven of privacy and calm as well as an escape from the endless stream of overcooked burgers, kebabs and spaghetti that were the standard fare of Baghdad room service.

The imposing pile stood back from a quiet side street in Karada, the most moderate of Baghdad neighbourhoods. Here, a mixture of middle-class Shia and Christian shopkeepers and restaurateurs enjoyed a quiet, comfortable existence, even as the rest of the city sunk into hell.

Our new residence was a classic example of nouveau-riche gaudiness, built on a scale found in places where people do not trust banks and sink all their cash into property and jewels. A sweeping marble staircase with polished hardwood banisters split into two wings above the hallway, and was crowned with a huge, crudely executed oil painting of a slave-owner's mansion in the antebellum South, with a woman in a Scarlett O'Hara ball gown exchanging sweet nothings with her top-booted beau as a thoroughbred trotted behind them. The furniture and faucets were done in worn gilt, the cabinets ponderous cliffs of dark wood frowning out over seas of marble flooring. It was like moving into the set of a 1980s soap opera, a conspicuous display of wealth in a street where almost every other home was a mini, walled palace. But after a few months of in-habitation by a rotating group of journalists and photographers, it bore less of a resemblance to *Dallas* than to *The Young Ones*, only with armed guards.

It was our translator, Thair, who found the place. Thair was a man in his late thirties who had spent most of his adult life working for the Information Ministry. He looked every inch the Baath Party apparatchik: heavy Saddam moustache, a bureaucrat's paunch and the pompous air of one who has always lived in a tightly controlled environment, knowing all the petty rules that prevail and the whims of one's superiors. He was confident of being able to inveigle himself on the side of power every time. Apart from his name – Thair means

119

'Revolutionary' in Arabic, as he was fond of pointing out to new arrivals, even though it made him sound like a German in 1945 boasting about being called Horst or Hermann – you could tag him as a Baathist by the way he never referred to the now disbanded ruling party simply as the 'Baath Party', as everyone else did, but insisted on trotting out its full title by rote: the Baath Arab Socialist Party. Even the eternal thesis he said he was working on for his PhD screamed blunt-instrument Baathist indoctrination: his doctorate was on American imperialism as portrayed in the films of Arnold Schwarzenegger and Bruce Willis.

Even after the Information Ministry was gutted and the dictatorship swept away, Thair remained stranded in the habits of a minor functionary in a highly stratified regime: pointedly jovial with his superiors, bullying to his subordinates and always on the lookout for a way to squeeze an extra buck out of both. Until we twigged to his game, he would ask us to give him the drivers' salaries to be paid by himself – he would then skim off half and threaten to sack the drivers if they complained. Everybody was in fact on the make at the time: it was too ingrained into a society that had been poorly managed by kleptocrats for so long.

In the case of renting our house, the Thair tax was particularly steep: he overcharged the company by around 6,000 dollars. The drivers said he had done so because he was sure they would be too scared of him to tell us. In fact, they did squeal, but begged us not to let Thair know they had told us what they had heard. Without any evidence against him, and needing a place to stay, we decided to overlook their accusations and to cough up. That cost us heavily; for the US administration, the accumulated cost of corruption would soon be running to around four billion dollars a year.

More disturbingly, as our staff and offices grew, we made the strategic mistake of appointing Thair as office manager. We rapidly learned the first serious lesson of post-Saddam Iraq: titles were a licence to lord it up over your subordinates and, in the case of many government ministers, line your pockets as quickly as possible. Mr Bremer was to find this out all too soon after he appointed what he thought was a multi-sectarian transitional government, but which turned out to be one of the biggest kleptocracies in history. Having established himself in a position of relative power, Thair instantly became a tin-pot pasha who set about sqeezing out the undesirable elements from our staff, cornering power and influence for himself.

Thair's skill as a manipulator far outweighed his ability as a translator. He spoke what I called 'Buddhist English' – in his translations, everything happened in a continuous present tense. A typical translation would be, 'He say his father die in bombing two weeks ago,' usually with a little editorial addition like, 'Fucking Yankees, they have no civilization, they are a new country, we are old and have much culture. Five thousand years we are here, you know . . .' It was easy to screen out the obligatory anti-American rant, given that his country had been bombed so recklessly and so many times by the US military. But the Tarzan-speak could get you down after a long hard day working in the sun.

For all his faults, Thair was actually one of the better members of the old guard to make it into the ranks of the post-invasion media. One former head of the Information Ministry's press office, a man who in his glory days before the war would threaten to block visas for western female journalists unless they went out on sleazy dinner dates with him, came sniffing round the major press agencies looking for work soon after the fall of Baghdad. He was blocked by the outcry of several women who had known him in the bad old days. Thair at least had been known to bend the rules for foreign journalists when working for *The Times* during the war, and had taken personal risks to accompany western journalists and photographers during the fighting.

But a new power struggle was already under way, in our house as in all levels of Iraqi society. We needed more translators and drivers to accommodate the swelling number of people we had working on such a huge story. There were around a thousand foreign media personnel in the city just after the invasion, plus aid workers and hundreds of thousands of American troops speaking not a lick of Arabic. For those Iraqis who knew English, there was a small fortune to be made working as translators, drivers, office managers or guards. And of course in such uncertain times, everyone wanted to look out for their own family and friends first.

So it was that Thair – who as our senior translator was assigned to our Middle East editor, Stephen Farrell – was asked to find me a translator. He puffed up with importance on hearing of the solemn task and promised me he would have an excellent interpreter, an A-grade student of English, with me the very next morning.

True to his word, the next day I came downstairs to find a dead-ringer for Nick Nack, the deadly midget sidekick of Francisco Scaramanga in *The Man with the Golden Gun*, waiting for me. I half expected him to produce a poison-dart blowpipe, but he seemed keen enough to help. 'Seemed' being the operative word – he barely spoke enough English for me to hold even a rudimentary conversation with him.

We set off anyway in Yassir the driver's Toyota, Yassir – who had passable English – happily explaining what Nick Nack was trying to tell me. My doubts grew swiftly as we drove past the enormous outline of a mosque Saddam had been in the process of building. I already knew that Saddam had hoped this Stonehenge of bare concrete pillars and jagged rebar pointing heavenwards would one day be the biggest mosque in the world, a morsel of knowledge that eventually allowed me to make sense of what Nick Nack was trying to explain to me.

'This more big large world mosque-wich,' Nick Nack informed me with a proud smile on his face.

'Hmmm . . . really?' I muttered, trying not to burst out laughing. Mosque-wich? Like a sandwich? I was frantically wondering.

That day in June 2003, I was trying to put together a story on the fate of Saddam's palaces, now either occupied by US troops or smouldering, stinking husks that were being rapidly dismantled, pipe by pipe and tile by tile, by looters. I asked Nick Nack who we could talk to about the palaces. He frowned in concentration, then suggested we talk to his university professor.

'Does he know about the palaces?' I asked, vaguely recalling that Nick Nack had studied sciences.

'Yes,' he replied earnestly. 'He is Palestinian.'

It took me a moment to connect the phonetic misfiring of synapses going on inside Nick Nack's brain. Palestinian . . . Palace-tinian . . . more big large world mosque-wich . . . you're fired, I decided immediately.

It was only weeks later that I discovered Nick Nack's true identity. It was a sweltering afternoon, and as usual I was waiting for Thair to show up for work after his extended lunch break. This time he was so late I stormed round to his house and knocked at the door of his flat. To my surprise – though I should by now have guessed – Nick Nack answered. Foolishly, I asked him what he was doing there. 'I am Thair brother,' he said proudly, as Thair suddenly appeared in his siesta *dishdasheh* to swat the tiny figure back into the darkened apartment. He looked mildly put out for a second, but then recovered himself quickly, deftly apologizing for his tardiness when we both knew why I was really standing there tapping my feet.

Finding reliable staff was a hit-or-miss affair in a country where most official records had been torched, government structures eradicated and the majority of businesses closed. Mr Bremer brought in crowds of exiled Iraqi leaders, who were instantly resented by the population they had left behind to the tender mercies of Saddam's regime. They were widely derided as having come home 'on the back of an American tank'. Journalists, on the other hand, had to rely on recommendations from the contacts we happened to have when we showed up in the country. Donald Rumsfeld said that 'you go to war with the army you have, not the army you want'; we generally started work with the translators we stumbled on by chance.

The officially established ones came from the now defunct ministries, most of them workaday functionaries with little ideological slant except a reasonable concern that their comfortable world had just fallen apart.

The other type was the young people just starting out, who spoke good English through their university studies or through an addiction to western films or music, and were keen to engage in the future of their country. Ali Hamdani, who would become a close friend of mine during a series of near-death experiences, was a classic example of the latter.

We found Ali a few days after I arrived in Iraq, in the lobby of the Sheraton Hotel. The sun-filled lobby was a sort of Rick's Bar of Baghdad, where everyone met over coffee or chilled Cokes: occupation administrators, American army officers, journalists interviewing robed clerics, Iraqi exiles touting their expertise, homegrown wannabes pushing their new-born political parties, or ordinary Iraqis looking for jobs, often with crumpled slips of paper bearing a handwritten recommendation from a US army officer they had helped in the previous weeks – 'You can trust this man. Signed, Captain Smith,

3rd Infantry Division.' (I even met a taxi driver once who showed me a scrawled note from a US major authorizing him to deliver a rocket-propelled grenade launcher to the nearest police station.) All of them were mixing with hotel flunkies, chain-smoking drivers waiting for their bosses and sweating aid workers hurrying around in their multi-pocketed safari jackets, emblazoned with the logo of whatever over-burdened NGO they worked for.

We were sitting drinking Turkish coffees by the high windows. I had just joined *The Times*, and was telling my new colleagues, as well as Thair and Haidar, the skinny young driver who had come with Thair from the Information Ministry, that I needed my own driver and translator team. Haidar, who spoke English like a stroke victim, slurring and forgetting words and struggling to make himself understood, offered his brother Yassir as my driver. Yassir was a former veterinary who had worked as a cameraman for Reuters and spoke reasonable English. Pleased to have made himself so useful to us and to have found a job for his brother, Haidar rushed off to find me a translator. He came back twenty minutes later with a fresh-faced, rather chubby young man with short hair and a goatee beard. He introduced him as his friend Ali. It was only months later that I discovered the two had never actually met before, but Haidar wanted to show off that he knew everyone in town. In fact, he had just bumped into Ali as Ali was saying goodbye to a Korean medical NGO he had been translating for. Ali had found the work easy because he was almost a doctor himself – he had been about to graduate from medical school when the invasion shut down all the universities. That was good news for us, since doctors were at a premium as translators. Iraqi medical colleges taught in English and all doctors spoke the language extremely well. They also had great contacts inside the hospitals, which was useful given the violence stalking the city. It also didn't hurt to have someone next to you who could patch you up if you were shot.

In addition, Ali was a cheerful and bright 25-year-old who also happened to be a computer whiz and a black-belt in full-contact karate. As a bonus, he played the oud – the Arab lute – and sang. In short, he was a perfect Swiss Army knife of a fixer. I didn't know it at the time, but his tribe was also to prove a key advantage in his future work for us: the Hamdanis, originally from the Aleppo area of Syria, are half Sunni, half Shia, which would be invaluable as the city began to divide under the weight of ethnic cleansing.

But that was still a long way off as we sat in the Sheraton that morning drinking coffee.

To test his English, I got him chatting about his experience in the war. Like most Iraqis, Ali's story was a startling example of how the incredible could become the everyday. His father, also a renaissance mix of linguist, computer expert and martial artist, had died of a heart attack a couple of months before America unleashed its invasion force, leaving Ali as the man of the house, responsible for his mother and two elder sisters. He did all those things that seem normal for self-sufficient Iraqis accustomed to wars, but which sound so alien to a pampered westerner – he dug a well in his back garden in case the water supplies were cut, then evacuated his family to a house in Hit, a desert town on the Euphrates in what would soon be known as the Sunni Triangle. The people they stayed with in Hit (pronounced, appropriately, 'Heat') were full of fraternal compassion for the refugees from the capital and refused to accept money from them, although Ali's was quite a wealthy family. There they could have ridden out the invasion except for one seemingly banal detail – Ali's brother, who worked for an oil company in Libya, had a Rottweiler that guarded the family house. Among Muslims, dogs are considered dirty creatures – the Prophet, I was told by Iraqis, had been a cat person and had a kitty that sat on his shoulder and even drank from his cup. But he hadn't liked dogs, and ever since then Muslims have considered them unclean. There was no way to take a Rottweiler with them. Besides, it had to stay and guard the empty house from looters. But it also had to be fed, and any neighbours who might have helped out had likewise fled the area.

So it was that Ali commuted every couple of days from Hit to Baghdad, past straggling convoys of Iraqi army trucks being blown to pieces by American missiles, risking his life to feed a dog. He didn't even like the dog much, but he had to feed it to safeguard the home and keep his brother happy. He laughed about it as he recounted the tale that day in the Sheraton, but it must have been a terrifying trip for a young man still grieving the death of his beloved father and risking his own life to fill up a dog bowl.

* * *

Hiring a bright young spark like Ali made perfect sense. Unfortunately, it also put Thair on the defensive. Ali's English was far better, he was able to fix our frequent computer problems and he had no party baggage trailing behind him – he was exactly the sort of person Thair distrusted, the new generation of Iraqi who could get ahead on merit alone, rather than through any skill at office politics. Ali wasn't scared of Thair either – he didn't really need the money and was far more interested in completing his medical training once the universities reopened than swanning around with the media. He immediately rubbed Thair up the wrong way by insisting we pay him directly, thereby sidestepping the traditional 50 per cent salary grab that middle management in Iraq always expected as its due. Thair also suspected Ali of sniggering at him behind his back. He was right on that one, of course: what he didn't realize was that we were all secretly mocking his pomposity and nostalgia for the good old days. Little did we know how soon the whole country would be looking back on Saddam's times as a period of relative stability.

Meanwhile, as Mr Bremer put together his Iraqi Governing Council to give some fragile appearance of autonomy, our staff continued to expand: as well as Thair, who was lording it around the mansion as office manager, and Ali, who was already proving invaluable with his hospital connections and Sunni university friends signing up for the insurgency, we had our drivers, the two Shia brothers Yassir and Haidar who came from a rough part of west Baghdad. Yassir was the older of the two, in his early thirties. He had given up being a vet since he didn't like any animals except sheep, and done a variety of other jobs. A slim and handsome man, Yassir was friendly and generally quiet, except when another driver cut him up in the terrible traffic jams: then he would start barking at them in English and Arabic, sounding like a furious dog and making a hand gesture that to me looked like an imitation of a woodpecker but was apparently insulting enough to the recipient's mother to start a tribal blood feud. Yassir was also very religious, in an unobtrusive way. In one of the first conversations I had with him, he told me how he had met his wife: he had gone to pick up his sister from the school where she worked as a teacher and spotted an attractive woman in the staff room, reading a copy of the Koran. He found out her name from his sister, then went to her house and spoke with her father. The two men chatted about the Koran for a while until the father was satisfied that Yassir was a godfearing young man who knew the names and honorifics of the twelve Shia imams and had a steady income. Then he called down his daughter and introduced her to the man she would marry.

As he recounted the story, I was desperately hoping Yassir would not ask how Lulu and I had got together. I dreaded having to tell him how we were out dancing one night at a club in Jerusalem, got very drunk and slept together the same night. I knew he wouldn't say anything, but he was sure to disapprove. Perhaps suspecting such infidel unpleasantness, Yassir was too tactful to ever ask.

Haidar, his younger brother, was the wild one. A skinny 24-year-old, he had the looks of a Bollywood film star but the fashion sense of a Ukranian teenager circa 1982, with cheap jeans pulled up almost to his chest and greased-back hair. He saw himself as a wheeler-dealer, a man of the world, forever boasting of street scraps he had been involved in, and always ready to pull out a wad of photos of women he was seeing. Most of them were sulky-looking trolls whose faces were hidden by an impenetrable mask of foundation and rouge, but I always forced myself to nod and said something complimentary. One day this would-be Casanova of Baghdad sidled up to one of our British photographers, and whispered proudly that he had finally lost his virginity. The photographer was surprised, and asked him about all the women in the photos, who he said were his lovers. Haidar admitted rather dejectedly that in Iraq dating was a frustratingly chaste affair, and that unmarried women would not have sex with their boyfriends. Almost all the women in his collection of snapshots were single, and he had been lucky to get a kiss off them. He had finally lost his virginity to a married woman, thereby courting deadly retaliation from the cuckolded husband and his family. He laughed off the danger with the bravura of an eight-stone Errol Flynn.

'I get my first gun when I am eleven year,' he told me in his quirky English. 'I 'fraid no one. No one.'

We often had guests staying in the house – extra reporters and photographers sent on special assignments, or visiting editors – so we frequently had to draft in more translators and drivers. Thair wanted to control this process for obvious reasons. But after the Nick Nack incident, I was wary of his choices. I asked Ali if he knew any more doctors willing to work with us, and he volunteered his brother-in-law, a practising anaesthetist called Mohanned. A friendly, no-nonsense father of one, Mohanned quickly became a regular, and as the situation deteriorated would bring back horrifying tales from the grim operating theatres of Baghdad's over-stretched hospitals. Once, after a particularly large suicide bombing, he ran out of IV bags – always a scarce commodity in Iraq – and knew that his assistant had thrown one away before it was completely empty. He reached in the bin to fish it out but instead came upon a severed hand that the surgeon had lobbed in there as he performed amputations on a production-line of patients. Peering inside, he realized the bin was an unlucky dip of severed human limbs.

Mohanned was a religious man, and would teach me about Islam's history and traditions as we drove around on assignments. Passing through the Shia town of Kufa one day, Mohanned told me about the first leaders after Mohammed, and how they squabbled over the succession – those who believed the Prophet's close companions should be the new leaders went on to become the Sunnis. Those who favoured a bloodline succession became the Shia. The two lines met briefly in Imam Ali, the Prophet's cousin who married his daughter Fatima, thus becoming his son-in-law. The two sides might have been harmonized, but for rumbling internal disputes which ended in Imam Ali's sudden demise.

'How did Imam Ali die?' I asked Mohanned as we crossed the palm-lipped Euphrates River on the edge of Kufa, where water buffaloes wallowed in the brown water.

'He was murdered by the Parisians,' Mohanned told me.

'What? Parisians killed him?' I gasped in disbelief.

'Yes, Parisians. You know,' Mohanned explained, 'from Persia.'

'Oh, Persians,' I laughed. 'God, I know the French have got a bad reputation, but that would take the biscuit.'

Like many devout Sunnis, Mohanned was rather disdainful of the Shia, and this could lead to spats with the drivers, both of them Shia. One day as we drove through Baghdad, Haidar was showing me yet another picture of a new love. I dutifully commented on her stunning beauty, and Haidar tucked the picture of the girl – who looked like Genghis Khan with lipstick – inside the Koran he kept on the dashboard, for safekeeping. This provoked a horrified rebuke from Mohanned, who told him it was blasphemous to desecrate the holy book with a photograph. Especially a photo of an adulteress, he might have added, but didn't. They spent the rest of the trip bickering in Arabic and English about whether Haidar was about to incur some kind of divine punishment. I figured that living in Baghdad was probably punishment enough.

Thair was not at all happy with Mohanned's hiring. He warned us that Ali wanted to fill the office with his own relatives, and would eventually try to drive him out. In retaliation, Thair tried to bring in more of his own people. That was how we found Saleh, an extremely mild and obliging man in his mid-forties who had worked in the Information Ministry's foreign newsgathering service. This meant, in effect, that he had watched CNN day in, day out, and told his superiors what was going on in the world from the American broadcaster's news bulletins. Like every other Iraqi, he had his share of chilling war stories.

During the first Gulf War, this quiet, unassuming Sunni had been in the military, teaching English classes at a naval academy in Basra. As US forces blasted the Iraqi army out of Kuwait, a Shia uprising swept the south, and Saleh decided that being a military man and Sunni in Basra was not a recipe for a long life. So he jumped on a train to Baghdad and was heading through the vast southern marshes – which would later be drained by Saddam to flush out the Shia rebels – when the train lurched to a halt. He heard shots outside, then a conductor came through the carriages and spotted Saleh sitting there in his uniform. The man told Saleh the train had been hijacked by rebellious Marsh Arabs who were going through the carriages killing Baathists and dragging off the women. He gave Saleh an engineer's overalls and told him to throw his uniform out of the window. That was how Saleh survived the 1991 intifada.

So it was that factions started to form in the house: at first it was Thair and a reluctant Saleh against Ali and Mohanned. Because the easiest way to hire staff was through people already on the payroll, the lines were further reinforced as we built our household staff. Thair found our two security guards – Ahmed, a stocky, energetic man who had been in the Republican Guard, and Ammar, a dreamy, slightly goofy ex-soldier with thinning hair who usually pulled the night shift, sitting in the kitchen with his Kalashnikov on the table and reading Plato in Arabic. He said he had been in the special forces, which I found it hard to believe at first – but then I reflected on Iraq's recent battlefield track record and figured maybe he was telling the truth. On the other hand, Ali hired our cleaner Ala, a bright kid of around twenty who kept the place spotless, although he couldn't read the washing instructions on our clothing labels and anything woollen ended up with orangutan sleeves. These battle lines would prove vital in the coming strife.

By the first Christmas after the invasion, the house was thriving, filled with an ever-changing cast of regular reporters, freelance writers and itinerant photographers, as well as our local Iraqi staff. We would throw frequent parties for friends and contacts in the Iraqi political parties and the occupation administration. Whenever we had a party, the street outside would fill with a motley selection of security guards, who had escorted our guests across town: Kurdish Peshmerga guerrillas in combat gear and webbing, toting Russian AK47s, would stand mutely next to British ex-special forces or South African mercenaries, jealously eyeing their brand-new MP5 sub-machine guns. Inside, coalition veterans already jaded by eight months in country would get drunk and bitch about the incompetence of other departments, while bright-eyed newcomers who had left their homes and their families to live in a sweltering Portakabin in order to build a new, democratic Iraq waxed enthusiastic about the bright future for the Middle East. If Thair was there, he would be earnestly advising perturbed officials that what was needed was the mass public executions of 'Ali Babas'.

'Hang a thousand of them from lampposts. That will bring order,' he would announce. They would laugh nervously, then look miserable as they saw he was not joking. It was a depressingly common view among Iraq's middle classes at the time – the local equivalent of Britain's 'short, sharp shock' prison sentences.

There was a good deal of socializing in Baghdad in the months before the roads became too dangerous and the bombers started to mobilize the hordes of Iraqis who had been disenfranchised by Mr Bremer's decisions to dissolve the army and sack all senior Baath Party officials. A couple of months after the invasion, I was invited to a surreal party in honour of the outgoing British envoy.

It took place at the old British embassy on Haifa Street, a handsome Ottoman mansion looking out over the sluggish waters of the Tigris. On the dusty pages of the visitors' book, soldiers from the Parachute Regiment had scribbled their names, the first to be inscribed since the embassy closed twelve years before, on the eve of the 1991 Gulf War. The compound, once the haunt of Gertrude Bell and T. E. Lawrence, was rather shabby, all balding lawns and peeling paint, and the staff worked out of three 'flat-pack' container offices erected on the old cricket pitch. Outside, there was always a group of Iraqi boys practising their English and unwittingly picking up whatever regional accent – Scottish, Geordie, Gurkha – the guardsmen on duty happened to have.

Haifa Street must have been very elegant once. Some of the handsome brick Ottoman houses still stood opposite the embassy. Most had been swept aside by high-rise concrete apartment blocks, where Saddam housed Palestinian refugees that Iraq had taken in. Between these towers, you could still wander along twisting lanes of crumbling mud-brick houses, a vestige of long-gone colonial Baghdad. But even by the time of the barbecue I attended at the British embassy one baking July evening, Haifa Street was already a place people avoided after dusk. Although it was only a few blocks from the Green Zone, criminal gangs were operating from the rotting netherworld overlooked by the 1970s tower blocks. Guerrillas were already moving in.

At the time, though, none of this seemed to bother the British embassy staff, as hardy and eccentric a bunch of diplomats as you could want to spend an evening drinking warm beer with. We stood in the gardens, sipping from our cans and eating burgers grilled to black carbon by an army squaddie. Christopher Segar, the head of mission, clad in baggy shorts from which two skinny white legs protruded, hopped bird-like from one foot to the other as he enthusiastically explained the cultural differences between northern tribes none of us had ever heard of. As he lectured us, a volley of pink tracer fire arced over our heads and across the river. Nobody flinched. One of the staffers, a grey-bearded man clutching an inedible hunk of meat, looked over his shoulder at Haifa Street.

'Oh that's just Ahmed. He's got a new gun, I think. He often test fires his weapons at night. I think there's some kind of turf war going on with a gang across the river. They won't bother us.' Everyone laughed and carried on eating and drinking, although the gunmen in the tower blocks were only a few hundred yards away, and could easily have strafed our jolly little party. I felt I had wandered into a remake of *Carry On up the Khyber*. A few months later, 'Ahmed' and his friends had become so violent that Haifa Street was a virtual no-go area where American and Iraqi troops battled almost daily with al-Qaeda-backed guerrillas, forcing the Brits into the relative shelter of the Green Zone. A few hundred yards from where we had our barbecue, three Iraqi election officials were dragged from their car and executed in the middle of the road in broad daylight by Sunni gunmen in early 2005.

For all its strangeness, our house was actually becoming quite homely. For Christmas, our Iraqi staff brought us a bizarre array of presents which were both touching and trashy: a plastic cigarette lighter shaped like a sailing ship, a bottle of Brut aftershave and a cheap watch that broke the same day. Ala, the friendly young cleaner, gave us a lurid rug with a portrait of Jesus, assuming that since we were westerners we would appreciate a picture of the Lord. We hung it on the wall next to a Shia flail I had bought in Najaf, the type used by processions of black-garbed men to flagellate themselves on holy days. We decided that with Christian and Shia symbols hanging on the wall, we needed to find something distinctively Sunni too. As Sunnis are strictly against icons, it was a tricky problem. But one day Richard Beeston, the visiting diplomatic editor, came home with a plastic toy AK47. We immediately hung it on the wall. The set was complete.

Christmas was the last time that Iraqis would enjoy such freedom of movement and careless partying. In their walled palaces, Mr Bremer and the generals had signally failed to identify the alarming rise of extremist factions, both Sunni and Shia, and the dream of a democratic Iraq was already ripping apart at the seams. The bombings had started to come thick and fast, although the nature of the violence still appeared random enough to allow us an illusory sense of security. Like frogs in slowly heating water, we were becoming inured to the horror. One morning we sped off to the scene of a truck bombing in Baya, a poor Shia area in the east of the city. A suicide bomber had tried to ram a petrol tanker filled with explosives into the district's heavily fortified police station. Hundreds of yards from his target, the kamikaze driver had accidentally collided with a minibus full of early morning commuters, triggering an explosion that ripped him and the passengers to pieces. Twisted wreckage littered the street as firemen doused the flaming carcass of the tanker with their hoses. All that remained of the passengers were tiny jelly-like scraps of human flesh rolled in dust. It looked disturbingly like Turkish delight. A few hours earlier, the jelly had been people with all their hopes, families and daily woes. A crowd gathered to view the carnage, some of them desperately asking if their own relatives had been among the victims. After about half an hour, we got back in the car and headed home.

But as we were driving through Karrada, we spotted a shop selling festive decorations. 'Yassir!' I shouted. 'Stop the car! We're going to buy a Christmas tree.' As we selected a small fir tree, it suddenly struck us what we were doing, Christmas shopping so soon after scraping dead commuters off our boots. But we bought the tree anyway. There was no point in not buying it.

As the rate of bombings and shootings increased, and the range of targets spread, we were forced to start securing ourselves. We already had guards as a precaution against the gangs of robbers roaming the city. One day our landlord's son, a hugely fat young man in a white *dishdasheh* and *yeshmak*, came bustling into the house with a tale that his father's shop had been raided by a gang of armed robbers. Incredibly, the father, who was even more obese than his son, had managed to escape. Now he wanted me to go to Paul Bremer and demand some action to safeguard his shop. I tried to explain that Bremer was rather busy running the country, far too busy to intervene in the individual travails of petitioners. But Saddam had practised the strongman method of governance, granting occasional audiences to plaintiffs begging for personal favours. It was a way of playing God, showing your absolute power to change a life, while simultaneously grooming loyalty at the grass-roots level. I told the landlord's son that things had changed now, that he should go to the police instead. But even as I said it, I knew it was pointless. Instead of coming under the rule of law, as the Americans had hoped, Baghdad was already succumbing to a new rule: every man for himself.

On New Year's Eve 2003, some friends at the BBC office held a party in their house on a closed-off street near the Palestine hotel compound. Lulu had been working all day at the Associated Press offices in the Palestine Hotel, and in the evening Yassir drove me over to pick her up before heading to the festivities. Just as she was getting in the car, a huge explosion echoed across the city. Behind me I saw a giant orange fireball, marbled with black smoke, rising into the night sky. Yassir spun the car round and we sped towards the bombsite, trying to work out what had been hit. There was mayhem in streets already crowded with revellers lobbing fire-crackers around, singing and chanting as they hung out the windows of their cars. Police vehicles, American Humvees and fire engines were forcing their way through the throng, and we navigated a path behind an emergency response vehicle until the road ahead was blocked by US soldiers near Arasat Street. Arasat Street was Baghdad's extremely cut-price answer to Soho, with restaurants still serving Lebanese wine and Basra shrimp. We jumped out of the car and ran down the street. American soldiers shouted warnings that the petrol tanks of burning cars were about to blow, that there could be more car bombs at the scene. But no one paid much heed, trying to get as close to the bombsite as possible and find out what had happened. When we managed to squeeze our way through, we saw what had been blown up: it was Nabil's restaurant, one of the swankiest eateries in Baghdad. In better days, just a few months before, it had been the haunt of UN officials, journalists and any coalition officials senior enough to have a private security detail that would enable them to leave the Green Zone. It was half collapsed in on itself now. American soldiers and Iraqi firefighters were milling around debris-strewn tables, trying to pull diners out of the rubble. One table had survived the huge blast intact, although the diners were gone: their knives and forks were still on their plates, while at the centre of the table there were dust-coated dishes of baba ganouj, hummus and lamb clustered round a bottle of Wild Turkey, in pristine condition but for the missing neck, smashed off just below the cap. In the flickering flames and flashing lights, soldiers gathered on either side of a prostrate woman half-buried in the debris. The scene resembled an infernal Nativity scene, a Book of Revelations tableau for dinnertime purveyors of democracy and modernity. Several western journalists had been eating there, one of whom lost an eye, but all the dead came from a house next door, where an Iraqi family had been sitting down to their New Year's dinner together. Their house had taken the brunt of the blast, crumbling to powder as the car bomb erupted in the street outside.

We stayed among the ruins until midnight, seeing in the New Year without even noticing its arrival. Then we went back to the office and filed the story before heading over to the BBC house to dance wildly till dawn, alive with the energy of simply being alive.

Several nights after the bombing, I woke up late one night with a jolt. Screeching tyres in the street outside had ripped me from my sleep. I had been thinking about how to protect our vulnerable house for weeks, but had been too busy working to actually do anything about it. As I shot bolt upright in bed, I cursed my stupidity: this is it, you waited too long, idiot! But it was just a careless driver, perhaps speeding to avoid the Ali Babas who prowled the city after curfew. The walls did not cave in on me and I lapsed back into a restless sleep. The very next day I ordered the house to be sandbagged and sheets of transparent plastic blast screens to be put up on all the windows to avoid splinters lacerating us during an explosion.

I told the guards to put the sandbags against the inside of the garden wall. Putting them up on the outside would have shown the world that we thought we were a potential target, which would have made us a de facto object of interest to the bombers. No one knew for sure why they had bombed Nabil's, but there were several obvious hypotheses – it was a place frequented by foreigners, it sold booze and it was what was known as a 'soft target'.

Our landlord had also given us two guard dogs to help protect us and his property shortly after we moved in. This had presented something of a cultural problem. The dogs were Doberman Pinscher pups, skinny little creatures with big ears, barely a few weeks old, the progeny of the terrifying hound of Satan that guarded the landlord's own house down the street. When Lulu and I saw them, we instantly thought they were incredibly cute pets, and allowed them into the house. This led to constant friction with the guards, who thought that these dirty, un-Islamic creatures could only be kept in a *halal* household if they served a strict purpose, like guarding the house. Consequently Ahmed, the former Republican Guard soldier who looked like a stocky prize-fighter, would lock them up in a small concrete alley at the side of the house whenever we were away, where they ate stale bread, lived in their own shit and barked if anyone came near them. Whenever we were there, they would have the run of the house and eat dog food we bought from a grocer's shop. Ticking Ahmed off was treading a fine line: you didn't want to piss off the people who were protecting you. But we ordered him to treat the dogs better, and he grudgingly did so. All the other staff hated the dogs too, and we could not rely on them to tell us what went on when we were away. So the dogs grew up schizophrenically, at times cosseted pets, at others caged beasts.

The upside of the Iraqis' dislike of dogs was that most seemed to be very scared of them. As the gangly puppies grew into burly guard dogs, we felt sure no one but the most determined attacker was coming through the gates.

The house seemed more secure against attacks, but inside the tensions were growing deeper. Intractable feuds would break out over something as trivial as road directions. Ali and Yassir fell out viciously over which road was the best way back from the south: the quick dash up the highway – with the ever-present risk of bandits robbing us – or the slower route through the various towns. Yassir, who stood to lose his car if we were held up, advised the latter, and we spent long hours stuck in an interminable traffic jam in Hillah, feeling just as exposed as if we'd been out on the freeway. They argued incessantly about it, with Yassir insisting that as the driver, he was in charge of security too. Ali insisted that he had a better sense of direction and had travelled more. I had to step in and tell them they should discuss the merits of each trip and I'd decide. But I hadn't realized that this was about more than just knowledge of road conditions – it boiled down to the pride of two Iraqi men, and which one could do his duty the best. It was almost existential. Yassir held his head up, too furious to look me in the eye as I told him to cooperate with Ali, while Ali threatened that he could not work with such obstinate people and was going to quit.

At the same time, Ali and Haidar had a huge bust-up. According to Ali, Haidar had decided that as the longest-serving member of the newspaper's staff – he had worked with us since the fall of the regime – he was entitled to order everyone else around, including Ali. Ali ignored him, which infuriated Haidar. Then one day Ali's car keys vanished. He had probably lost them, but in the light of the dispute with Haidar, he said they had been stolen as part of a harassment campaign to drive him out of the office. One day, I heard them shouting at

145

each other in the television room while I was working next door in the office. They were screaming insults at each other in Arabic, but oddly enough switched to English as I arrived. They were about to come to blows so I stepped between them, wondering if it was such a good idea putting myself in the middle of a black-belt at full-contact karate and a street fighter who was always boasting about his scraps. They shouted at each other, calling each other liars and otherwise impugning the other's integrity until I shouted at them both to just shut up. They did, but the tensions simmered on.

Thair was getting more and more complacent, even as his ability to do the job declined. The days of simply interviewing victims of bombings were gone – he was having to translate complicated issues such as the drafting of a constitution or legal matters, and his English was not up to it. He became irritable and increasingly garbled, often leaving me confused as to what the interviewee was trying to say. Yet none of this seemed to ruffle his sense of self-importance. When I was appointed bureau chief, he smugly, but foolishly, confided to one of the other correspondents, 'Ah, James, he will do whatever I tell him to.' The correspondent told me what he had said: my patience with him had by then worn out, and since I was now the sole correspondent, I decided I only needed one translator. The obvious choice was Ali. So we gave Thair his marching orders, and he eventually left, although not after a sad, begging speech to me which began, 'James, we are like brothers . . .'

It was only later, after things had died down inside

the house, that I discovered what dramas really had been going on behind the scenes. It was like *Upstairs Downstairs*, Iraqi-style, and came out quite by chance, while I was sitting in a sheikh's antechamber in Karbala with Ali, waiting for an interview. Killing time over the obligatory cup of sugary tea, Ali told me what he had heard from Ala, the cleaner. One of the other members of staff – whom I shall not name – had apparently been sitting in the kitchen, plotting with another employee about how to get rid of Ali. Ala had been cleaning the floor and listened to the two of them discussing hiring a gang of thugs to waylay Ali as he drove to work. They would steal his car, maybe even have Ali kidnapped. But then Ala stepped up to the plotters and told them that if they went ahead with their plan, they would have to reckon with him and his tribe. Apparently he came from a pretty big tribe, as his warning was enough to stop them in their tracks.

Again, it was impossible to know whether all this was true. It was the account of the cleaner, who spoke no English, relayed to me by Ali, the victim.

'What do we do about this?' I asked Ali.

'Nothing,' he said: taking action would incur the risk of tribal retribution against either him or me, in a city where there was no functioning police force.

I knew other journalists were having similar problems. An English colleague of mine had unwittingly allowed his driver to recruit two of the neighbourhood's worst criminals to be his guards. The two men did nothing except sleep in front of the television, and the journalist was too afraid to sack them in case they killed him. The driver used all sorts of tricks to manipulate the poor correspondent, even telling his neighbours that since he didn't work on Saturdays – he worked for a daily, and had no paper to write for on Sunday – he was Jewish. He then told the reporter the neighbours thought he was a Jewish spy, and should rely on him for protection.

The driver was also threatening any translator who got too close to the journalist, so he could never keep an interpreter, no matter how much he liked them. Eventually one of the translators plucked up the courage to tell him what was going on, so the correspondent sacked the driver. The driver told his tribal leader about the insult, and a blood feud was started. At one point, the translator had to hide in a kitchen cabinet when an armed gang from the driver's notoriously tough tribe arrived to kill him. In retaliation, he kidnapped the former driver and held him until a fragile truce was arranged. That was Baghdad's labour law.

We promoted Ala from cleaner to guard. His brother Mohammed became our cleaner, as well as doing guard duties. They both liked dogs, too, and for a while all seemed well: the staff were happy, we had rooted out the troublemakers in our midst, and the dogs were free to run around the garden.

But it didn't last. One morning in March of 2004, Mohammed the guard/cleaner came up to me in the kitchen and told me that the previous night, while we were having a dinner party inside the house, a car with four men had pulled up outside the gates. One of them had called out to him, 'You'd better be really careful soon,' and then the vehicle sped off before he had time to fetch his gun from the porch.

Given the wave of kidnappings sweeping the city, it seemed a fairly clear warning. Things were already extremely tense: one morning several weeks earlier, as I was interviewing a priest who was worried about American evangelists coming to Baghdad to steal away his flock of Chaldean Christians, I received a hysterical call from Lulu.

'Thank god you're OK,' she half sobbed. Apparently someone had come into her office at the Palestine Hotel and told her I'd been murdered, together with Ali. In fact, an Iraqi translator for *Time* magazine had been shot dead that morning, and on the scrambled grapevine of Baghdad raw news, the rumour was spreading that *The Times* journalist had been killed. It was unnerving to have your death reported to you, though: I quickly wound up the interview and scuttled back home.

But it is a tough decision to leave your home at the drop of a hat, especially if the threat is not explicit. Lulu and I were discussing whether we should leave when Ali came in. He had been talking to Mohammed, who had told them that in fact the same thing had happened a week before, too, only he had not wanted to tell us. He was afraid we would leave and they would all lose their jobs. Which is exactly what happened. We decided to leave the house immediately. It was a heart-wrenching moment though – we had to give the three guards a month's notice, say goodbye to the dogs and move back into the grim compound of the Palestine Hotel. The guards understood, and we said our sad farewells. We gave the keys back to the landlord. A few hours later, like refugees, we were wheeling a barrow with all our possessions – clothes, duvets, computers, helmets and flak jackets – through the winding barbed-wire check-points of the Palestine. Lulu was crying. That night, as if to add to our general misery, a mortar was fired at the hotel. It missed narrowly, but we shot out of bed as the explosion shook the building, leaping for cover in the bathroom.

'Jesus Christ,' I shouted out of the window. 'You've driven us out of our house. Can't you leave us alone even in this shitty hotel?' And we both started laughing, sheltering in the darkness of our hotel bathroom.

Whoever it was that drove us out of our house, we would ultimately have to thank them. Within a few weeks the whole country was in rebellion, and everyone we knew left their houses to move back into the fortified hotel compounds. Several of those who ignored the warning signs paid for it with their lives.

Months later, I was driving through the old neigh-bourhood and told Yassir to stop by the house. The dogs were still there, huge and feral and locked up in the alley beside the house. They had become everything Ahmed wanted them to be, ferocious, frightening and unloved. They barked when I approached the gate, and that is when Ahmed himself came to see who was there. He seemed pleased to see me and invited us in to look around. The place was a mess, being renovated and divided into separate offices to maximize the landlord's profits. He still seemed to think that the violence would be over in a few months, and was planning for the good times on the other side of the gathering storm. I have no idea whether it eventually engulfed him, or whether he managed to get out in time.

And in June 2004, a few days before the American occupation authority was due to return sovereignty to a hand-picked Iraqi government, I was invited to a very hush-hush meeting deep in the Green Zone. Far behind the razor wire and the soaring concrete blast walls, a few of us crowded into a small room where, to our surprise, we witnessed a rushed ceremony: Mr Bremer signed a document and handed it over to Iyad Allawi, the new Iraqi prime minister. It lasted barely fifteen minutes, but when it was over Iraq was once again, nominally, a sovereign nation. The procedure had been held prematurely and in secret to avoid any rocket attacks that might disrupt it, even here in the relative safety of the Green Zone. Immediately after signing away his authority, Bremer dashed to Baghdad airport and un-ceremoniously leapt on a plane, never to return.

IN BABYLON'S HALLS

Tourism under Fire

See how its ramparts gleam like copper in the sun.
Climb the stone staircase, more ancient than the mind
   can imagine,
approach the Eanna Temple, sacred to Ishtar,
a temple that no king has equalled in size or beauty,
walk on the wall of Uruk, follow its course
around the city, inspect its mighty foundations,
examine its brickwork, how masterfully it is built,
observe the land it encloses: the palm trees, the gardens,
the orchards, the glorious palaces and temples,
   the shops
and marketplaces, the houses, the public squares.

The Epic of Gilgamesh

Iraq is, as Iraqis will never tire of telling visitors, the birthplace of civilization. It was here that wild animals were first domesticated, and writing subsequently invented to keep tabs on which goats belonged to whom. But it was also the birthplace of many of civilization's woes. Living in war-torn Baghdad, it was easy to imagine that the first clay tablet written in spiky hieroglyphs in fact spelled out a death threat, telling some hapless Akkadian family they had two days to leave Nippur or be killed.

If the echoes of Mesopotamia's long abandoned gods have reverberated down history to fashion our present-day holy warriors, the more material seeds of the Iraq war were also sown in those long-ago civilizations scratching out their tallies of wheat, goats and chickens on the wet, alluvial plains of the Tigris.

Animals were first domesticated around 10,000 years ago in the Zagros mountains, in the north of modern Iraq. That was the first step taken by mankind away from the time-honoured practices of hunter-gathering tribes to become property-owning farmers. The Mesopotamian climate was milder and wetter back then. Today's inhospitable stretches of desert were then green pasturelands, perfect for hunting or herding. It is telling that the ancient Semitic name for these rolling green lands was *eden*: it may well have been paradise for the small family groups roaming the area, with few natural predators and plentiful food. Telling also that in the Bible, the punishment of Adam and Eve for stealing the fruit from the tree of knowledge was banishment from the pastoral Garden of Eden and a lifetime of toiling the land. Was this an allegory for the discovery of the technology that shackled man to the unending grind of agriculture, lured away from the freewheeling life of the hunter-gatherer society?

Down in the valleys of the south, these bands of

nomads found that the clumps of wheat growing along the flood plains of the great rivers were easily harvested bundles of carbohydrates, vast reserves of energy waiting to be gathered. The first fields may have grown from stashes that the nomads buried for safe-keeping, then found sprouting into new reserves when their wanderings brought them back to the same spot months later.

In Baghdad, a battered copy of the *New Yorker* magazine reached our house in autumn of 2003, crumpled and leafed through by half a dozen different journalists before us. In it was an article by Richard Manning, entitled 'The Oil We Eat'. For me, it was a real revelation.

Manning explained that while most plants concentrate their energy in putting down deep roots and coexisting with other species to create a rich and sheltered environment as a survival tactic, wheat gambles on concentrating all its resources into fat bundles of energy, or grain, and thriving briefly in homogenous clumps on land cleared by natural catastrophes, such as flooding. Its long-lasting seeds are then carried to other areas cleared by nature's catastrophes and spread there. Agriculture – clearing the land of competing species, cutting down the crop every year – is an artificial recreation of these natural catastrophes that favours man's preferred plant. The same would happen with other crops: rice gave birth to the vast civilizations of Asia and corn fuelled the rise of Meso-American cities.

As agriculture grew in scale, it required more

organization to build and maintain irrigation systems, bring in harvests and defend the yield against the marauders still roaming the prairies beyond the new farming settlements. Storing food also led to a concentration of power: the most powerful members of the primitive societies controlled access, ensuring their descendants were stronger and healthier. Personal wealth had been created for the first time in history, and with it hierarchies – those wretches who toiled in the fields day in, day out, those who accounted for the harvests, the priests and scribes, those who processed the reaped goods, such as bakers and tanners, and those who had kicked and fought their way to the top of the pile, the early kings. Scientific examination of skeletal remains from those earlier settlements shows that for the average farmer, the new lifestyle was actually worse for the health than the age-old gamble of hunting and gathering. But it was too late to go back – the first palaces and temples were already emerging, priests were reinforcing set views of the universe and its hierarchies, and the people toiling in the fields were paving the way for countless generations whose labour has benefited others far more than themselves. This was the dawn of civilization that Iraqis love to boast about, the famous Fertile Crescent we all learn of in history classes.

The new ability to raise and store food, and no longer be at the whim of wild animals' migration habits, allowed populations to grow. Out of the vulnerable hamlets of mud hovels and reed huts, whose exact replicas are still scattered across southern Iraq to this day, grew the first cities: Uruk, Larsa, Ur, Girsu, Lagash,

Eridu, places so old their names do not even register on our consciousness today.

They were constantly at war with one another. Larger populations enabled leaders to raise bands of warriors, and eventually armies, to attack their neighbours, and steal their transferable riches too. While they fought their petty wars over the millennia for supremacy over this or that stretch of the Tigris or Euphrates, the new technology sped ahead of them. The knowledge of early agriculture broke through the chain of the Zagros mountains in the north and burst out upon the fertile European plain. The genie was out of the bottle, and nothing could stop the agricultural revolution. Within just three hundred years, the farmer-settlers had conquered the whole of western Europe, killing and displacing the Cro-Magnon hunter-gatherers who had roamed the wilderness before them since time immemorial. Anthropologists believe only one pocket survived in the mountainous reaches of northern Spain, and that they are the forebears of the modern-day Basque people.

On these fertile plains, stretching from France to the Urals, the population of Europe would swell massively over the coming centuries, tempered by bouts of famine, disease or the wars between peoples competing for the vast wealth of so many toiling peasants. When Europe discovered the New World, the explosion started all over again. As the world became a global community, the rampant wheat empire mixed with the corn and rice societies to produce the vast monocultures that now dominate global agriculture.

Eventually, however, the amount of cultivable land ran out, and dust bowls and depressions were the result of intensive over-farming. That is until agriculture was once again revolutionized by new technology: in the twentieth century, nitrogen-based fertilizers, tractors and combine harvesters massively increased yield once again, but at the cost of turning agriculture into an industry. The new technologies all had one thing in common, too: they required vast quantities of oil to keep going. When the columns of American soldiers rolled into Baghdad in April 2003, they were in effect closing a circle of expansion that had started 10,000 years before. The struggles of Ur and Eridu had returned to Mesopotamia, a kind of historical karma in the imposing shape of Abrams tanks and Bradley fighting vehicles. So it would make me laugh when my Iraqi friends would look at the US soldiers sweating in the streets and sneer, 'These Yankees have no civilization. They've only been around a few hundred years, while we've been here for five thousand.' And I'd tell them the American soldiers were simply surfing the crest of a wave that started here, in Iraq, all that time ago.

The fresh-faced American soldiers were sniggering at the bricks of Babylon when I first visited that ruined city in June 2003. They weren't amused by the ancient bricks bearing the inscription of Nebuchadnezzar, one of the world's first emperors, who embroidered his glittering city on the Euphrates and boasted in cuneiform etched into the palace walls of his triumphs and conquests. No, they were amused by the Arabic inscriptions in the more recent bricks built into the restored walls that Saddam Hussein had erected on the sagging foundations: the glazed words, dating back only to 1987, bragged, 'This was built by Saddam Hussein, son of Nebuchadnezzar, to glorify Iraq'. Other bricks bore Saddam's invocation of Allah to protect his realm from the infidel invaders who now stood around, loose-limbed warriors turned camera-toting tourists. That's why these tanned kids, looking like extras from a Norman Rockwell painting, got such a kick out of the etched lines: it was they, and no one else, who had toppled the tyrant who had hitched his name to this eternal city.

Our tour guide that blazing day was also a military man, a sprightly middle-aged navy chaplain whose divinity studies had kitted him out with all the Biblical legends needed to accompany his walks around Babylon's halls and wide boulevards. At the blue-glazed Ishtar Gate, the traditional entrance to the inner city, where a looted souvenir shop stood empty, Lieutenant Commander Thomas Webber greeted his groups of thirty or so off-duty conquerors – soldiers and marines, grunts and pogues – while a toothless Iraqi guide gazed on in disdain, trying occasionally to sideline one of the soldiers and lure him off on a private tour. With only a few words of pidgin English, his attempts were inevitably brushed aside.

'This is probably one of the most conquered cities in the world,' Webber explained, apparently without any sense of irony, as he launched into his historical explanation to the youthful conquerors. He led his charges – thrilled to have survived their own once-in-a-lifetime adventure into the history books, and relieved just to have a day off from the dull post-conquest routine of traffic policing and kit maintenance – through the triumphal procession routes, past the wall carvings of the god Marduk, a taxidermist's practical joke made up of a dragon's head, snake's tail with scorpion stinger, the front paws of a lion and the hind legs those of an eagle. The soldiers, who all touted digital cameras, snapped their way through the ruins, past bat-fringed storage cellars and the desiccated Hanging Gardens – once a terraced palace of lush trees and flowers irrigated by flowing streams pumped from the Euphrates, one of the original wonders of the world – and round the crumbling statue of the Lion of Babylon, just like any normal tourists, except in desert fatigues. It was a topsy-turvy world, where the invading army left the traditional looting of the realm to the locals, and instead took time to do the sights, like Florida tourists visiting Machu Picchu.

Webber led his group into a vast room, his voice echoing off the soaring brick walls as the soldiers gravitated towards the pools of blue shade. The place was believed to have been the banqueting hall where Daniel – he of the Biblical lion's den – had been summoned by the drunken king Belshazzar in 539 BC. The king was white with fright – during a bacchanal with his court, he had used sacred Jewish ceremonial bowls as wine goblets, prompting a disembodied hand to emerge from the wall and write a message in a strange language. Belshazzar sent for Daniel, by now a wise old advisor taken from Jerusalem as a teenage hostage when Nebuchadnezzar conquered the Judean capital thirty years before. A renowned interpreter of dreams, Daniel had no trouble deciphering the script since it was in his native tongue, Hebrew.

'You have been weighed in the balance and found wanting,' the ghostly hand informed Belshazzar. According to the legend, the king was killed that same night by his sons and invading Persians swarmed into his kingdom, ending the Babylonian empire.

Webber's audience oohed and aahed and laughed at poor dumb Belshazzar and his hapless boozing buddies. Little did they know how prescient the tale of garbled messages and Persian infiltration would prove to be: while some of America's crack forces were wasting their time looking for non-existent weapons of mass destruction, Iranian agents were already crossing Iraq's wide-open borders, making contacts in its towns and cities, forming alliances and funding militias that would bring the country to its knees. It would only be a few short years before the planners of the Iraq war would be 'weighed in the balance and found wanting'. Unlike Belshazzar – and fortunately for them – they were far from Iraq by then.

The US military was oblivious to this at the time, still flush with victory. Webber, a trim and fit man in his late forties, with a lined but boyish face under a floppy desert hat and huge shades, was fond of recalling the vainglory of Saddam, whose giant palace of Babylon stood like a wedding cake on a hill overlooking the site. Now that Saddam was on the run, the entire area had become a marines base, with olive-green tents under the palms fringing the river and lines of Humvees parked in the shade of Babylon's ruins. It looked like a surreal theme park, a cross between Disneyland and Vietnam, as marines in shorts and sweatshirts jogged in the unbearable heat or lifted weights in open-sided tents in the shadows of ancient Babylon's walls. Just beyond the wire, where the camp met the main road heading south, a tourist souk had sprung up where the conquerors could buy vastly overpriced and not very high-quality rugs, Iraqi army bayonets or any of the thousands of army badges and decorations that had been pinned to the chests of proud officers who had never won a war. The Iraqi vendors were taking in more money than they had ever thought possible, selling war mementoes to an army that had stormed into Iraq so quickly it hadn't even had time to pick up its own.

Webber would point to the time-eroded mud bricks creaking under the weight of Saddam's reconstructed walls, an archaeologist's nightmare, and tut-tut at the sheer vandalism the dictator had visited upon his own heritage. Now that the marines were there, he promised, the site would no longer be looted by scavengers making off with Nebuchadnezzar's bricks, or even just the dusty replica antiquities from the tourist shop.

But with time, the new victors would wreak their own havoc on the ruins. Military camps and archaeological sites do not mix well. The constant rumbling of two-ton Humvees crushed brick pavements almost 3,000 years old, the thump of helicopter rotor blades destabilized fragile structures, and the 2,000 US marines who passed through scooped vast amounts of sand and dirt containing fragments of historical relics into their defensive sandbags, or gouged trenches through the sediment of thousands of years of history. The US military later described the untold damage as 'regrettable'.

But the ruins survived yet another conquest and occupation. It is impossible to say whether all the tourists that day made it home, but they soon stopped going to Babylon. The roads became too dangerous for such frivolities. The brief interlude was over, and the eternal war that seems to hover over the area was already cranking up again.

'I gotta poo,' yelled Lieutenant Simon Wlodarski at the top of his lungs, hunkered down in the ruins of some forgotten city. Even with mortar rounds flying overhead, he caught me snickering at him and quickly added, 'God, I hate that acronym.'

'Poo' is military jargon for 'Point Of Origin'. It is called out by a spotter – usually one slightly less self-conscious than the marines reservist officer I was lying face down with in the half-buried ruins of an Akkadian city, around thirty miles south of Baghdad – to indicate where indirect fire is coming from. As it happened, he didn't have a poo, and the squad of marines ducked and weaved for cover among the dune-choked remains of Sippar, once the proud home of the temple of the sun god Shamash, from whom the Arabs derive their word for the sun, 'shams'. Luckily for those on the receiving end, ruined cities provide very good cover from in-accurate mortar fire, and Shamash was kind to the marines that day. They sheltered in deep excavations and ran along trenches that had once been streets filled with Babylonian merchants from across the tiny surface of the known world.

That was 3,000 years ago, and this was October 2004. Local guerrillas from the area around the small town of Yusufiyah had hidden their weapons caches in the ruins. Kilo Company – part of the marine expeditionary force charged with pacifying the area, which had slipped back into the hands of guerrillas in recent months – were clearly getting warmer in their weapons hunt. We couldn't see our assailants, but the mortars crumped intermittently into the trees and dirt around us for hours as we stumbled through the lost city and flattened ourselves in the surrounding groves of date palms.

The ruins themselves were a strange moonscape, a low mound that rose above the lush fields and palm-fringed canals like a dun carbuncle. The city was so ancient that even its name seemed to have been erased – the marines only ever referred to it as 'the ruins' – but I was later able to identify it as Sippar, one of the capitals of King Sargon of Akkad. King Sargon had built the template for empire-building, carving the first-ever imperial domain out of his Semitic fiefdom and the conquered Sumerian city-states to the south in 2334 BC. Sippar had been a shrine city, much like Najaf and Karbala are today, rich with the pilgrim trade and divine tributes, which as a cult centre had been passed on from one empire to the next for millennia, before eventually being taken by the Elamites – the forerunners of the Persians – in the sixth century BC.

Historians believe that Belshazzar, far from being murdered by his sons as the legend claimed, died fighting the invading Persians close to Sippar. The city appears to have been abandoned several hundred years later when the followers of Alexander the Great built brand-new cities in the land they had recently vanquished. Now, in the still, warm days of October, it was a vast pile of dust, looking as if the contents of a giant vacuum cleaner had been dumped in the green land. It was topped by a thin crust moulded by wind and rain that the marines' boots crunched through as though they were walking on sugar frosting.

In places where excavations had been carried out over the previous century, walls protruded and the shapes of buildings could be discerned. Before the mortar men started lobbing explosives at the expedition, I watched in amazement as two marines with a metal detector scanned the area for hidden weapons, then used their entrenching tools to dislodge bricks that had stood since the dawn of history. Their metal detector was constantly buzzing, and they hacked around for half an hour before realizing that the bitumen the Akkadians and Babylonians used instead of cement to hold the bricks together was probably triggering the alarm.

Ironically, it was the sudden shout of 'Incoming' followed by the dull thud of mortars that interrupted this insouciant vandalism. The mortar fire was more of a nuisance than a serious hazard, since whoever was firing was way off target. But every ten minutes or so there would be a thud, a wild shout of warning and everyone would duck behind a wall or jump into a pit.

Eventually, harassed, sweating and finding nothing, the men of Kilo Company moved their search to the palm groves that fringed the site. There they struck lucky with their own excavations.

Just outside the archeologists' locked-up wooden huts, they spotted a more recent mound which someone had tried to camouflage with dead palm fronds. The marines quickly dug it up and finally found what they were looking for: row after row of Chinese rockets, about five feet long and buried to a depth of about six feet. The marines crowed in victory, happy that these weapons at least wouldn't be made into roadside bombs. At the padlocked gate of the site's wooden hut, they shouted for someone to come out and explain what these rockets were doing buried right outside. No one showed up, so they reversed a Humvee through the gate, smashing it to the ground. They walked in and found an old man, either too deaf or too scared to come out, guarding wooden barracks containing shelves of broken pottery shards and stone relics. The marines tried to question him, but none of them spoke Arabic and the old man seemed oblivious to every question posed in English. Eventually they gave up, and left the old man with his antique rifle to guard the relics that were even more exposed to theft now that they had smashed the gate down.

Outside in a nearby field, the troops poked about and found even more buried treasure troves of grenades, mortars and rockets. I wondered how many more there were out there, and whether the men who had buried them were still alive. If not, these weapons too might sit in this dry earth for millennia, together with the bronze spearheads of the Akkadians, waiting for future generations to dig them up and put them in their museums.

The marines radioed for trucks to come and remove the huge stash of weapons they had unearthed. A crackling voice told them none was available. It was getting dark now and we had been under mortar fire for hours. The company commander was worried that his men could be ambushed if caught out after nightfall in this treacherous landscape, deep in what had become known as the Triangle of Death for its endless butchery. With its canals and exposed raised banks running through verdant palm groves and rice paddies, it looked very similar to Vietnam. Instead of removing the weapons, the commander decided they would have to dispose of the cache in situ. That meant finding a convenient place to blow it all up. The captain looked around, chatted with his explosives expert. I saw them pointing at the vast mound of dirt and ordering the men to start moving the rockets there. I had a sinking feeling as I realized they were about to blow it all up on top of the archaeological site.

I went up to Lieutenant Wlodarski. It was starting to get dark, and he seemed distracted by the increasing possibility of his men being ambushed. In future years, this would be the place where American soldiers were attacked by superior forces on several occasions, and several captives beheaded and mutilated.

'I think this whole mound is an archaeological site,' I told him, reluctant to interfere in military matters but unable to let the destruction of a historical site pass by without saying a word. I felt it was my duty to at least raise the issue.

'I really don't think it's a good place to blow all this stuff up,' I told him.

Wlodarski eyed me with suspicion, suddenly realizing the drawbacks of having an independent observer in a combat zone as complex as Iraq.

'We aren't the Taliban. We're not blowing up Buddhas,' he barked, clearly annoyed at my interference.

'I know that,' I said, 'but I really think you're about to blow up an important historical site.' Of course, I had no proof that this was actually anything but a huge pile of dirt, which is what it must have looked like to most of the marines.

Wlodarski shook his head and stomped off. I found the company commander, Captain King, and told him my fears. He nodded and muttered something about 'trying to limit the impact on the site'. Behind him, a marine was already sprinkling C4 explosives packages on the rockets like a chef throwing croutons on a Caesar salad. Then we were ordered to mount up the Humvees and drive a half mile to safety. It was dark as we sat in the vehicles, waiting for the blast. When it came, it was deafening. I watched as a huge fireball rose over buried Sippar. In the gloom, I heard one of the young marines quipping about the sheer vandalism of the act.

'The Hague, here we come,' he laughed softly, referring to the international criminal court based in The Netherlands. Someone gave a short bark of a laugh. We drove back in the dark, subdued but still ever alert for the guerrillas who had spent the day trying to kill us.

*   *   *

Back in the makeshift camp in Yusufiyah, it was easy to imagine the last days of a dying civilization. The marine expeditionary force had only moved into the little market town a week earlier: before that, the area had been under the nominal command of the US army, who had decided months before that their presence was only exacerbating the violence and so pulled out, handing security over to the local police force. The police, hopelessly ill-equipped and barely trained, did not stand a chance. Sunni insurgents, from their shifting bases in outlying farms and hamlets where no law reached, had raided Yusufiyah in the summer and taken all the policemen prisoner. They locked the officers in their own cells and blew up the building, with them inside. Half a dozen policemen were slaughtered. Since then the insurgents – a mixture of former soldiers and Baathists, al-Qaeda fanatics and Syrians – would occasionally swoop into town on market day, publicly behead any Shia suspected of spying for the Americans or for a Shia militia, and leave the rest of the population cowed and in shock.

When the marines took over control of the area, their commanders decided the situation was unacceptable. Kilo Company had been sent in to restore order and back up a new police force, no sign of which was visible anywhere. Forward Operating Base (FOB) Saint Michel was built around the ruins of the destroyed police station and a commandeered girls' school. In between the two buildings, sweat-streaked American mortar teams squatted in sandbagged dug-outs: one, which was manned by skinny teenagers stripped to the waist in the heat and who looked too young to be out of high school, had a cardboard sign outside their foxhole with the motto 'We shell, you yell.'

The drains of the school outhouse were blocked, and someone had spray-painted on the walls: 'Piss only.' Outside, there was a camping chair with the seat cut out and a plastic trash bag underneath for anyone wanting to take a crap: as soon as I saw it, my bowels obediently seized up for the entire duration of my stay in Yusufiyah.

Kilo Company was under constant attack by guerrillas and weapons smugglers whose rat runs snaked through the palm-shaded canals and fields, bringing men and arms out of the Saudi desert to the southwest and up to the Sunni Triangle to the north. As I drove in with a supply convoy on the first morning of my assignment to cover the reconquest of the Triangle of Death, purple smoke drifted across the camp's muster yard, summoning a medevac helicopter. A marine sat clutching his bleeding and bandaged arm as a towering gunnery sergeant, known as RPG Head, told the medic to keep talking to him. 'Don't let him go into shock,' he ordered. There was a constant thump of mortars – most of them outgoing, but some landing around the camp – that went on day and night, rattling everyone's nerves. The mortars started to follow the marines every time they left the rudimentary protection of the base to patrol the dirty streets of Yusufiyah, where mute locals watched the heavily armoured American marines walk past with a mixture of suspicion and terror. No one would tell the Americans anything – they had no guarantee that these soldiers, like the last ones from the regular army who had been replaced by the marines, would not just up sticks and leave them at the mercy of the psycho-killer beheaders lurking out there in the shady farmlands.

The Triangle of Death was to murder what the Fertile Crescent had been to farming, a testing ground where inventiveness and opportunity provided a constant crop of bodies killed in increasingly macabre ways. Sunni hardliners preyed on the Shia community until corpses clogged the blue canals: soon, Shia militias would start wreaking their own revenge. Even the dead weren't safe: on several occasions, Shia families taking relatives slain in Baghdad's daily bombs to the vast cemetery in Najaf were attacked by guerrillas who would open the wooden casket, behead the corpse and then decapitate several of the mourners for good measure.

There were no limits on the horrors perpetrated in the area, and the barbarity would eventually seep, like a miasma, into the American ranks stationed there. More than a year after I left, a group of American soldiers at a checkpoint near Yusufiyah decided to get drunk and make their way to the house of a pretty local girl they had seen passing their position on several occasions. They broke in and shot the girl's parents and five-year-old sister through the head. They then gang-raped the fourteen-year-old girl before murdering her and setting her body on fire to destroy the evidence. A few months later, an Iraqi gang from Yusufiyah took revenge by attacking another US patrol, killing one soldier and kidnapping two others. The captives were tortured and beheaded, their mutilated bodies left booby-trapped on the roadside to maim whoever came to retrieve them.

The marines I was stationed with were all reservists, weekend soldiers flung into one of the most vicious and deceptive combat zones in Iraq. They had the same basic training as regular marines, but all had jobs and lives back home beyond the military discipline of the Marine Corps. I heard one, a drama student, bemoaning the fact that he had to keep his hair so short for military service. 'You know, in theatre you have to have long hair,' he told his comrades, an ill-judged remark that drew a chorus of derisory guffaws. Their commanding officer was a major who looked like a 1940s B-movie matinee star, with a reddish trimmed moustache and the harassed look of a leader failing under siege. His will was implemented by the huge gunnery sergeant I had encountered on my arrival, a man who must have stood at least seven feet tall. This giant would stalk around the base with a pump-action shotgun in his paw and milk-bottle glasses strapped to his dirt-streaked face, shouting orders that always ended with a threat. 'Go do it now, or I'll kick you in the fuckin' nuts,' was a typical moti-vational device. He looked like Frankenstein's monster made up of the left-over parts of Steinbeck characters – the men had unaffectionately nicknamed him RPG Head for the conical shape of his skull, discernable even under his helmet.

The reservists, despite being generally better educated than their regular comrades, seemed to have little idea of cultural sensitivity: their call sign, 'Crusader', was also painted on the sides of their Humvees, just in case any of the locals could read English and were looking for extra reasons to mistrust the armed foreigners who came and left at will.

But then you had to wonder how far cultural sensitivity would have got them by that stage anyway: graffiti scrawled on the walls of Yusufiyah warned that anyone caught defacing pictures of Saddam Hussein would have their head cut off or have their hands amputated; terrorists went through the town handing out price lists detailing what they would pay for the deaths of local Iraqi police officers. While I was there, the head of the National Guard in nearby Mahmoudiyah was chased through his own town by gunmen in black BMWs, barely escaping to the relative safety of his base. A local political party leader wasn't so lucky – gunmen hunted him down through the streets and pumped him full of bullets. It was clear that what had passed for civilization in the intermittent periods of calm over the past 5,000 years was at an historic ebb.

At night, kept awake by the thump of mortars as I lay shivering with cold on the floor of the abandoned school, last year's exam papers still littering the corridors, I tried to picture the last stand of the Akkadians here, soldiers trying to hold the line against the Persians and the imminent collapse of their civilization. Could they have been any more confused and scared than these young Americans, thousands of miles from home and bewildered by the viciousness all around them? I very much doubted it.

*   *   *

When I was eleven years old, in my first history class at secondary school, my teacher drew a stunning picture of the ziggurat of Ur of the Chaldees on the blackboard. The stepped pyramid and the exotic names – Sumer, the city of Ur – rising out of a desert civilization I had never heard of, and which was far too old for my young mind to grapple with, fired my imagination and forever entranced it with the ancient world. For a long time I became obsessed with the Pharaohs, Biblical history and the wars between the Greeks and the Persians. I don't believe childhood obsessions ever quite fade away, just as the imprint of those lost worlds is still delicately traced across the minds of modern civilization.

So when I stood on top of that self-same ziggurat in June of 2003, looking out on the American airbase that had, like the marines encampment around Babylon, mushroomed round the ruins of a vanished people, I felt an electrical tingle of excitement run up my spine. I tried to imagine all the ambitions and dreams of the people who had lived here on the edge of time and on this ancient shore, the lives they led and the elaborate stories they wove around heroes, gods and monsters. Those legends were meant to bind them together, to help them cling to their fragile new civilization and prevent them sliding back into the primitive life of the hunters and nomads they saw all around them, out there on the plains. Gilgamesh, where are you now? According to the legend – the first epic ever to be recorded on clay tablets – the wayward, conflicted king had dived into the Persian Gulf four and a half millennia ago to search for a plant that bestowed immortality, somewhere near this site. A serpent had eaten the magic plant while the returning hero slept, condemning the son of King Lugalbanda to dust. In the intervening time, the sea had retreated far from Ur's shores, leaving the port city stranded in the desert outside the city of Nasariyah. Italian soldiers in snappy uniforms and Armani shades were stationed in the town now, and several had taken the morning off to visit the ziggurat, a hulking platform of brick and bitumen that was surprisingly intact. Steep flights of steps led up the front to a crumbling summit that resembled a wild hilltop.

Officially, I was tracing the route of the invasion from the Kuwaiti border to Baghdad to see what had really changed in the two months since the US and British forces sped across the sand berm on the frontier. But having driven from the capital to the southern port of Umm Qasr, the scene of the first battle of the war, I had been told by London to file my entire odyssey in just six hundred words, a ridiculously small amount of space for such a sweeping piece. So I treated the assignment as a personal sightseeing trip, testing the mood for my own interest and taking in as much of the country as I could.

In Basra, I saw the joy of liberation from the oppressive Saddam fermenting into fury as the summer temperatures soared and even basic commodities such as drinking water evaporated in the heat and chaos. Beetroot-faced British squaddies, in full battle armour, swayed in the heat haze as they stood guard over petrol stations, unable to stay out in the 60 degree Celsius heat for more than twenty minutes at a time. Inside their Land Rovers, medics gave them IV drips to rehydrate the soldiers quickly enough to return to their duties, while outside Iraqis raged that they were having to fetch water from the river, shouting their fury that the clock had been turned back centuries in a few brief months.

In Umm Qasr, the docks stood empty of shipping and the dust blew through streets where people still marvelled at the novelty of DVDs and refrigerators. On the wall, someone had sprayed the words 'God job Pliar and Boosh', which, after a minute of staring, I realized was actually a compliment to the work of Tony Blair and George Bush. But here again there was no water in the pipes, the electricity pylons had been toppled by looters and many of the DVDs were of religious sermons by the Shiite leaders who would soon turn the area into a fundamentalist battleground.

In Nasariyah, the mood was positively festive: the city on the Euphrates had seen some of the hardest fighting of the war, but now the restaurants and cafés were open. The streets, where during the 1991 uprising thousands of people had been lined up and shot, were still full of trash but were bustling with men, women and children tasting freedom for the first time in decades. Even the electricity had improved, the grid having been rerouted to provide some of the local power that had formerly been sent off to Baghdad, where it kept Saddam's support base sated. I smoked a *narguilah* on a rooftop café, where people smiled and waved and came up to greet me, as though I personally had liberated Iraq.

*　　*　　*

Strange as it seemed later in the war, when even the shortest journey in Baghdad involved military-level planning, chase cars, escape routes, gunmen and the constant threat of a vile death, there were days after the invasion when touring Iraq's ancient sites constituted a pleasant break from the grind of work.

In October 2003, I planned a day trip to mark my first anniversary with Lulu. Haidar drove us to Aqargouf, a jagged diamond of eroded mud-baked bricks rising two hundred feet over the palms on the road from Baghdad to Fallujah. We parked outside the locked-up site and found a hole in the fence. There was not a soul to be seen on the paths that wound among the ruins, the palms and the eucalyptus trees. We poked around semi-restored temples and royal storehouses and ascended the steps to the ziggurat, once the exclusive preserve of priests and kings, closed to plebs like us. The ziggurat, perhaps built as an outpost of the early Babylonian empire, was a shapeless lump, blasted by three and a half thousand years of sandstorms and rains into something resembling a free-standing cliff, riddled with holes gouged by generations of pigeons for their nests. Only the parallel striations that bisected the crumbling mud face indicated that the structure might be man-made.

The base had been rebuilt to its original splendour, a huge platform of neat yellow bricks that lifted it above the plain. The ziggurats must have been a wonder to behold when all the other buildings on earth were mud huts made of sun-dried bricks and reed thatch.

After wandering the abandoned palaces in awe for an hour, we drove back into Baghdad. It was a lazy Saturday afternoon and I had arranged to go to one of Baghdad's most renowned restaurants, Khan Mirjan, close to the copper bazaar and the city's teeming street markets. The restaurant had once been the place to go for the handful of tourists who dared to visit Iraq. It was built in the thirteenth century as a caravanserai, one of the inns for camel trains crisscrossing the deserts from Syria to the Arabian peninsula, ferrying spices and cloths from China and Samarkand along the Silk Road. The size of a modest medieval cathedral, its brick vaulted ceilings soared above wooden galleries where merchants once sat over sweet tea and haggled over the price of nutmeg and coriander, cinnamon and silk, when Baghdad, known across the Muslim empire as the 'city of peace', was the richest and most civilized metropolis in the world.

I had not made a reservation, but that was no problem. The place was empty. As we walked into the cavernous gloom, it was not even clear whether it was actually inhabited, except for the few cats that stalked among the rows of empty tables. But then an elderly man stepped out, surprised to see anyone in his restaurant. In his rudimentary English – he explained he had once been an English teacher, but had rarely had the chance to practise with native speakers – he invited us to sit down and gave us menus. The choice was basic – chicken, lamb, rice and vegetables. We ordered a couple of beers. He said he didn't have any, then called over a boy – possibly his son. The kid scampered out and came back five minutes later with two warm tins of Turkish beer. The waiter came back and we ordered, only to discover there was in fact only one item on the menu. So we both ordered that one 'dish of the day': meat kebabs with flat bread and parsley. Again, the boy darted out and returned fifteen minutes later with our food, bought from a street vendor. The man was clearly struggling to keep this famous eatery open. As we sat washing down our gristly kebabs with warm lager, we gazed around us at the musty, sepulchral building, the cats wandering in and out of the kitchen at the back, and decided it was in fact much better that nothing we consumed had actually been prepared on the premises. As we paid the bill, a paltry amount, the elderly waiter seemed keen to chat, after years of waiting to practise his English. We talked for a while, but in fact his English was so rusty, and my Arabic so poor, that he seemed to understand very little of what we said. We walked out past a medieval seminary and into the bright evening, where vendors and hawkers filled Rashid Street as they had done since the caravanserai had been built.

Not all of Iraq's ruins were ancient. The war had left plenty of gutted buildings, but the spectacular relics were the endless monuments to Saddam's vanity. On top of his Republican Palace, in what had suddenly become the American nerve centre of the Green Zone, stood six vast metal heads of the dictator wearing the pointed helmet of the Kurdish warrior Salahedin, who had been born in Saddam's hometown of Tikrit before growing up to achieve what Saddam also boasted he would do – conquer Jerusalem. The statues were twenty-five feet high and for a long time after the fall of Baghdad scowled down on harassed Pentagon officials struggling to cope with the country they had vanquished. It took months before they could even get round to organizing a crane to topple the vast busts.

The palace itself seemed to have had a charmed existence since its construction during the relatively peaceful interwar period of British hegemony, having survived unscathed both the hail of cruise missiles and the subsequent looting. Oddly enough, inside the marble entrance hall, past the steps where the nineteen-year-old King Faisal II was gunned down in the 1958 coup d'état, was a model of the palace in a glass case. Someone had reached inside the case and crushed the roof of the plaster model – it always reminded me of a sort of picture of Dorian Gray in reverse.

Less than a mile away, other effigies of the dictator still survive – Saddam's wrists were used as the models for the giant hands rising from the parade ground, holding aloft two massive sabres that form an arc over the long ceremonial driveway. Spilling out of the netting of the swords' pommels were the helmets of Iranian soldiers harvested from the battlefields two decades before. Some had been embedded in the parade ground's tarmac for Saddam's tanks to symbolically drive over during the annual march past. Now the helmets were covered in American soldiers' graffiti – 'Mike Adamson, North Bend, Washington' – an added humiliation to those long-dead Iranian troops, and an extra layer of sediment in a land with too much history for its own consumption.

But of all of Saddam's follies, the most spectacular was the enormous mosque he almost finished building in Mansour, the expensive district of central Baghdad where all the embassies stood, and where all the return-ing exiled political parties were busy purloining the residencies of fleeing Baathists. The mosque consisted of a monumental central cupola soaring into the air and surrounded by four smaller domes – all quite capable of holding thousands of people – sitting in a huge empty construction site. It looked like a giant, alien space station that had crashed into the heart of the city and half buried itself in the sand. Its domes were so high they dominated the entire city skyline. On my first evening in Baghdad, I stood on the roof of my hotel across the city, drinking a beer and watching a blood-red sunset behind the mosque: smoke from some smouldering government ministry drifted in front of those huge globes of concrete, and two Apache helicopters buzzed around it like angry wasps defend-ing their hive. It is one of my abiding memories of Baghdad.

A few months later, I was showing my foreign editor, Martin Fletcher, around Baghdad on his first trip to the city. I took him to the mosque and he suggested we break in. It was poorly guarded, and the fence was down in several places. Up close, the empty building inspired a medieval kind of awe, as it was no doubt meant to. As we approached, I heard Martin reciting a poem:

'I met a traveller from an antique land
Who said:—Two vast and trunkless legs of stone
Stand in the desert. Near them on the sand,
Half sunk, a shatter'd visage lies, whose frown
And wrinkled lip and sneer of cold command
Tell that its sculptor well those passions read
Which yet survive, stamp'd on these lifeless things,
The hand that mock'd them and the heart that fed.
And on the pedestal these words appear:
"My name is Ozymandias, king of kings:
Look on my works, ye mighty, and despair!"
Nothing beside remains: round the decay
Of that colossal wreck, boundless and bare,
The lone and level sands stretch far away.'

'What was that?' I asked in my literary ignorance.

'Ozymandias,' said Martin, who had clearly been to a better school than I had. 'Percy Shelley. All about the transience and vanity of power. Fits this place perfectly.'

I gazed up at the huge domes in front of us and had to agree.

For every modern ruin, there were hundreds of ancient ones to explore. There were cities such as Nineveh, once the capital of the Assyrian empire and now a vast blanket of grass spread across the centre of Mosul. These places were so old they'd been dug up by European archeologists a century ago, excavated, and were now gently slipping back into the eternal dust again, as though the effort of emerging to face another war were too great. The best pre-served of these were in the north, in or close to Kurdistan, which was in the process of slowly breaking away from the rest of the country. The area was generally safer than the Arab lands to the south, and I took great delight in exploring these lost places, so far from any tourist route, on my trips to the north.

Above the winding alleys of Kirkuk's age-old markets, I discovered an entirely deserted citadel that rises towards the windy blue sky, apparently forgotten by the city below it. We strolled under the tarpaulins and corrugated-iron rooftops of the souk to emerge into a lost world of crumbling Ottoman palaces, vacant mosques with beautiful coloured tiles still peeking through the dust, the abandoned mansions of the city's once-proud governors. Marco Polo had passed through these streets in 1294 AD, on his way from China. Somewhere deep beneath my feet were the remnants of the seventy-two defensive towers built by King Sluks during the Roman era, when the city was known as Kergi Sluks: somewhere below them were the walls that Assyrian King Nasirbal ordered constructed in 884 BC to protect this outpost of his empire. The entire hillock made up of all these buried civilizations had itself risen from the remains of a Sumerian city, whose only surviving trace was a calf statue and a few copper tools excavated years earlier. My local guide told me the citadel had only been finally abandoned twenty years earlier, after millennia of occupation, when Saddam's jet fighters were bombing Kurdish rebels holed up here. We climbed staircases that disappeared halfway up minarets whose tops had been lopped off by shells, and stood in dusty halls where Marco Polo might once have dined.

A faint breeze blew from the plains below, where oil had been discovered in the 1920s, making Kirkuk one of Iraq's most important cities. Out there in the higgledy-piggledy streets below us, Kurds, Turkmen and Arabs were quietly struggling for control, murdering and threatening and driving each other out of their homes as they vied for the dark, viscous soul of the oil city. The Kurds and the Turkmen each insisted the place was part of their timeless heritage: the Arabs had no such claim, having been implanted here by Saddam in the 1980s when the dictator tried to strengthen his grip on the city by ethnically cleansing the Kurdish majority who claimed it as their capital.

As if to remind me of the bitter struggle still going on, the sound of gun shots rang out somewhere below the citadel. The guide said it was not safe to stay, so we quickly made our way out of the ruins. We had no desire to become part of the long and painful history of the place.

The roads of Kurdistan lead through the stunning ravines and mountain crags of the Zagros range, where man first domesticated animals and set in train the agricultural revolution. This had once been bandit country, although the age-old fighting had died out recently. My chain-smoking driver was called Zurian, a lean and rugged ex-bodyguard of the Kurdish leader Massoud Barzani. Zurian had been wounded many times in the Kurdish civil war a decade before, and was fond of telling war stories as we sped in his black BMW along the road between Arbil and Suleimaniyah. I had come north after a colleague of mine, Rory Carroll of the *Guardian*, had been kidnapped by the Mahdi Army, and Baghdad suddenly became too difficult to operate in. A trip north sounded like a good idea.

On the outskirts of Arbil, Zurian pointed out a neighbourhood we passed through that had experienced combat so vicious and prolonged in the Kurdish civil war of the mid-1990s that both sides had ended up using knives on each other in hand-to-hand, gladiatorial fights carried out in the backyards and houses.

A few miles on, he waved to the mountain crags where Barzani's Kurdish Democratic Party, based in Arbil, had been fighting Jalal Talabani's Patriotic Union of Kurdistan, out of Suleimaniyah. The hardy Kurdish mountain guerrillas – who still wear their traditional baggy jumpsuits and waist sashes, as well as keffiyahs wrapped high on their heads like turbans – had slogged it out for years, Talabani forging an alliance with the Iranians, Barzani taking the dramatic step of allowing Saddam's hated troops into the safe haven to attack his rivals. I told Zurian my knowledge of Kurdish history was shaky at best, and asked why exactly the rival factions had waged such a bitter war. He puffed on his Miami cigarette and shrugged.

'I don't know, it was just fighting,' he said, stubbing out his cigarette in the BMW's ashtray and instantly lighting another, as though this curt answer explained the years of pain and suffering. Perhaps it did for many people.

Along these empty mountain roads, life seemed to

have changed very little over the millennia. Women herded goats and geese along mountain streams, tiny hovels sheltered from the sun in the lee of the towering rock faces. On the arid steppes, many still marked with little triangular signs warning of landmines, men on donkeys watched over flocks of sheep. It was easy to see in my mind's eye the Persian king Darius, in his bright silk robes, galloping away across these plains with his entourage as they fled the carnage of Gaugamela, the battlefield near Arbil where Alexander the Great routed the massed Persian army. Darius took refuge in the citadel of Arbil, which archaeologists believe is the oldest inhabited site in the world. While staying in Arbil, I had taken advantage of the novelty of being able to walk around outside without being automatically abducted, and strolled through the narrow lanes of the citadel. It was clear that life hadn't changed a great deal since those first settlers moved there. The crest of the 7,000-year-old hilltop fortress, known as the Qalal, was ringed with splendid biscuit-coloured facades of Ottoman palaces, but the interiors had long since collapsed and the poor denizens had carved tiny huts out of the remains, facing muddy streets with narrow sewage channels snaking down the middle. Rough wooden logs held up the roofs of the baked-brick hovels, yard fences were made out of empty cooking-oil cans. If you half-closed your eyes, for a fleeting moment you were back in ancient Mesopotamia.

Down in the city itself, things were starting to change. The bazaar, where merchants sold honeycombs and goats' cheese and pistachio nuts in a hive of crumbling alleyways, was slated to be pulled down and replaced by a vast shopping precinct of four thirty-storey buildings, providing 6,000 retail spaces. Money was flowing into Kurdistan as investors tried to get in on the ground of this oil-rich country, while avoiding the terrors of the Arab regions just to the south. Even the labourers building the new motorways, bridges and gated residential communities were mostly Arab refugees who had fled the killing fields of their hometowns. While war and looters swept away the historical vestiges of the Arab lands, success was doing the same work in Kurdistan.

Not that there was much sentimentality for the passing of the old ways. This was a far cry from England, where heritage is all important and everything ancient is preserved. In the souk, I bumped into a retired teacher called Ahmed Abdelhadi, working at his son's shoe shop to make ends meet. He was full of satisfaction at the development.

'We feel really happy watching our city being rebuilt,' he told me. 'It used to be just sewage in the streets.' I felt a twinge of sadness, knowing that soon all of this would be gone, but it was hard to blame them. Nostalgia for history is all very well, but only when such a brutal history is not so close behind you.

ANCIENT FEUDS

A Festival of Blood in Karbala

All night I could hear the drums and chants, the hubbub of more than a million people milling around between the shrines. Unable to sleep for the noise, I'd look out of the hotel window at regular intervals. No matter what time of night it was, there was an endless vista of people in the huge square below me, come to Karbala to mark the martyrdom of the Prophet Mohammed's grandson, Imam Hussein, almost 1,400 years before. Throngs of people were knotted around the mighty cauldrons handing out free rice, beans and meat to hungry pilgrims, others bunched around the cohorts of bare-chested men whipping their backs with metal flails under arc lights or slapping their chests red-raw with their open palms, to the tinny cries of CD-recorded imams.

The clamour went on all night and through the milky-grey dawn, when the crowd thickened and swelled again, more pilgrims squeezing into the already packed plaza between the two mosques dedicated to

Imam Hussein and his companion in death, Abbas. It was Ashoura, the festival of the Shia martyrdom, and the first time so many worshippers had been free to come from across the Muslim world and worship. In the square near the Imam Hussein mosque, a fountain spurted a geyser of red-dyed water to commemorate the blood that had once flowed so copiously here, when Hussein and his band of seventy-odd companions joined battle with the Caliph Yazid's army. In a few hours, hundreds of men would jog round the two mosques beating their heads with swords until their scalps opened and their faces were masked by blood, an act both of commemoration and contrition, for the Shia of 680 had failed to rally to their hero's side, allowing him and his band of followers to be butchered and beheaded. Hussein's head rests to this day in an outsize tomb in the Ummayad mosque of Damascus, taken there as a trophy by Yazid's generals, and as proof that the dangerous rebel was dead.

I had arrived in Karbala the night before, March 1, 2004, with Lulu, my Sunni translator Saleh, and Terri, our photographer. It was far and away the most enormous gathering of people I had ever seen: perhaps one and a half million Shia had descended on the city sixty miles south of Baghdad, on the edge of a desert that swept southwest into the empty wastes of Saudi Arabia. The pilgrims had come from as far afield as the mountains of Afghanistan and Pakistan, from the Gulf states and from all across Iraq for the festival. As we drove out of Baghdad late in the afternoon, we navigated an endless stream of devout Shiites walking resolutely southwards, carrying their green and black flags and banners and bearing aloft portraits of the imam, looking like a dashing 1920s matinee movie idol in a green cape, with thick ruby lips framed by a rich black beard. Saleh tut-tutted: Muslims were not supposed to tolerate such graven images, and Sunnis likened these Shia practices to idolatry. But the mood among the Shia was unmistakably buoyant and festive. The year before, they had run to Karbala during the time of Ashoura, flocking to the city built on the ancient battlefield to celebrate the blood-soaked rites that Saddam had for so long banned. But the rites had been ad hoc and as much a celebration of Saddam's recent overthrow as a religious festival. This year's massive turnout was determined to mark the ceremony in full honour, and to show the world that Iraq's Shia were, for the first time in living memory, flexing their muscles as the country's majority community.

The pilgrims on the roads were so multitudinous – endless men, women and children, on foot, in cars, packed into banner-streaming buses, the lame pushed in wooden market carts by younger relatives, trails of dust rising into the smoky spring sky as they moved – that our progress was excruciatingly slow, eventually grinding to a crawl as we approached the lush, green villages on the fringes of the city. All along the roadside, people were cooking up cauldrons of rice and beans, grilling kebabs, all to offer to the pilgrims, to help their brethren on their way to Hussein's city but also to help themselves on the road to heaven. Helping pilgrims was a sure way to curry favour with the Almighty. As we trundled through one of a string of villages hung with sparkling fairy lights in the rising darkness, a young boy skipped up to the car and offered us lamb and parsley kebabs: I accepted gratefully, not having eaten since morning. It was delicious. At one point we stopped to go to the toilet by the roadside, mingling with other travellers relieving themselves in ditches: in the dusk, with the dust rising from the tramping feet of the pilgrims, the coloured banners catching the last sunlight, I felt transported to another century. When we finally reached Karbala itself, the road was blocked and the fields around had turned into a giant parking lot where people were happily debussing and heading into town, many of them singing and clapping hands. We managed to persuade a policeman to allow our car in, and wended our way through the throngs towards the centre, where we parked and walked on towards the soaring domes and minarets of the twin shrines.

We strolled through the heart of the city, where the feast was in full swing. The main street leading up to the shrine's plaza was swarming with people giving away food from steaming vats, selling yellow-fringed prayer shawls in Islamic emerald green, vendors hawking slices of a caramel-like sweet known in Arabic, with unabashed honesty, simply as 'fat'. Others were offering prayer beads, as well as the brutal equipment of Shiite devotion: metal flails for self-flagellation, swords for auto-mutilation in honour of the slain saints, and round tablets made of holy clay for the faithful to bow their heads to when making their daily prayers, which mark the truly devout with permanent grey scars on the foreheads.

The streets were lit up with strings of bright lights, and were all but impassable due to the herds of people streaming in from every corner of the Islamic world, nearly all of them clad in the traditional black costumes of the Shia. Karbala, run down through decades of deliberate neglect by Saddam's government, and badly damaged in the 1991 uprising when the government sent in tanks, is not a pretty town, but its cancerous concrete buildings and sewage-tainted streets are generally redeemed by the bustle of the religious markets catering to famished travellers and pilgrims. That night, the city was transformed into something fabulous, the mood of rejoicing tangible wherever we went.

'This is all very free now, all the people are free to say what they want to say,' said Mohammed Najar, an enthusiastic pilgrim taking his fill of the rice that was also free that night. 'Ashoura is only the beginning,' he beamed at us, reflecting the sense of buoyant optimism that infected the city that evening.

In the jostling crowds we heard the Shia discussing what glories the future might hold for them: some wanted Islamic law, which they said would bestow freedom on all Iraqis, not like in Iran. 'Iran is different to Iraq; we have Shias and Sunnis and Kurds and Christians. We mustn't obey the laws from Iran,' insisted one pilgrim. Others merely wanted the Shia to claim their rights as Iraq's majority, citing the democracy that the Americans were touting at every opportunity. But most simply rejoiced that this night, for the first time in a year, there were no American or coalition troops around, that Iraqi security guards were the only force in town. They were doing it on their own, and sovereignty was coming soon to these proud people.

'In the past, we had to stay at home and say our prayers in secret,' recalled one man, standing in a knot of fellow travellers near the mosque plaza. 'Many people were killed here by Saddam's forces,' lamented another. A third man in the group, who identified himself as Amar Taleb, a former army colonel of engineers, said solemnly, 'Today is a great day. We get our freedom today.' His friend Abbas Hussein was exhilarated by the sense of liberty, so long a stranger in these impoverished streets. He uttered words I had never heard in Iraq before, and have never heard since. 'We only want whoever can offer us freedom today, be he Muslim, Christian, Kurdish or even Jewish.' I wondered how long a Jew would last here, even one offering freedom.

We headed for the Hotel Moon, where some colleagues had secured a floor by booking early. Accommodation elsewhere in the city was impossible to come by, and thousands of pilgrims were simply unfurling mats and blankets and bedding down in the noisy streets. With the police force still barely functional, the local political parties had ordered their militias to conduct security operations. As we approached the huge square where the domes of the two soaring mosques glittered in the bright lights, we were forced into separate lines to be searched: Saleh and I into the men's line, Lulu and Terri into the women's. It was then I remembered, to my horror, that Lulu had a bottle of red wine stashed away in her bag. We had packed it that morning, planning to share the Lebanese plonk with our friends in the hotel that night. Like total green-horns, we had failed to consider the fact that there would be such strict security, or that our hotel might be right at the hub of the ceremony. I looked round at Lulu, a mild panic rising: it was too late, she was already being searched. I froze at the thought: we were about to smuggle a bottle of booze into one of the holiest sites in Shia Islam during its most sacred festival. Not only that, but an infidel woman was the perpetrator of this heinous crime. I saw Lulu was trying to hide the bottle under her radio equipment, but for once the guards were being professionally thorough. Inevitably, one of them pulled out the offending item, a look on his face like he had found a sewer rat reciting the Talmud in Hebrew. There was an instant explosion of outraged babble from the others: faces turned in the crowd, people perhaps thinking the guards had unearthed a hand grenade. All I could understand in the increasingly high-pitched squawks of shock was the word *haram*: for-bidden. I cursed our stupidity and watched as a group of outraged men quickly congealed around Lulu. Lulu rather unconvincingly tried to argue that the dark red liquid inside was water. I pushed back through the crowd – which was growing at an alarming rate – with Saleh. I told him to tell the guards that we were Christians and we needed the wine to celebrate our own religious services. It was a long shot, and they didn't buy it any more than the water excuse. They probably knew more about Christianity than I did anyway.

Voices were now being raised to sub-mob decibel levels as heated denunciations flew over our heads. The fact that the guard was waving the bottle of Chateau Infidel around in the air was only attracting more angry Shia, as he probably knew it would: if mob justice could be dealt out, he would be absolved of having to do anything about these insolent kefirs and their bottled Beelzebub. Saleh very bravely tried to argue that it was his bottle, and they were about to drag him off when Lulu and I insisted it was definitely ours, playing our only remaining trump card – dumb foreigners, very sorry to have unwittingly insulted your fine religion, take the bottle and we'll be on our way. Luckily for us, the guards decided at that point to turn the whole thing over to the police, and led us away like guilty schoolchildren to see the force commander, who like a dutiful leader of men was sitting in a nearby café, sipping tea with a bunch of cronies. Our escort explained our heinous offence: the police commander looked us over angrily, but clearly didn't want to deal too harshly with westerners, whose country after all still occupied his. He ordered one of his officers to expel us from the city on the spot. This was a great stroke of luck for us: as soon as we were out of sight of the commander, Saleh, with the consummate ease of all adult Iraqis, offered the policeman a bribe of 5,000 dinars – around three dollars – not to throw us out of town. Our escort immediately agreed. Sensing he was on a winning streak, Saleh offered him another 5,000 to sneak us through the back streets to our hotel, avoiding the security cordon and the offended guards. Again, his offer met with instant approval. For six dollars, we avoided the shame of expulsion and a missed story, and we got to walk unmolested to our destination. I was all for offering him a few dollars more to see if we could get our bottle back, but the others figured that would be pressing our luck. So we arrived, slightly elated at having dodged disaster and emerged victorious, at the Hotel Moon, a three-storey concrete block right on the edge of the bustling sea of humanity that had inundated the main plaza. We quickly discovered that several of our colleagues had likewise been rumbled on the same booze-smuggling ruse before us. The police were doing a brisk business in sober journalists that night.

From the third floor of the Moon, the view was stunning: between the shining domes of the twin shrines, various processions cut through the endless mill of pilgrims. To the beat of a goatskin drum, a phalanx of men in black, green bandannas wrapped tightly round their heads, slowly advanced towards the Imam Hussein shrine, taking one step, stopping, then swinging chain-link flails to scourge their backs before taking another step to the hypnotic beat of the drum. Others were singing and beating their chests in time to their hymns, the slaps of a thousand people at a time resonating across the throngs. Some overzealous groups of men were already beating their heads with swords, although the actual procession of self-mutilation did not begin until after sunrise. Saleh, standing next to me on the narrow concrete balcony, looked down in disdain. 'This is not Islam,' said the devout Sunni – possibly the only one there that night. 'Islam forbids you from mutilating or harming yourself.'

In fact, the square we were looking down on had been the tectonic plate for the age-old schism between the Sunnis and the Shias. When Imam Hussein rode into battle against the Caliph Yazid, the seeds of the split had already been sown for a generation. Yazid was the son of Caliph Muawiyah, whose ascendancy to power had been sorely disputed: those who would later be known as Sunnis ('the companions') believed that the Prophet Mohammed's succession should rightfully fall to his close companions. Mohammed had died without appointing an heir, and in the confusion surrounding his death, the Muslim leaders elected his closest companion Abu Bakr as the first caliph.

However, the sect who would become known as the Shia (which literally means 'the followers') believed that Mohammed had in fact designated his son-in-law Ali, who was married to his only daughter Fatima, as his successor. By the time Ali became Caliph, his claim to power was disputed by Muawiyah. When Ali was assassinated, Muawiyah claimed the throne, and was then succeeded by his son Yazid. In the mounting civil war that surrounded the power struggle, Ali's followers looked to his son, Hussein, to fight for the position of Caliph. However, when Hussein, his brothers and seventy-two companions showed up on the field of battle in the place that would eventually become Karbala, his supporters deserted him, and he and his men were slaughtered. With this bloody death,

Hussein's status as a saint was secured and the Shias' long obsession with martyrdom kick-started. In penance for their betrayal, the Shia beat themselves, just as some extreme Christians in the Philippines will still have themselves nailed to a cross at Easter for mankind's failings to their lord. The defeat in 680 was more than just another bloody afternoon in an unforgiving part of the world: it was also the start of an irreconcilable split in the religion, with hardcore Sunni groups, such as Salafists, refusing to even see the Shia as Muslims, regarding them instead as apostates. That feud was about to be refreshed with much new blood on this age-old battlefield.

We rose before dawn and blearily slipped into the sea of humanity. Lights were on in all the buildings, and the noise level never dipped below the ambient roar of a million people praying and talking as they bowed to the ground or strolled in groups looking for breakfast. Gradually, the mass of humanity compressed itself inwards towards an area sandwiched between the shrines of the Imams Abbas and Hussein, which gaze at each in mourning over several hundred yards of paved open ground dotted with trees. Even on normal days, this stretch of the plaza would be traversed by arthritic old women on their hands and knees, only their lined faces visible under billowing black *abbayas*, crawling past the market vendors from mosque to mosque like dying crows, paying penance for untold sins. That dawn, they had been replaced by scores of men dressed in white shrouds and bearing swords in their hands. They had already started to wander in a circuit between the mosques, slapping and scraping their heads with scimitars and knives as they went. Some screamed out 'Haidar' ('the lion'), one of the many names attributed to Imam Ali, Hussein's father. Some of them started running as they hit their heads: more and more flowed into the swift parade, until we found ourselves in an island of spectators, watching as on either side of us the devout derby surged between the shrines, their faces painted by blood, the incessant beating of the swords tearing through their scalps. Some winced in pain with each blow, others appeared indifferent as the trance of expurgation of age-old sin sealed them off from the world of the senses. Their white robes became tie-dyes of blood, and occasionally one would pass close enough to spray the spectators.

'It's nothing, just drops of blood,' one man from Baghdad told me as I pushed backwards to avoid the scarlet drizzle. 'It's an old tradition, practised since the days of the martyrdom of Imam Hussein.' In fact, many Shia religious authorities now discourage the drawing of blood in Ashoura, an attitude shared by at least one woman I spoke to, who shielded her young daughter's eyes and muttered to me, so that no one around could hear, that this was not the intelligent way to show dedication to the Imam. 'The Shia are strong and peaceful, we don't need to do this to show our devotion to Imam Hussein.'

But most appeared to see some kind of vindication in the ritual. 'I think nowadays it is better than in the past, now we are free to beat ourselves,' smiled Dawoud, a twenty-year-old jobless labourer who had walked two days from Nasariyah in the south to attend the ceremony. He had offered to join the bloody procession – men selected according to their health and ability to endure such abuse – but had been turned away as the organizers said they already had too many volunteers. 'I feel happy when I see this, it makes me feel closer to Hussein,' he smiled.

After about an hour, the gory procession seemed to lose steam. Relatives led their bloodied menfolk away to recover, many of them blinded by the blood running into their eyes.

The festival started winding down now that the main event was over, but still the masses milled around the city centre. I had come here suspecting that after the recent spate of bombings in Baghdad, this was the next logical target. Relieved, however, that nothing had happened, we returned to the hotel to pack our bags and leave. With Terri's photos of the event – the first full Ashoura since the fall of the regime – we had a good story already. It was time to head back to Baghdad and file. We had left Yassir on the edge of the city centre – he hadn't wanted to leave his car, worrying that it would either be mistaken for a car bomb and destroyed, or stolen by some opportunist in the anonymous crowd of black-robed pilgrims. He had slept in the vehicle, so we checked out of the Hotel Moon and headed off to find him again. Outside the hotel, we walked by a group of pilgrims gathered near a cauldron to get their free breakfast, then passed a little staged tableau of a desert scene, replete with a very sedate camel, presumably representing some episode from Imam Hussein's life. On our right was the giant blood fountain, still gushing out its geyser of martyrdom. We were just walking back down one of the main streets to the edge of the city centre when we heard a muffled boom. We froze.

'Was that a bomb?' I asked. Nobody seemed sure. There was another diffuse percussion. This time I was sure it was an explosion. I looked at the crowd: a ripple of confusion caused people to stop and turn their heads, but no one seemed quite clear about what they had just heard, if indeed they had heard anything. There was a moment when that swell of people appeared to waver, some deep herd instinct communicating itself wordlessly through the black throngs. I shouted to the others to get behind an iron railing on the corner of the street, fearing that a stampede was about to break over us. Almost every year, hundreds of pilgrims die in a panicked crush in Mecca during the Hajj, the sheer force of numbers alone sometimes the only reason for the stampede. But something that day prevented this crowd, which had such good cause to flee, from doing so. Perhaps it was the knowledge that so many carried in their hearts, that no true harm could come to them here, on this day. Inner peace, or the draw of martyrdom, who knows. As soon as we realized they were not about to surge for safety, we headed back towards the mosque plaza.

It was not easy going. Close to the explosions, the calm we had marvelled at further out in the sea of people was gone and we struggled through crowded, narrow alleys against a storm surge of fleeing, startled pilgrims, their religious calm stripped away by the horrors they had just witnessed. Some stopped long enough to give us snatched reports of what had happened: pieces of meat raining from the sky, arms and legs scattered on the ground. Many were bleeding, making their way as fast they could towards what they imagined was safety. But there was no safety that day. The terrorists had sent in at least nine suicide bombers, the police later concluded, to mingle with the crowd and spread their mayhem as broadly as possible. Perhaps they wanted to compound the death toll from the bombs with a massive crush: just over a year later, when the country was fully in the grip of a remorseless terror, more than a thousand Shiites were killed in a stampede on a Baghdad bridge after Friday prayers. And that day in Karbala, as people ran to the blast sites to tend the wounded, or flee the bombers, they ran into the explosions of yet more kamikazes. Police officers tried to block off streets and shepherd people away, only to direct them straight into the killing zone of yet another suicide bomber. No one knew where to run, or even what exactly was being used to cut them down in their dozens: for a long time, it was unclear whether we were being attacked by mortars, hidden explosive devices or suicide bombers. An Iranian pilgrim called Fairuz, who spoke broken English, pointed at a pile of rubbish and told me the bombs were hidden there. I shouted to Lulu and Terri to avoid the piles of trash, then realized how pointless that was: the streets were lined with the detritus of a million people in a city with no functioning garbage disposal service. We decided we had to return to the hotel as quickly as possible, get off the streets before we were caught in the next explosion or set upon by terrified pilgrims. Already people were starting to vent their rage against anyone they thought looked suspicious, and in Iraq, that usually means foreigners. Any foreigners will do in a crisis. Many of the people in the streets were still holding the swords they had beaten themselves with during the dawn frenzy. There was little chance they would be rational enough to understand we were just journalists, even more scared than they – after all, we didn't have the consoling thought of Paradise awaiting us as martyrs, just a body bag and a distraught family back home.

For twenty minutes, the city centre echoed to the din of explosion after explosion, with hundreds of people scrabbling down side streets, not knowing where or when the next detonation would be. To be in the centre of it was bewildering, but we had no time to fully take in the fear or the horror, trying as we were to piece together what had already happened and how to survive what was yet to come. As we emerged from a grimy, seething alleyway, the crowd suddenly thinned and we stumbled out again on to the main plaza, next to the Imam Abbas mosque with its lofty, emerald-tile walls. Wooden handcarts laden with bodies were being pushed through the wreckage. A woman's corpse lay near the shrine, wrapped in a black *abbaya*. A security guard picked up her severed head and placed it on her back as ambulances struggled through the remaining pilgrims to evacuate the dead and wounded. An elderly man scraped together gobbets of flesh in one of the plastic food trays that minutes before had been laden with rice and bean handouts. By a blown-in restaurant door was what remained of a man I presumed to have been a suicide bomber. His body had been reduced to a pond of jam-like pulp, atop which sat his head, eyes closed and lower jaw sheared clean off. I stared at the intact head in grim fascination, grabbed Lulu's sleeve and pointed it out to her, utterly transfixed by the sight: Lulu groaned in horror, and looked away. Nearby, some men were hassling Terri for having taken photos. We pushed them away and dragged her off. Saleh warned us that the crowd was becoming increasingly belligerent towards us.

Returning to the hotel was far harder than expected, as two of the explosions had occurred very close to it. In fact, the route we had taken fifteen minutes earlier had led us right past two of the suicide bombers, who must have been standing in the crowd, waiting for their cue and muttering their final prayers or curses, as we had passed by. Outside the desert tableau we had passed was a lake of blood marking where the spectators had stood. The camel remained in place, frozen in shock, as though stuffed. The rice cauldron we had walked by outside the hotel had been another target. On the roof of the hotel I later spotted what appeared to be a small lump of human entrails, perhaps one of the hungry stomachs that had been waiting in line as we went by shortly before. The road outside the hotel was closed, so we ducked around the back: I heard another boom, closer now, up ahead. We were jogging by this time, the fear starting to kick in: forget the story, forget the photos, just stay alive. Finally we rounded a corner and saw the hotel ahead, standing on an almost deserted street looking up to the square. We ran up, but a plainclothes security guard from one of the militias tried to stop us, shouting something in Arabic. We tried to reason with him, but he was screaming that we had to turn back, even though we were so close to safety. At that moment, a member of the hotel staff appeared at the door and, recognizing me, held out his hand and pulled me in. I grabbed Lulu's hand, she grasped Saleh and he dragged in Terri: we daisy-chained to salvation.

Or so we thought. When we got back inside, an Italian photographer told us the hotel had been stormed by the mob after a hue and cry went up, with frenzied agitators swearing that the building was full of suspect foreigners. An angry crowd had burst in and beaten the staff and guests, several of whom were sitting now in the lobby and corridor, having cuts and bruises patched up by the harried receptionists. Most of the journalists inside the hotel at the time had locked themselves in their rooms until the pack receded, fanning out to find easier victims. Everyone was shaken, not least the Italian photographer Marco, who had been blown to the ground by one of the first explosions, then attacked by a furious crowd immediately afterwards. One of the incensed pilgrims had even pulled Marco's own pocket knife from his belt and tried to stab him with it: only the swift intervention of his translator had saved him. Elsewhere, Andrea Bruce Woodall, a *Washington Post* photographer, had been too conspicuous with her blonde hair even under a headscarf, and had been dragged by the camera straps round her neck by the mob before her quick-thinking colleague Anthony Shadid, an Arabic-speaking American journalist of Lebanese descent, could calm the people down by claiming she was his wife. The lesson was clear: don't mix with furious, shell-shocked Shiite pilgrims to whom anyone with a different skin hue is a suspicious outsider. Even as we made our way up to the roof to survey the scene from relative security, the police outside were rounding up Iranians and Pakistanis, anyone who didn't look Iraqi. Yassir, our driver, was briefly dragged off to the police station merely for standing by his car, which none of the local shopkeepers recognized.

From our vantage point on the roof – where most journalists were now gathering, avoiding the lump of human meat baking in the morning sun near the parapet, and wondering whether we would be stormed again and pitched to the street three floors below – we could see the tattered, bloodstained crowd slowly re-forming. In the centre, the men had even started a kind of religious run, sprinting in a large pack from mosque to mosque. I was amazed: there were still reports that the rubbish piles were filled with bombs, and here they were continuing regardless, even though the police had had no chance to search for more explosives. It was hard to tell who had been injured and who was covered in blood from the morning's savage devotions. I decided it would be a good idea to continue my reporting from inside the hotel, for the time being. Already, people claimed to know for sure who was behind the attack, which had killed more than a hundred people.

'I think it was Wahhabis and Sunnis,' said Khalid Qaddum, one of the young waiters hovering among the shell-shocked guests in the hotel lobby. 'They think if they kill three Shias they'll go to heaven.' But for the Shias, he insisted, it was their dead who would go directly to heaven, while the bombers would go to hell. It was a logic I remembered from Gaza.

In the almost deserted hotel restaurant, I bumped into Sheikh Mohammed al-Sayyidi, a student of the powerful al-Hawza school of Shia Islam, who told me his cousin had been among the first to run to help people caught in the very first explosion, only to be blown apart by the second. I offered my condolences and said he must be very sad.

'Do I look sad?' asked the 35-year-old, smiling calmly. It was only an hour or two since he had witnessed his cousin's violent death, but he was clearly unperturbed. On the contrary.

'I'm jealous of him, he has gone straight to heaven. His father is happy but we haven't told his mother yet. I'm sure my cousin is being hosted by Imam Hussein even now.' He swore that the Shia were ready to die for their faith, which was why they could never lose this ancient battle fought at the gates of paradise. 'They want to provoke a civil war, but we hope to be martyrs. If they know this, they'll stop,' he said. His prediction was to prove all too hollow, however. The Karbala bombings were only the start. It would soon get much, much worse.

After the sheikh had returned to join the festivities, we bribed another police officer to escort us back through the solid wall of Shias, packed tight as penguins in an Antarctic blizzard, to our car and made our painstakingly slow getaway through the masses, already parading their defiance to the bombers and announcing their willingness to die.

CITY OF BROKEN MOSQUES

How the Spiders of Allah Defeated the US Marine Corps

Lieutenant Colonel Brennan Byrne, commander of the First Battalion, Fifth Regiment of the US Marine Corps, stepped out of his briefing room and gazed happily up at the sky. 'God, that sound gives me a stiffy,' he laughed. 'Don't quote me on that!' he added, spotting three journalists standing outside, pens poised over notebooks and waiting for an update. We laughed too. After all, he was a friendly, helpful officer with a sense of humour. About a mile away, however, people were being vaporized by a wall of bullets.

The otherworldly howl and burp of the Spectre gunship continued to reverberate across Fallujah, the mournful cry of a shambling monster satiating itself on human life. By a trick of acoustics, the eerie *waarrrp* sound of a hundred bullets per second leaving the aircraft's chain gun was audible only after the bass *buuurrrrr* of their impact on disintegrating Iraqis. The fact that the AC130 was such a large, unwieldy aircraft –

an airborne platform rigged with Gatling guns and cannon – made it seem all the more sinister. Like a mythical dragon fishing over some human pond, it scarcely bothered to exert itself, yet was still able to unleash carnage with practised indifference. But as I stood outside the colonel's headquarters hut on Iraq's newest front line, I knew there was nothing we could do about the killing around us.

For the past seven days in April 2004, the marines in Fallujah had seen some of the harshest urban warfare since they had sweated it out for control of Hue City during the Tet offensive, back in January 1968. In the streets, dogs picked at the bloated corpses of Iraqis who had died in the fighting. Hundreds of people had been killed, though due to the ill-defined nature of the battle, no one was ever quite sure who they were, who had killed them or how many they numbered. The figure we did know, on the other hand, was that around 60,000 people – a third of the city – had already fled as the marines fought their way in, block by block. More Fallujans left every day, if they could bypass the fifteen-mile-long, six-foot-high earth wall that the US forces had bulldozed round Fallujah like a tourniquet to prevent the rebellion leaking out.

Byrne, a tall, lean man in his forties with a grey short-back-and-sides but a youthful, animated face, had at his command hundreds of men from the 1/5 Marines, a battalion with a long history of success, peppered with the odd near-disaster. It had fought the Germans at Aisne in 1917, driven the Japanese out of Guadalcanal and Okinawa in the Second World War, battled against vastly superior numbers of Chinese at the Chosin Reservoir in Korea and slogged it out in the jungles of Que Son to attack the Ho Chi Minh trail, where it took heavy losses. Now it had flown in from Japan to take on the toughest task in America's latest military venture: the pacification of Fallujah.

This was Byrne's first major combat command, a chance to cover himself and his battalion with glory by crushing what his boss, Marine Major General James Mattis, referred to as 'Joe Jihadi' – the Islamic fanatics and Baathist thugs who exerted their ruthless grip over this small, benighted city on the Euphrates, just west of the capital. A vigorous and charismatic commander, Byrne was itching to fight this battle and win, but he regularly took time out to sit down and brief the small coterie of journalists who had made it this far into the battle zone. He would pull a cold MRE, or Meal Ready-to-Eat, pouch out of the pocket of his pixellated 'digi-cam' uniform and eat the unappetizing, often unidentifiable, chunked meat with a plastic spoon as he elaborated on how his men were the 'credible ability to coerce' that made any diplomacy with the rebels possible. Or he'd describe the stashes of pilgrims' money belts packed with explosives that his men had found hidden together with uniforms of the Iraqi Civil Defence Corps, a local militia who were supposed to be on the Americans' side.

But if his nether regions were stirred by the mournful hunting call of the AC130's feeding frenzy, it was with good reason: Byrne's General Patton moment of glory against Joe Jihadi was rapidly souring. Political meddling, both from back home in Washington and Baghdad, and a surprisingly dedicated resistance would eventually hand a stinging victory to the tribal zealots across the lines.

From the very start of the occupation, Fallujah had been the epicentre of the incipient insurgency. Its citizens proudly called their hometown the City of Mosques, a description that made it sound much grander than it actually was. Sure, there were plenty of shiny mosques (or at least, they had been shiny before the mortars and machine guns chewed up their minarets until they looked like used toothpicks). But otherwise it was a run-down, forbidding den of haughty and staunchly religious tribesmen, perched on an ancient smuggling route from Jordan to Baghdad. It was a city steeped in tribal honour, with all the brutality and human suffering that that entailed. The men of Fallujah, I was told, would pull their guns on each other for trying to jump a petrol queue. Proud and devout, with a hair-trigger response to any slight upon their manhood, the city's population of 300,000 was entangled in a web of centuries-old blood feuds into which the American army – the largest, newest tribe on the block – had stumbled. The men of the city had a frightening disregard for the fighting capacity of their occupiers, matched only by a flagrant indifference to their own deaths. Their fate was in Allah's hands: their task was to defend only their honour and their families, in that order. Fallujah had often been described as a hotbed of support for Saddam. Closer to the truth was that even

Saddam had been wary of these ferociously insular desert berserkers and had co-opted them into his Republican Guard regiments, subscribing to the old adage that you should keep your friends close, but your enemies closer.

The buildings were the same washed-out non-colour as the dusty flatlands that limped off to the horizon, as though one of the seasonal dust storms had long ago been frozen by some capricious djinn into the shape of houses and streets. The merchants' homes were walled mini-fortresses, or sprawling neo-Babylonian displays of gaudy opulence, with every possible combination of stone colonnade, Swiss gable and Roman palisade available to the kitsch-loving ranks of Iraqi sheikhdom. Aside from the vicious dignity of its occupants, the city's other claim to fame was the best kebab restaurant in the entire country. Hajji Hussein's was an eatery short on interior decor but full of pot-bellied men who filled themselves with greasy meats topped by globs of glistening white lamb fat. I had not eaten at Hajji Hussein's in a long time: the city had become increasingly hostile to any outsiders, even to Iraqis from outside the city. The last time I had plucked up the courage to walk through the market in Fallujah, while on a trip there a couple of months before, a small boy had called out to me, 'Mister, mister.' When I looked at him he mimed firing an imaginary RPG at my face. I smiled nervously and walked quickly back to my car, the market stallholders staring at me impassively as I left. A few weeks after that, a group of American security contractors working for the firm Blackwater drove past the kebab shop, apparently diverted off their route by US forces operating on the highway. Their vehicles were ambushed by local clansmen, raked with machine-gun bullets and blown up by rocket fire. Then a howling, capering mob came out and beat the burning bodies with sticks, tied them with string to the rear bumpers of cars and dragged them down Fallujah's main street, to a steel girder bridge built by the British in the 1940s. They strung two of the mangled bodies from a steel span at the eastern entrance to the bridge, then stood on a donkey cart and beat them again with sticks, causing the blackened corpses to emit small puffs of smoke.

Byrne's marines were ordered to shave off the wispy moustaches they had been told to grow as a token of respect to the local tribesmen. They launched a large-scale 'cordon and knock' sweep of the city for the killers, but almost instantly ran into a well-prepared guerrilla force. Lulu, who was with the marines, was pinned down by rocket and machine-gun fire with her embed unit and had to be extracted by armoured vehicles. She phoned me in my Baghdad hotel room the same night and told me to get down to Fallujah as quickly as possible.

Unlikely as it had seemed even a week before it happened, the American military had lost control of the main highway leading west from Baghdad to Jordan in that first week of April 2004. Right on the outskirts of the occupied capital, gunmen pinned down US supply convoys with roadside bombs and rocket attacks, the terrified ex-military drivers hunkered by their stalled

18-wheelers, clutching carbines and waiting to be kid-napped or killed. The sinews of the occupation were snapping fast. Although the capital itself seemed on the brink of collapse, I desperately wanted to get down to Fallujah.

It took a week of badgering the marines via satellite phone and email before they agreed to fly me and a few other journalists to the fighting. They clearly didn't want too many press people down there, getting in the way just as things were going badly. Lulu was working from her end to get me there, too, although with an ulterior motive. Like the marines, she too had thought the operation would last only a day or two. Now it had flared into a full-scale siege, and the marines were fighting their way in, block by block. Consequently, she had run out of clean underwear, tape-recorder batteries and all sorts of other kit. As I headed to the helicopter land-ing strip in the Green Zone clad in body armour and with a bag full of Lulu's knickers, I felt pleased that our joint efforts had paid off eventually. It was only when we lined up in the dark at Landing Zone Washington that I saw exactly why the marines had agreed to the press transport. As we introduced ourselves and shook hands in the darkness, a man in camouflage fatigues stepped forwards. I thought at first he was one of the military press officers escorting us.

'Ollie North, Fox News,' the man said by way of intro-duction. Oliver North was, of course, the former marines colonel who in the 1980s had colluded with Panamanian dictator Manuel Noriega to sell US weapons to the American-hating Iranians to help secure the release of US hostages in Lebanon, and who had then funnelled the proceeds to the right-wing Contras in Nicaragua to subvert the government there. And while Noriega was now in a Miami prison, North was working for Fox News. He was greeted like a rock star by the young marines, who had arranged a special flight into Fallujah for him, and who begged for his autograph wherever he went. They laughed politely at his lewd and unvarying jokes about his cameraman having some kind of venereal rash.

As North regaled the ground crew with yet another reference to STDs, I was forced to ponder my unusual predicament: not only was the city we were headed for in the hands of Islamist and nationalist guerrillas and their local gangster allies – kidnappers with a mean streak and a penchant for shooting down helicopters like the giant Chinook I was boarding – but I was worried that if we crashed, my body would be found next to a burst rucksack spewing out bras and panties. And if we somehow survived, here I would still be not merely laden with women's lingerie but accompanied by the man who had illicitly sold weapons to the Iraqis' sworn enemies, the Iranians, on behalf of President Reagan. I tried not to dwell on it too much.

Helicopters in Iraq always flew in tandem for security reasons, but because we were flying with lights off, we couldn't see our fellow chopper. The Chinooks wheeled out over the rooftops of Saddam's palaces in the small hours, the roar of the engines and twin rotors deafening. All we could see were the lights of Baghdad through the open rear hatch – whole neighbourhoods swathed in electrical blackout suddenly gave way to brightly illuminated sectors where the grid was working, the lights of homes and mosques shimmying through the heat haze of the Chinook's engines. A marine hooked up to a safety line sat on the open hatch, rifle ready, scanning the blackness below for any trace of enemy activity. Two other marines manned heavy machine guns poking out the side doors at the front. The helicopter spun and swooped crazily to avoid any fire from the ground. After about forty minutes we landed in total darkness, to be shown off the 'copter again by the ever-mute loader.

Camp Fallujah was a vast terrain that had once housed the Iranian Mujahedin Kalk (MEK), an opposition guerrilla organization in exile that Saddam had sponsored, which, in absentia, had been condemned to death en masse by the ayatollahs back in Tehran. Now listed as a terrorist organization by the coalition government who had taken over Iraq, the 3,500 members of the organization – a bizarre mix of Marxist and Islamic fundamentalism, a third of whose fighters were women – were living in limbo, under close watch in another former military camp out near the Iranian border, since nobody had the faintest idea what to do with them.

Camp Fallujah was a huge complex. Complex was the right word to describe a place made up of the former MEK terrorist cult's base, an ex-Iraqi military camp and, rather incongruously, a walled former holiday camp called Dreamland (not exactly Disneyland, it offered some rusty swings and slides, a muddy lake and a few parched, peeling birch trees that partially obscured the newly added machine-gun towers). Together, they had agglomerated into a vast US encampment just beyond the eastern fringe of the town itself. Ironically, the place seemed more like a holiday camp in its new incarnation as a US military base than it had ever been as an Iraqi resort: it now had a large internet café, several gyms equipped with Stairmasters and treadmills, a games room complete with air hockey and pool tables, a shop and a chapel, which had once been the auditorium where MEK officers listened to speeches in Farsi about contemporary terrorist techniques.

The sprawling camp was like a small city, and probably larger than many places that claimed such a title in Iraq. At the core was a well-preserved sandstone complex that had been the MEK headquarters, and showed the softer side of a covert guerrilla organization: a well-tended lawn grew outside the buildings, and a small series of ponds connected by a tinkling stream was caringly lined with pansies and a rock garden. Around the complex were several other low-rise accommodation blocks. In almost every space in between were large tents, lines of porta-johns, parked ranks of US armour, and marines milling absolutely everywhere: marines jogging in grey sweatshirts, marines puffing away in the allotted smoking areas (which invariably featured a cautionary picture of a soldier with a huge red nose like a melting toffee apple, warning all personnel to use insect repellent against the risk of leishmaniasis, a parasite spread by sand-fly bite). All around us there were plodding columns of Humvees, Amphibious Assault Vehicles and Light Armoured Vehicles kicking up trails of dust on the marines as they flip-flopped to washroom trailers in shorts and T-shirts, flak jackets on and towels flung over their shoulders. Every so often a huge boom would make new arrivals jump nervously: the vets would look at you disdainfully and shrug. Outgoing. I later realized that few could actually tell the difference between outgoing and incoming. As I leapt under a ping-pong table one night after a particularly loud bang, a soldier called out a useful tip. 'It's only the one you don't hear that you have to worry about.'

Going into a combat zone is like moving through the concentric circles of hell – at each stop you're increasingly jittery, but when you reach the next one down the line, you realize how much better off you were before. Back at Camp Fallujah, I had jumped whenever I heard outgoing artillery, as well as the odd incoming rocket. Now, driving out in a convoy of Hummers along the bumpy track, a cloud of dust announcing our approach for miles around, it seemed as if we were leaving behind the safest place in the world.

The drive took us between the high breezeblock wall of Dreamland and a scrapyard of stripped-down Iraqi army vehicles abandoned from previous wars, then on to a road leading straight into town, a couple of miles away. The marines in my truck were friendly and chatty, but once we left the safer area by the camp walls, they became taciturn and stared out the sides of vehicle, rifles at the ready. They were remarkably relaxed, I thought, as I surreptitiously lowered myself on to the floor of the open-backed and recklessly unarmoured Humvee. But then they knew what I didn't yet, that the part of town we were heading into was largely controlled by US forces: the next circle of hell was further down the line.

At first glance, everything remained the same from my visit a few weeks prior, when I had driven in to report on the lynching of the US contractors. That journey with Lulu had been terrifying, not knowing if we too would be burned and strung up by the locals. We had stopped only briefly to speak to a few vendors selling goods on the roadside. A man flogging petrol from jerry cans spat his hatred for the Americans.

'I'd have done even worse to them if I'd been here yesterday,' he boasted. I wondered what could be worse than having your burned corpse hung from a bridge and beaten by kids, but I was sure if anyone could think up something, it would be a Fallujan.

The streets had still been quite busy then. Now there was no one, except a few marines at a sandbagged checkpoint where we dog-legged off to the left, southwards, into the industrial zone. While it was generally called the 'industrial zone', this term was in fact quite misleading, conjuring up images of a light industrial estate with aluminium-sided warehouses and neat redbrick sales offices. This place, on the other hand, was a mass of low-lying, crumbling car repair shops, grimy little tyre vulcanizers and scrapmetal yards, the owners' names painted in faded, dribbled paint. A metal frame with a crude, blue-painted onion dome on top marked the mechanics' local mosque. The marines had been forced to battle hard to take the zone because one of the main industries here had been the manufacture of rockets, car bombs and homemade mortars, welded together and hidden behind decaying car parts. Understandably, the guerrillas had been reluctant to relinquish their armoury. Now, cautiously guarding their newly won turf, marine snipers crouched on rooftops, keeping anyone from sneaking across the highway leading from the north of town, which remained under rebel control.

We bumped along a dirt track where wild dogs ran barking at the wheels of the Humvees, then skulked back to their lairs in abandoned buildings. The quiet of this once bustling city of 300,000 was unsettling. I was relieved when we pulled into the soda factory where the marines of the 1/5 had set up their Forward Operating Base.

The soda factory had previously been one of the few functioning, legitimate businesses in Fallujah: it had turned out local, highly sweetened variations of Fanta and Coke, as well as a pithy, thick nectar called Rani, which was much treasured by the sweaty and dehydrated troops who now preyed on the sugary trove. The quartermaster had tracked down the owner of the factory and handed over 15,000 dollars for all the pop that the parched marines were swigging down. The American fighters lounged on the factory conveyor belt or crashed out in bivouacs strung among the wooden pallets. Communications centres and command posts were squeezed into every nook and outhouse. Wiry young men stripped to the waist milled around, baring huge tattoos of crosses, demons and busty blondes on their backs, arms and chests, the sooty night-camouflage still smudged across their drawn, youthful faces. Hooches had been strung up all over, rifles stacked in black metal stooks. The place reeked of body odour and Coca-Cola. One skinny young man, wrapped only in a towel, hopped awkwardly about as he tried to pull on his underpants, an odd touch of modesty in the teeming display of virulent, beef-fed American manhood.

In the front yard of the factory compound, the troops of Weapons Company had set up their bivouacs in shell scrapes and slit trenches in the mud. From there, they ran their dangerous sorties to rescue downed helicopter crews and ambushed supply convoys. In between times, they lounged on their packs in whatever shade they could find, comparing porn mags their girlfriends had sent them.

'Any girl who sends you *Butt Man* is a girl you can marry,' sagely reflected one bespectacled trooper. Another lamented the fact that the women in the magazine his girlfriend had sent were, in fact, lady-boys. 'Chicks with fuckin' dicks,' he spat as his comrades hooted with laughter.

Naked girls weren't, however, their sole source of satisfaction: I saw one nineteen-year-old marine, a complete gun nut, marvelling at a weapon that had been confiscated during a raid. 'Un-fucking-believable,' he moaned ecstatically as he recalled handling a rare

221

Second World War German MG34, a collectors' item which had, by a bizarre twist of casting, been the weapon used by Chewbacca in the original *Star Wars* movie. Seeing the antique machine gun had made the whole battle worthwhile for the kid, who spent his down time conjecturing as to how it might have ended up in Fallujah. He joked that the guerrilla who had used it probably had had no idea that it was worth close to 20,000 dollars. Another marine showed me a home-made weapon straight out of *Inspector Gadget*: a plastic helmet that had two rocket tubes attached to the top of it, presumably so the user could fire over walls without being shot.

'I hope the guy never used it, 'cos the back blast would have broken his neck,' the marine said, chuckling with glee at the thought. 'Come to that, I hope he *did* use it.'

The front line was officially called Phase Line Violet on the marines' map. The men on the ground had a different name for it: Bullshit Boulevard. If it had an Iraqi name, I never learned it. There were no Iraqis around, except the dead ones lying in the street and among the purple bougainvillea. On the eastern side, the marines of Alpha Company sat in the metalsmiths' workshops and carpenters' ateliers of the industrial quarter; across the road, in the lush gardens of the emptied merchants' quarter, the holy warriors and tribesmen of Fallujah waited.

Bullshit Boulevard was a fifteen-minute drive from the soda factory through the ghost town of the industrial zone. I looked out across the no-man's land through the window of a sniper's nest. Across the road, in the drive of a large villa, stood a burgundy Mercedes, its windscreen splintered by bullets. Rotting next to it was the body of its owner. Further along the street, by a lawn of green, well-watered grass, a man in a black *dishdasheh* lay dead on the pavement, his hands in his pocket. Next to me stood the man who had shot him dead a few hours earlier.

Corporal Ryan Long was a chatty, friendly 26-year-old with a keen interest in dirt-biking. He had woken up that morning at dawn in a shabby, abandoned loft wallpapered with faded blue Disney characters from the 1960s, roused from a broken sleep by his best buddy, Lance Corporal Ryan Deady. Deady was still young enough to joke about how he had gotten into trouble in his last stint back home for under-age drinking. There had been a lot of shooting that night, though in a period of calm a deer had wandered down the deserted street, nature moving in as men moved out.

Deady, dressed in a T-shirt emblazoned with the regimental slogan 'Make peace or die', had shaken Long awake and pointed out an Iraqi man walking down Bullshit Boulevard. The man's hands were hidden suspiciously in his pockets. Long told his friend to fire a warning shot. The man kept on walking, resolutely, despite the shot.

'So I said, "Let me do it,"' Long recounted calmly, no evidence on his face of the strain of making a life-or-death decision after just a few hours' sleep.

The eternal question: what did he feel afterwards?

Long was honest: his best friend, Lance Corporal Blake Wofford, had been killed just a few days before.

'Now one of my best friends is dead, I'm thinking maybe this is the guy who got him. Last year I'd have never shot a guy without a weapon. But I'm a demolition expert; you can hide a lot under your clothes.'

He paused a moment. 'It feels numb now,' he said. Long had clearly thought about it, despite his air of unworried professionalism. 'I don't know if that's good or bad. But the sooner we get one of these bad guys, the sooner we can go home.'

He had seen enough to make any 26-year-old jaded. During a recent gun battle on Bullshit Boulevard, he saw an Iraqi ambulance screech up to a wounded man. It was accompanied by soldiers from the US-trained Iraqi Civil Defence Corps. Instead of retrieving the injured man, the three men in the Red Crescent ambulance fired rocket-propelled grenades at the marines, then sped off as the ICDC men gave them covering fire.

'We walked into this thinking there'd be good guys and bad guys. Then you get here and have men in ambulances firing RPGs at you,' Long sighed.

Outside, the occasional whoosh-bang of an RPG swept down a nearby street as the guerrillas tried to manoeuvre for position. No one seemed too concerned about the menacing sound. In the shade of a destroyed car, a puppy that the marines had adopted was rummaging through used MRE packets for food. Around its neck someone had tied a canvas collar with a cardboard name tag that read 'Nasty Fucker'. I walked next door to where the rest of the unit lounged. On the roof, in a brick outhouse, a marine lance-corporal lay on his belly and viewed the streets and houses along the barrel of a .50-calibre machine gun. He said he sang to himself to pass the time. Again, the question that every journalist wants to ask any soldier in combat, ghoulish and voyeuristic: 'What's it like to kill people?'

He didn't look up. 'I don't even think about those people as people,' he said frankly, after a moment's thought. In the distance, I could just spot figures moving around in the guerrilla-controlled zone, carrying white cloths or T-shirts tied to sticks, heedful of the truce terms. Without the flags, they would quickly cease being people in the war-hardened eyes of the young man beside me and become mere targets. In his remarks, made without ever lifting his gaze from his weapon's sights, was all the sadness of this battle: people who were trained to feel nothing as they took another person's life, fighting to the death – for what: oil, freedom? – with people raised to feel that kinship was the sole preserve of their clan and their deity. Both were a million miles from ever knowing who the other was, and, more tragically yet, even caring.

I was just pondering whether this was a professional defence mechanism for the fighting man or a disturbing case of heartlessness when I almost got an Iraqi killed myself. I was amazed to see a man in a white robe come out of his backyard barely thirty yards away. He had no white flag, just a bundle of sticks clutched between his hands. A few yards away from him lay the corpse of a dead neighbour, yet the man appeared to be gardening. I laughed in pure disbelief.

'That guy must be crazy, doing his gardening on the front line!' I said. The lieutenant I had come on to the roof with clearly hadn't seen him.

'Where?' he asked.

'Down there,' I said, 'just up that street leading off the main road.'

To my horror the lieutenant suddenly barked out to one of his men: 'Sergeant, shoot that man!'

I felt a surge of utter panic at what I'd done. 'No, no, he's just doing some gardening.'

It didn't even strike me how ridiculous that sounded, standing there on the front line. 'Look, he's just got some sticks in his hand.'

The lieutenant clearly thought the man was covering up an IED – which he may well have been, although he might just as well have been clearing up his yard. People do odd things when armies are entrenched outside their houses, and perhaps he was trying to inject some normality into the chaos around him. The fact that a reporter was there made the lieutenant think twice.

'Fire a warning shot,' he ordered. The sergeant took aim and fired a bullet down the street. The gardener almost jumped out of his skin. To my great relief, he bolted like a jack rabbit back into his house. I made a mental note to watch what the hell I said out here.

The battle was a stop-start affair, with politicians in Baghdad and Washington dithering over whether to level Fallujah or try to talk to the fighters in town. New marine units would be deployed for attack, only to be stood down as a fresh ceasefire was called. Despite these truces, the firing never stopped for more than a few hours at a time, and the American troops would still send out units into the grand houses along Bullshit Boulevard, running across the open space to avoid sniper bullets, then throwing themselves panting against walls as the local madman, a leathery, toothless lunatic left behind by a family that had fled the city, would casually stumble up and talk gibberish at them in Arabic.

Most of the houses the marines searched belonged to wealthy merchants or tribal sheikhs who had locked their valuables inside one room or another for safe-keeping. The marines blew the doors off, often finding nothing more than a stash of embroidered cushions and bedding, or a jewellery box. Staring at a huge living room, a marine I was with couldn't help comparing it to the sweltering concrete workshop where he slept, in the thick dust from the stone cutter's marble engravings for Fallujah's mosques.

'Pretty nice place,' he remarked angrily. 'These people live better than we do, and they're complaining.'

Another outraged marine from New York came up to me and held out a cigarette lighter engraved with an airliner crashing into the World Trade Center. I told him these souvenirs were sold by the hundreds in any of Iraq's street markets. But for him, it seemed to confirm the unfounded suspicion that what they were doing was somehow linked to the September 11 attacks.

'I'm taking this to show the people back home,' he

said as he tucked it into his webbing. Outside, marines sat by ornamental fountains under orange trees, catching their breath before the next house, the next street, the next sniper attack. Their faces looked boiled in their own sweat. Other times, they would hunker down behind the parapet on a rooftop and listen to the shrapnel from a mortar round zipping overhead.

Interspersed with days of sniping and vigilant, sweaty boredom were episodes of pure terror. I heard about one such episode that had been fought along the line by Bravo Company, so I hitched a ride with the supply convoy and sought out the sergeant who had almost seen his unit wiped out.

A few days earlier, Staff Sergeant Ismael Sagredo had found himself in charge of fourteen men facing imminent annihilation after his Amphibious Assault Vehicle had become lost in the labyrinthine alleys across the line from Bullshit Boulevard. His vehicle had been one of two AAVs trying to trap insurgents who had just ambushed a US supply convoy near the front line. But as the two armoured vehicles trundled down parallel alleyways, Sagredo's unit came under fire from rocket-propelled grenades. The AAV was taking direct hits but the lane was too narrow to turn the behemoth around. So the officer in charge, Lieutenant Christopher Ayres, ordered his driver to charge their attackers.

'I've never seen so many RPGs. A lot of them were propped up against the walls with extra rounds,' said Sagredo, the 35-year-old son of Mexican migrant fruit pickers who worked their way through the states and seasons. All his siblings had been born in different parts of the country. Sitting in a ratty chair in an otherwise bare room in central Fallujah as he recounted the tale, he barely seemed to register the regular explosions just a few blocks away, as mortars landed or his comrades detonated guerrilla weapons caches. At one point, I was half-blinded by a flash of light from a blast, but Sagredo, a twelve-year veteran of the corps, remained calm and earnest throughout the interview.

After being forced to follow a dog-leg in the alley, Sagredo's unit found itself driving into unknown territory. They turned another corner and saw hundreds of guerrillas ahead of them. The Iraqis were apparently as surprised as the Americans to find a lone Marine Corps vehicle in their midst. They quickly gathered their wits and sprinted frantically for their weapons as the marines opened up with M16 rifles and machine guns. Rockets started smashing into the AAV. One pierced the armour at the front, taking a large chunk out of Lieutenant Ayres's leg. The rocket did not explode, however, but instead hit the engine, setting it ablaze.

Still under intense fire, the driver swerved south along a route known to the marines as Shithead Alley, desperate to find a turning back to the east, towards their own lines. The gunner was already dead from enemy fire, and several men had been knocked down by the incessant volleys of missiles slamming into armour. Sagredo saw that the blaze from the engine was rapidly spreading towards their own stockpiles of grenades. Then the engine gave out completely. With the motor dead, the rear gate would not open. The men had to climb out of the hatch one by one, still taking small-arms fire. Luckily for them, their dash down the gauntlet of Shithead Alley had left behind their attackers, who may have numbered up to six hundred men. The respite was only brief, however.

'When we stepped out I was relieved. At least I wasn't going to burn,' recalled Lance Corporal Abraham McCarver, the machine-gunner, when the survivors gathered in the yard to tell their story.

But they saw that Lieutenant Ayres, blinded by pain and the smoke, was crawling blindly back towards the fire. Sagredo and McCarver pulled him back, but his webbing caught on a rack. They were still taking fire, hearing the zings of bullets chunking into the vehicle around them, and were very conscious of the fact that the vehicle could explode at any moment. Then Ayres's webbing ripped, and they carried the wounded officer to the nearest house, kicking down the door. The marines took up firing positions on the roof as more than a hundred and fifty Iraqi gunmen swarmed down Shithead Alley towards the small house.

'All the Iraqis surged south to join the festivities,' Sagredo deadpanned, his face smooth and impassive, in contrast to his men, who laughed at their brush with death like the school kids they had so recently been.

Sagredo now found himself in charge of an impossible situation. Scenes from the movie *Blackhawk Down* flashed through his mind. 'It did remind me of that soldier being dragged through the streets back then,' he said. Sagredo was also aware of the almost identical scene of medieval brutality that had been played out with the bodies of the four US contractors just streets away, only a couple of weeks before.

Outside, the marines could hear the shouts of the Iraqi fighters, could see their feet shadowed under the front gate. 'I opened a window because I heard voices and I thought it was Americans,' said Corporal Koreyan Calloway. 'There was a guy in a headscarf with an AK47 standing there looking at me, so I shot him.'

The attackers were darting down narrow alleyways beside the house, and lobbing grenades from neighbouring rooftops. 'They were running across our line of fire like we weren't even shooting at them,' Calloway said, the disbelief still visible on his face. Luckily, the house had bars on the windows, so the attackers could not climb inside.

'It was just like a range, we were just shooting them down,' said Corporal Jacob Palofax. In the midst of the firefight, with the armoured vehicle's munitions blowing up, an ambulance pulled up. The marines thought they were being rescued. Instead, a dozen men with RPGs jumped out and started firing. The Americans were almost out of bullets: none had more than two magazines left, Sagredo was down to his last four bullets. An Iraqi round hit a kitchen pipe and gas started whistling out as RPGs slammed into the building. A guerrilla burst through the front gate with an RPG and was shot dead. Another tried to follow and was wounded. For Sagredo, in whose hands the lives of his men now lay, it was crunch time.

'It was in my head, we just got to go. Whoever makes it back, makes it back, those who fall, fall,' he said. 'That was the decision I'd have had to make, and I'm glad I didn't have to do it.'

He was saved from ordering that mad dash to oblivion by shouts from his men on the roof. In the midst of all the gunfire and shouting, Palofax screamed down that he could hear the rumble of tanks. Suddenly, the rescuers appeared, but to Sagredo's horror the first one went straight past. So did the second. Sagredo got on the radio and told them to back up. They did. A rifle muzzle appeared through the gate, and Captain Jason Smith came through shouting, 'Marines, marines, friendlies!' It took an hour for the tanks to hook up with the burnt-out vehicle, but they were determined not to leave the dead marine behind inside it. Once they had cleared the area, an F16 air strike was called in. I watched it from the rooftop of the soda factory: the fighter dived in over Shithead Alley, cannon squalling, then flipped upside for a second to see what damage he had inflicted. The plane swooped several times, twisting like a swallow over the smoking rooftops. Intelligence reports later said around a hundred Iraqi bodies were counted in the street.

Sagredo spoke quietly, with great self-control. He and his men had not even been pulled off the front after their terrifying ordeal. I wondered whether he expected to get a medal for shepherding his men to safety, but he just shook his head.

'A decoration would only remind me of what happened. This is something I want to forget. Unfortunately, if it doesn't affect me now, I know it will haunt me later.'

*　　*　　*

As the marines were sniping and blasting their way through the streets of the run-down industrial zone of Fallujah, a strange, new belief was being fomented across the front line among the Mujahedin waiting to enter paradise after a brief passage through the hell of a US military onslaught. That freshly minted legend was the spiders of God. For all that it sounded like a David Bowie song, Allah's arachnids had apparently arrived, and were pouncing on American soldiers like monsters in the movie *Eight-Legged Freaks*. (Ironically, the giant-spiders-attack-smalltown-America flick had originally been called *Arach-attack*, but the producers had been obliged to change the title because it was released in the run-up to the war and the title sounded confusingly like 'Iraq attack'.)

The genesis of this latest belief lay in a newfangled little gizmo that had taken the country by storm after the Americans arrived: the internet. Through wires and satellite pulses, the pictures that would spawn the legend had arrived on both sides of Fallujah's front line, strung out between sniper nests and rocket-blasted mosques that snagged along the edge of the industrial area.

While I was living with the marines in the soda factory, I received the first spider picture from my sister Claire. I can't stand spiders, and the picture made my skin creep: Claire had known I would get a macabre, arachnophobe's kick out of them. Two huge camel spiders, the size and colour of boiled pullets, were hanging from a helmet that was being held up gingerly by an

American soldier in front of the camera. One of the foul beasts had its fangs embedded in the helmet's camouflage cloth covering, while the other appeared to be eating the abdomen of its mate, dangling by its jaws.

The marines with me had fought their way up through the desert the spring before, living in rough hooches and shell scrapes, and confirmed that such unsavoury creatures really were out there. One marine I spoke to had seen a camel spider first-hand, and had only been prevented from squishing it underfoot by the intervention of a nature-loving chaplain.

The marines had plenty of tales about the camel spiders: they were the size of dinner plates and could run, screaming like banshees, at twenty-five miles an hour to leap on to the underbellies of camels, which they then anaesthetized with a toxic bite so they could chew their way into the victim's flesh. Hence the name.

Clearly, though, the claim that they were vicious killers which no man could outrun was slightly undermined by the photo of a soldier examining two of the monsters without apparent threat to life or limb. A little on-line research revealed that the marines' tales were in fact Arab urban myths. While still far too big and disgusting for my liking, camel spiders can actually only move at around ten miles per hour; they prey upon scorpions and crickets, not camels and unsuspecting foreign armies.

What I didn't know at the time was that across town in Fallujah, cut off from the outside world by a military cordon, an internet café was still up and running, using a diesel generator for electricity and a satellite dish to connect with the outside world. The picture my sister had sent to me was already doing the rounds on the web. In besieged Fallujah, the Mujahedin were staring at the same images, and something more than an urban myth was being born: the resistance leaders were detecting the divine hand of God.

I've always wondered about the origins of myths: there must be some grain of truth or fact behind the glistening pearls of legend. Did the Gadarene swine really jump into the Sea of Galilee and drown when Jesus drove the demonic spirits of the possessed into them, or did one panicked pig stumble into the water during all the wailing and screaming of an exorcism? Did plagues of locusts and frogs really swamp Pharaoh's Egypt, or was there just a natural population boom in a particularly wet year? What actually happened?

In Fallujah, the genesis of legend was transparent. As the spider picture spread among the tribal fighters – many of whom had never even left their town, and believed implicitly every word of their ferocious preachers – so did the stories of chair-sized arachnids, whose poisoned hairs could make a human body turn blue and explode in a shower of corrupted blood. The spiders were clearly allies sent by Allah to see off the evil infidels. The picture was printed out and plastered on the walls of mosques with the title 'Miracle of God in Fallujah'.

'The soldier says that it runs fast – about 40 kilometres per hour. It is poisonous and it makes a screaming sound,' claimed the posters, which the fighters latched on to with all the desperate hope of the doomed. From there, the stories quickly spread and fed off each other: fighters had seen the mighty spiders emerge from nests near the railway tracks along the northern district of Jolan, where the al-Qaeda leaders were said to be holed up. The toll – sixty US troops dead, no less. The marines' urban myth had morphed into the guerrillas' miracle of God.

But it didn't stop there. Fallujah fighters later claimed that flocks of white doves would hover above the positions of marine snipers along the front lines, betraying the sharpshooters' positions. (I later spent some time with marine marksmen and saw not even a sparrow, let alone a flock of white doves, overhead. Instead, there were several dead Iraqi bodies sprawled in the street marking the American snipers' line of fire. The marines also said they had found little bottles of antipsychotic pills on rooftops deserted by the retreating Mujahedin, which might explain how the myths were fuelled.)

Other Fallujans reported seeing gigantic, ghostly knights of yore mounted on white steeds, magically appearing to hack down the American troops. Whenever the much-feared Cobra helicopters fired off withering bursts from machine guns and missed, some fighter would be convinced he was cloaked in a veil of invulnerability fashioned by the almighty. Even those who failed to dodge the bullets were sacred martyrs, and reports circulated that the bodies of slain holy warriors were not decomposing, but smelled instead of sweet musk. The ones I saw reeked of rotting flesh and had been gnawed by wild dogs.

Several months later in Najaf, my translator Ali was with Shiite militiamen who were battling American troops outside the holy shrine of Imam Ali when he heard a grizzled veteran tell a greenhorn colleague not to bother aiming his rocket-launcher.

'Imam Ali will direct the rocket to its target,' he said, before the missile shot off into the side of a building.

Back at the soda factory, Colonel Byrne was becoming increasingly frustrated that his assault was going nowhere in those early days of April. He knew his men could take the city, if he was just given clear instructions to do so. But the instructions never came. Instead, the marine commanders, who initially advised against Washington's determination to invade the city, knowing what a bloody price would be paid, were ordered to pull back and train a local force of ex-army officers from Fallujah to police the city. It was a disastrous decision. The Fallujah Protective Force, as it was known, turned out to be little more than the same guerrillas the marines had just spent a month trying to defeat. And the Mujahedin, gloating at the withdrawal of their seemingly unstoppable foe, declared a miraculous victory for Allah, and for the giant spiders that had implemented His divine plan.

If it was a stinging climbdown for Byrne and his men, it was much, much worse for the people of Fallujah. The real nightmare was just beginning for them, as their city became a mini-Taliban state of beheadings, beatings and summary executions. Fallujah also quickly became the Detroit of car bombs, with the workshops of the industrial quarter once again put to use in churning out explosives-rigged vehicles destined for the Shia markets just up the road in Baghdad.

As if foreshadowing this new season of impending violence, I found a group of marines standing around a boom box outside the soda factory on my last night in Fallujah. They were relieved to be getting out, despite the anger of failure, and danced a sort of hip-hop shuffle to the beating rhythm. I recognized the song. It was 'Bombs Over Baghdad', by Outkast. Only this time, it wouldn't be the Americans bombing Baghdad, but the men they were ceding Fallujah to.

TWO IN THE HEART, ONE IN THE MIND

Battlefields of the Soul

The American girl looked young, maybe twenty-one or twenty-two. She had red hair and big-rimmed glasses, and was too pretty for a soldier. In fact, she told me she'd been a drama student before signing up. She was bouncy and extroverted, and giggled with excitement as she came up to me, standing near the Strykers parked inside the gate of a military outpost in Mosul.

'I made a grown man cry yesterday,' she boasted, with a happy chuckle.

'How?' I asked her, and she looked at me coyly, a look that journalists often get around soldiers. *Wouldn't you like to know?* the look says.

'I work in the interrogations,' she said, as chipper as if she'd announced she worked in the mergers and acquisitions department of a successful corporation. She had heard the Strykers rumbling in from a mission in the city, and was hoping to find some fresh Iraqi prisoners she could practise her newfound interrogation skills on. She asked me if any detainees had been brought in.

I told her there had been two men, one young, one middle-aged. They had been brought in from a raid I had gone on, to a grain warehouse somewhere in Mosul, though I really couldn't have said where exactly as I was stuck in the back of an armoured vehicle and couldn't see a thing. We had sped off, the young soldiers nodding their heads to Def Leppard's 'Pour Some Sugar On Me' on the speakers rigged up in the back, then the ramp had gone down and we'd all leapt out into a reeking pile of manure. The soldiers had spent a sweaty hour hefting heavy sacks of grain, finding nothing. Two men inside the warehouse were pushed to the floor, flexi-cuffed, and empty canvas sandbags were put over their heads. When we arrived back at the forward operating base, the soldiers had sat the two prisoners down on the weights bench of their jerry-built gym and snapped their pictures with them, making silly faces and rabbit ears over their sandbagged heads. It was as if the Iraqis had been arrested by a well-armed frat house involved in freshman hazings rather than an occupying army. The MTV generation goes to war.

The young woman did nothing to dispel that impression.

'Rats,' she cussed when I told her the prisoners had been hauled off to another base. 'I wanted to have fun with them.' Then she bounded off to find something else to distract her. I later heard the two men had been released. One of the officers in charge of the raid had stern words with a man in a ski mask, who I learned was the informer who had given the Americans bad intel, possibly to settle some personal grudge.

Later that day I disembedded from the unit and moved into a cheap hotel overlooking the Tigris. It was spring 2004: no one had any idea yet about the abuses of Abu Ghraib, the scandal that was just weeks from breaking on the world and sweeping away whatever last hope the Americans had of winning over the people they had come to save. It was a slow week, and I had a couple of days before I had to get back to Baghdad. I decided to track down a spectacle I'd been hearing of since I arrived in Iraq, and which had sparked my growing interest in strange religious rituals: the Sufi ceremony of self-impalement.

Sufis are a mystical sect of the Sunni branch of Islam. I had long been a fan of the Pakistani Sufi musician Nusrat Fateh Ali Khan, whose haunting rhythms and plaintive chants are designed to induce the trance state necessary for Sufi devotees either to push long metal spikes through their cheeks, ears, arms and sides or to whirl like the fabled dervishes of Turkey and Syria, the most renowned practitioners of the sect. I was curious to see the strange rite for myself, and Mosul was one of the principal centres of the practice in Iraq.

There was one problem, though: the leading sheikh of the Sufis in Mosul had recently been arrested by the Americans and, in his own words, 'humiliated'. He never specified what this humiliation was – for Iraqis, being slapped with a sandal is a mortal insult, while for the American guards at Abu Ghraib it could be stripping men naked and forcing them to simulate sex with each other. Whatever it was, the sheikh was furious and refusing contact with any foreigner. Ali, my translator, spent hours with him while I was still embedded, cajoling and commiserating, before the sheikh would even agree to see me, let alone allow me to witness his people's private ceremonies. I would have to use the narrow opportunity of interviewing him to schmooze my way into a self-impalement session.

Inside the *diwan* at the small Sufi mosque, I was greeted by a fuming giant. Sheikh Hassan al-Bedrani must have been at least seven feet tall, with a huge boulder of a head and hands the size of boxing gloves. Presumably he had suffered from an overactive pituitary gland when he was growing up. In his plain white *dishdasheh* and matching *yeshmak*, he loomed over me like a galleon's sail, billowing with righteous anger. He was also remarkably pale for an Iraqi, lending him an intimidating, ghostly air that was only bolstered by his evident distaste for me as an unmannered western infidel. The sheikh immediately launched into a litany of complaints, how the American soldiers had burst into his mosque, refusing to remove their boots, had handled him roughly and dragged both him and his wife away for questioning, stealing her Syrian passport along the way.

Listening to his furious speech, I couldn't help thinking of the young American woman I had met the day before at the US camp, and wondering if at some point this tall, dignified man had passed through her hands. For her, it was fun, something new for her to chalk up on her CV and tell her drama school pals back in the states: 'How I made grown men cry in the war.' For him, on the other hand, it was a mortal humiliation, one for which he could never forgive America. Honour had been insulted, and fighting was the only way to expunge the tarnish.

Sipping tea in the *diwan*, I politely pointed out to him that armies tend, of necessity, to be rough and ready, and that he should not judge an entire country by the actions of a few jittery men and women in a combat zone far from home. I remembered the marine's dark joke about winning over Iraqi hearts and minds: *Two in the heart, one in the mind*. I did not mention this to the sheikh.

Angry as he was, the sheikh was also an intelligent man, and slowly nodded his giant head. I told him I would ask the Americans at the Mosul palace if they could locate his wife's missing passport. He smiled and thanked me: I was in.

The ritual was a strange, intense spectacle: around twenty men and boys sat on cushions lining the walls of the domed mosque. Several of the older men were visiting sheikhs from Syria. They were friendly to me, owing to my acceptance by Sheikh Hassan, but I was not totally surprised that the Americans had been suspicious of them, given the cross-border flow of jihadists and weapons from Syria. However, Sufis are far from the mainstream of Sunni Islam, and their rites would likely be considered sacrilegious by al-Qaeda, something the average American officer carrying out raids from Mosul palace was unlikely to know.

We were served coffee and a strange honeydew confection that tasted a little like candy floss. Ali struggled to find the word to describe it: 'You call it manna? Like in the Bible?' he said.

'Manna from heaven?' I asked. He nodded, and told me it was secreted by sap-sucking bugs living on desert plants, rather than strung on bushes by God. It was rare and expensive. I was being honoured, it seemed.

The drums started slowly, accompanied by the mournful, hypnotic chant of the men doing the drumming; as the rhythm accelerated to a frantic pace, one of the men sitting across the domed hall leapt up and pulled off his *dishdasheh*, revealing a lean body stippled on the sides with grey pockmarks. He picked up a straight metal skewer from a stack by the wall and, after a few deep breaths, plunged the three-foot rod through the loose skin above his hip. He didn't flinch, but picked up a second one and pierced the other side of his body. Then he pulled them out again – there was no bleeding.

'This is truly a miracle from God, is it not?' mused the giant Sheikh Hassan, peering intently over at me.

I nodded, although I was actually thinking that putting the stake through his head and surviving would be a miracle – stabbing your love handles hardly seemed to prove the existence of an all-powerful deity. But I kept such doubts to myself.

'I've never seen anything like it,' I said diplomatically. 'Very impressive.'

The sheikh smiled approvingly at my answer, and signalled for the ceremony to continue. A series of men stepped up to the floor, one after the other, and started harpooning themselves. At one point, one practitioner's son, a boy of about six, was pulled into the middle of the room and had narrow spikes put through his earlobes. He didn't seem to mind. Only once did I see a trickle of blood flow from the small puncture wounds in a man's side: he quickly wiped it away, as though ashamed.

Towards the end of the proceedings, Sheikh Hassan invited me up to feel the metal stake under the skin of a young man's stomach. As I gingerly felt it, the sheikh put his hand over mine and forced it hard on to the skin-sheathed stake, as he vigorously sawed the metal back and forth with his other hand to demonstrate that the devotee felt no pain. I couldn't tell if he did, but he was puffing in and out rapidly like an athlete preparing for a sprint. I was invited to pull the stake out of the wound myself: it came out smooth and steady, with a slight resistance, like pulling a shoelace through the eye of a new boot.

The sheikh, it turned out, also had a dark sense of humour: seeing me grimace at extracting a metal stake from a man's body, he suddenly declared that he had taken to me so well that we would do a 'special' together.

'What's that?' I asked nervously.

'You and me together, on one stake,' he announced gleefully. 'We'll be like a kebab! We can put some onions on too!' He started trying to unbutton my shirt, as I politely but urgently protested that there was no way in hell I was going pillion on a metal pole with a seven-foot sheikh. It was not clear he was really joking. Yassir, my driver, leapt up and urged me, 'Do not do it, Mr James!'

'Too bloody right I'm not doing it,' I said. Seeing Yassir's earnest distress, Sheikh Hassan suddenly burst out laughing and wrapped his long arm round my shoulders. We hugged like old friends. The diplomatic dispute between east and west was over, for the time being at least.

Now here's an important question. Think carefully about it, as your life may depend on the answer one day. Should a goat wear underpants?

As crazy as this may sound, this was a policy point for the newly declared Islamic State of Iraq, the reborn caliphate proclaimed by al-Qaeda in Iraq in early 2006, whose main policy goal was to take the Sunni lands of central Iraq back to the good old days of the Prophet Mohammed in seventh-century Arabia. A similar project to turn back the clocks had been tried in Afghanistan by the Taliban and their al-Qaeda allies, and had for a while succeeded in creating a miserable, brutal place, much as Arabia probably was 1,400 years ago when Mohammed and his neighbours were fighting over which imaginary deity should be revered as ruler supreme of the universe. Their safe haven ruptured after the US invasion of Afghanistan, the Sunni extremists – a mixture of fundamentalist strains such as Wahhabis and Salafists, collectively known as *takfiris* – were establishing the same model in the green farmlands just north of Baghdad.

I first came across this brand of off-the-chart extremism in 2005, while reading a local news report in Baghdad about a grocer's shop that had been blown up. The four people who worked there were executed in front of their vegetables before the TNT was set off. I didn't realize that they had been murdered because of their vegetables.

'Now what the hell have people got against greengrocers?' I asked Ali, who was sitting in the office, fiddling with a broken computer. I already knew that hairdressers had been targeted for more than a year because fundamentalists objected to them giving western hairstyles, especially US military-style buzzcuts. Most barbers, threatened with death if they shaved beards in un-Islamic styles, had packed up shop or operated in secret in their homes to a discreet clientele. And of course alcohol sellers had been blown up by Shia gangs since just after the invasion. Recently, gunmen also had taken to shooting mobile-phone vendors who sold western pop jingles as ringtones. And a few satellite dish salesmen had also been slaughtered for allowing western programmes into the pure Muslim lands. But greengrocers?

Ali was giggling at my question. 'You know, you'll think this is crazy, but I heard that the Mujahedin have issued a fatwa that tomatoes and cucumbers can't be displayed together.'

'No way! Why? Because cucumbers look a bit like a cock and tomatoes look like breasts?'

'Yeah, basically,' he said. 'Tomatoes represent femininity and cucumbers . . . well, you said it,' he laughed.

This really took the biscuit, even in a war being waged in the name of such bizarre ideals as rebuilding a seventh-century desert empire. I rushed next door to the office of National Public Radio, and told a friend of mine this new gem of utter ridiculousness. He too was amazed, but his translator Saad, a Shia who had lived in western Baghdad until being recently chased out of his home, just nodded.

'I've seen the leaflets,' Saad said. 'Tomatoes and cucumbers cannot be displayed together. You can still sell them, but they can't be seen together.'

It was astounding in its stupidity and barbarity. I knew these guerrillas were manically repressed sexually, but this had descended to a juvenile level comparable only to Benny Hill. It reminded me of the worst Victorian prudes who would have covers made for their table legs because legs of any sort were suggestive of sexuality. I didn't know the most extreme examples were yet to emerge, however.

As Iraq effectively fragmented into its constituent parts – a Kurdish north, a Shia south, Sunni west and centre, with a lethal maelstrom of mixed sects killing each other in Baghdad – al-Qaeda and their local affiliates had decided to take advantage of this centripetal force and declare their own breakaway caliphate in 2006. Now they had started enforcing their brand of puritanism in Diyala, a province of verdant farms, canals and rivers just northeast of Baghdad. It was perfect guerrilla warfare territory, and it was here that the jihadists concentrated their efforts to carve out an Islamic state.

There was no public decree of the new laws, but soon everyone seemed to know them. In Iraq, there was a constant swirl of rumours and speculation, repeated from neighbour to neighbour, town to town, so one had to be careful about what to believe. But I knew a freelance Iraqi journalist operating in Diyala who had reliable links to both Sunni and Shia militants, so I asked him to find out what the new rules in al-Qaeda-controlled Iraq were. When he got back to me a few days later, I realized that the country really had gone through the looking glass.

From Baqouba, just north of Baghdad, to Samarra, halfway to Mosul, vegetable sellers had not only been warned against selling cucumbers and tomatoes side by side but had also been cautioned to sell bananas only in plastic bags to avoid offence. In addition, the production and selling of ice – which had been a boom business for years, with electricity in such short supply – had also been banned. The reasoning was that in the Prophet's day, there would have been no ice in Arabia and he would not have drunk chilled water. So nobody now could have any, which was unfortunate, since anybody so afraid of bananas was clearly so sexually frustrated that putting some ice down their trousers might have helped matters.

Also, the Mujahedin had gone one further along the no-alcohol line by banning smoking. This was not strictly for health reasons (as shown by the punishment, which wasn't a giant nicotine patch but instead involved inserting the smoker's index finger into a metal pipe and snapping the digit at the knuckle), but because

Muslims are not supposed to harm themselves: clearly there were plenty of people out there ready to do that for them. Tobacconists had their shops torched and smokers had to have a quiet puff at home if they couldn't give up. Quitting the habit was not so easy in such trying times, either.

But the granddaddy of all the crazy edicts concerned the goats. Our man in Diyala confirmed a persistent rumour that goatherds had been ordered to put underpants on their animals for modesty's sake, as clearly an inflamed young jihadist who had never seen an unveiled woman might feel unduly aroused by the site of a goat's nether regions. Sheep, it seemed, were exempt since they have big flat tails that cover their genitals.

It was too weird for it to be true, I thought, so I asked Mohanned the translator to ask around independently to see what was really going on. Mohanned had a friend working as a doctor in Baqouba hospital, and asked him if he had seen any strange ungulate fashions in the fields of Diyala. As it turned out, the doctor had experienced a potentially deadly brush with goats' underclothing.

The doctor had been travelling in a taxi minibus from Baqouba through the rich, guerrilla-controlled farmland to Baghdad. Passing through one village, he had spotted a goat wearing a pair of boxer shorts.

'I started laughing,' he recalled over the telephone, asking us not to divulge his name. 'It was a goat wearing boxer shorts. And a very nice pair of boxers they were too. But then the other people in the taxi van said, "Stop laughing, or you'll get yourself killed." ' Facing such a choice, he quickly managed to contain his mirth, and lived to tell the tale.

In 1843, Karl Marx famously described religion as the opium of the people (or, as Joe Strummer put it more lyrically in 1980, 'The message on the tablet was valium'). I have nothing against that: everyone needs a little opiate now and then to relieve the heavy burden of consciousness, the knowledge that one day we and everyone we know and love will die. Even baboons have been known, in times of plenty and with no predators around, to escape boredom and baboon angst by chewing on natural herbs that give them a slight buzz.

It is when the mild opiate of mainstream religion is distilled into the crack cocaine of fanatical fundamentalism that the problems really start. Iraq was quickly becoming ideology's answer to a vast methamphetamine factory in the desert.

It seems that when American military planners pondered how quickly democracy would take root in Iraq, allowing them to declare victory, bring their troops safely home and start pumping the country's huge oil reserves to lubricate the global economy, they failed to consider that Saddam's Iraq was a carefully constructed vacuum in which perceptions of reality – except the reality of the daily struggle not to starve, be tortured or be killed – had been completely warped. When the thin needle of American steel burst the bubble, a pandemic of weird ideologies, long-suppressed fears and carefully nurtured paranoia erupted. Thus it was that before too long you could be murdered for the wrong hairdo, risk your life for a Greek salad or be forced to put panties on your livestock.

'Custom is king of all,' wrote Herodotus in *The Histories*, his compendium of tales of strange customs in the Aegean and eastern Mediterranean two and a half thousand years ago. In some respects, little has changed – there are still weird and colourful communities living according to time-worn tradition, barely touched by the industrial sheen of modernity. Understanding their stories is often vital to knowing what makes them do the things they do, and how they may react to new influences. This is known in the jargon of international studies as 'a strategic narrative', the story we tell ourselves – and our enemies – of who we are, what we want and what our society deems acceptable, desirable and reprehensible. These stories, often distorted and almost always written from the victor's perspective, give us a sense of self.

Somehow, America's war planners seemed to have ignored the warning of *The Histories* and assumed that ancient Mesopotamia, crisscrossed with one of the longest, most violent histories in the world, was a blank slate on which they could freely write their own history, as their forebears had liberally rewritten the conquest of the Native Americans as a thrilling adventure tale. They were wrong.

Worse, George Bush apparently thought the Middle East was a Gordian knot to be hewn in one brief, decisive stroke: he did not realize that intervening in the region's politics is akin to performing brain surgery, in which any false cut of the scalpel leads to scar tissue and a violent reaction elsewhere in the body politic.

Had the Americans shown a little more interest in Herodotus's bizarre tales, it might have helped them in Iraq. It might also have helped them see the similarities between themselves and the country they were fighting for.

For al-Qaeda did not have the monopoly on fire-and-brimstone rhetoric. Shortly before he unleashed his massed army from Kuwait, President Bush was forced to dismiss the man he had appointed as Deputy Undersecretary of Defense for Intelligence, Lieutenant General William G. Boykin. The devoutly Christian general had made the mistake of publicly admitting his religious interpretation of the battle he had fought in Somalia with a Muslim warlord a decade before.

'I knew my God was bigger than his. I knew that my God was a real God and his was an idol.' Which is essentially what any adherent of a monotheistic faith has to believe.

General Boykin lost his job for merely being honest about what he believed. I once heard a marine lieutenant in the unit calling themselves the Crusaders express exactly the same view, while we were being mortared in the ruins of an ancient Assyrian city in the Triangle of Death. And he really believed it. Probably Mr Bush believes it too. After all, he once told Palestinian Prime Minister Mahmoud Abbas that he was under marching orders from God.

'God would tell me, "George, go and fight those terrorists in Afghanistan." And I did, and then God would tell me, "George, go and end the tyranny in Iraq," and I did,' he said, according to senior Palestinian officials. Mr Bush didn't say exactly how God was communicating with him, whether it was voices in his head or if the decree came in the form of writing on the wall. Either way, when he described his 'war on terror' as a 'crusade for liberty and democracy' shortly after the September 11 attacks on the United States, it didn't take the Muslim world long to decide that this was more than a mere metaphor.

But then, such sentiments were far from uncommon in the Middle East. Iran's president, Mahmoud Ahmedinejad, and Iraq's first elected prime minister, Ibrahim al-Jaafari, both claimed to be acting on God's instructions.

Just as Iraq was the cradle of our often brutal, over-acquisitive civilization, it was also a key birthplace of myth. The imaginations of the ancient peoples who worked the land were just as fertile as their silted flood-plains, and their deities have hardly been dimmed by age and mutation. It was here, some 5,000 years ago, that the Sumerians, dwelling in the world's first mud-brick cities that had recently sprung up from the fertile alluvial plains of Mesopotamia, imagined the original pantheon of gods, together with the legends of creation.

In their theology, the Goddess Nammu, personifying the mysterious, primeval ocean (now known more prosaically as the Persian Gulf), gave birth to a male sky and a female earth. These two got together and spawned the air-god Enlil, a brat who caused his parents to divorce but who in turn begat all the land's living creatures. The names of the gods varied from one city-state to the next, and the story was embroidered over millennia to push to prominence the favoured deities of whichever mini-state or empire was on the rise. Thus, Sumer's Enlil was eventually incorporated into Babylon's Marduk, who in turn morphed into Assyria's Ashur. At some point, according to legend, a man called Abraham left ancient Ur and migrated northwards up the Euphrates, through the hills of Syria and south into Canaan. The ideas he took with him slowly transformed into a new belief in the land he settled around Hebron. There they slowly evolved into Judaism, Christianity and Islam.

The early Sumerian stories reflected the way peasant societies imagined the dawn of time, which largely resembled the dawn of their working day as they headed off to their fields to gather the wheat and barley that had fuelled the growth of those early cities. As the sun rises, sky and land are separated in a misty day-break, just as land and sea are divided. Many of the gods were simply embodiments of the elements: there was Apsu representing the fresh waters, Tiamat the salt waters, and Mummu for the clouds. Given the vital importance of the annual floods that terrorized but also nourished the lands, they even had two specialized gods of silt, Lammu and Lahamu.

The gods milled around and bickered a bit, as ancient gods were wont to do, before Tiamat, the salt-water prom queen, became pregnant by Apsu, her sweet-water sweetheart. But the babies in her belly were irritatingly noisome, so she decided to kill them. The other gods were outraged, so they killed Apsu. There was an inevitable power struggle between Tiamat's son Kingu (who rather surprisingly sided with his mother, despite her attempts to abort him) and Marduk, the off-spring of two of the principal gods. After a dreadful battle, Marduk defeated Kingu, who had headed an army of sharp-fanged dragons and serpents. Marduk caught Tiamat in his giant fishing net. The young god blew the four winds into her mouth, fired an arrow through her heart and smashed her head in with a mace. In order to make sure she was really dead, he then cut her open 'like a shellfish', thus setting a bloody precedent for untold generations on how to dispose of unwanted rulers in Iraq.

Kingu was also executed, and from his blood Marduk fashioned the first man: an ominous genesis for us poor mortals, carrying the seed of original sin, a theme Christianity would one day return to. Marduk was pro-claimed King of the Gods at a drunken celestial banquet, and the great temple of Babylon was erected in his honour. This was man's first recorded attempt to explain the universe and his place in it. Fantastic as it may sound, this theological interpretation of events dominated civilization's cradle for a good 3,000 years, far longer than any other theology since then except Judaism. This was no fly-by-night sect. And before it is written off as ancient nonsense, it is worth bearing in mind that a revised version of it, carried by Abraham, the son of Ur, to Canaan – that god created the earth out of nothing and then fashioned man to populate it – was being debated during the latest Mesopotamian conflict, in 2005 in a courthouse in Dover, Pennsylvania, where America's powerful Christian lobby called the story 'intelligent design' and insisted it be taught to the country's schoolchildren alongside (or, preferably, instead of) Charles Darwin's evolutionary theories. The case was eventually thrown out by the judge, but not before it had been accorded serious legal consideration.

The battles between the modern and the medieval are not just fought in dusty foreign lands.

DEATH IN THE VENICE OF THE EAST

Three Summers in Basra

I went to Basra looking for an uprising, but found instead an old man my grandfather had worked with on Iraq's railways during the Second World War, sixty years before.

Leonard Goodsir was a fit and jovial man in his eighties when I met him in the shabby lobby of the Merbid Hotel. Outside, in the suffocating heat of August 2004, Basra teetered on the brink of war.

Despite his age, his leathery arms were still full of a steam-engine stoker's corded muscles, and his sharp mind retained a crystalline memory of the city and the rail routes during that long-ago war, when he had worked – still a fresh-faced teenager – on the railways of the dying British Empire.

Leonard was the son of an Anglo-Indian family that had settled in this teeming port city on the Persian Gulf, back when Basra was still renowned as the Venice of the East. It was a thriving commercial hub, built on well-trodden spice routes from the Far East and looking out on the palm-shaded Shatt al-Arab waterway, as vast and sluggish as the Mississippi. The slatted windows of merchants' sprawling, wood-shingle *shinashil* houses, their ornate wooden balconies a testament to centuries of Ottoman craftsmanship, overlooked winding canals that snaked through the city and out into vast date-palm groves before emptying into the Shatt al-Arab, itself a confluence of the Tigris and Euphrates, which met upstream at Qurna, the mythical site of the Garden of Eden.

Now the houses were falling in on themselves, the canals transformed into reeking open sewers and the date palms decimated by artillery and air strikes in the war with Iran, the hardiest survivors transplanted to the northern farms of Saddam Hussein and his cronies. Upriver, the Garden of Eden had been drained and concreted over, and was now patrolled by Danish peacekeeping troops.

Sitting in the lobby, Leonard pulled out a handwritten list of names he had prepared for our meeting. It was a record of all the British Army engine drivers he had worked with. I scanned down the old-fashioned-sounding names and saw 'Ted (?) Hider' written halfway down. My grandfather Edward had spent his entire life shunting trains about an east London gas works, except for a few brief years in the early 1940s when he manned an anti-aircraft gun in a field in Kent before shipping out to Basra. From here, he drove trains laden with arms and ammunition up through Persia to supply the beleaguered Russian army as it fought Hitler for control of the Caspian oil fields.

'I remember it was Christmas, maybe 1941 or 1942, when they had a party for us young apprentices in the mess rooms,' said Leonard, who had retained a fluent English with a hint of an East End accent inherited from the train drivers he once sweated alongside: he claimed he could also remember some pidgin Urdu picked up from the Indian troops who had been posted to Basra. 'A man dressed up as Santa Claus climbed up a ladder and in through the window and gave us all presents from the bag he was carrying. That man was your grandfather.'

I had hardly known my grandfather, even though he had died when I was nineteen and therefore easily old enough to have evinced some interest in his wartime past. But like millions of other British soldiers of that epic era, Edward Hider hardly ever spoke about his years in this distant corner of the empire. Instead, my memories of him were of stifling summer holidays at my grandparents' home in Kent; the tarry smell of freshly creosoted fences and compost heaps behind the bungalows that were slowly stretching out into the cabbage fields of Thanet; my pasty skin burning in the 1970s heatwave on the beaches of Margate and Ramsgate where he and I went with my grandmother. Both of them were working-class Londoners from the East End, for whom this life was retirement heaven. For me, it had been a claustrophobic suburban wasteland, planting the seed of wanderlust that eventually brought me to the far-off place where he had spent years dreaming of quiet Metro-land pubs and green parks back home in England.

To be sitting here with an old man who remembered him when he would have been about my age touched me deeply. How would Edward Hider, posted here in the middle of a global war against totalitarianism, ever have conceived that his grandson might one day be sitting here, in the midst of a new, sprawling and ill-defined war, chatting with the lean Iraqi kid he had instructed on the workings of the steam engine? I wished I had talked to my grandfather more – or at all, to be honest – and I remembered with shame how little interest I ever showed in the slightly built, quiet old man as a person. Why did he never want to tell us about it? Perhaps because so many people had been through it, or because he thought his time as a humble train driver didn't match up to the heroics of the front-line veterans. I will never know.

I had only discovered my family's longstanding connection with this crumbling city near the Kuwaiti border the year before, standing on the rooftop of the same hotel in August 2003. I had just filed a story from my satellite phone about the death of a British soldier, killed by a roadside bomb not far from the port. The spot was marked by a metal lamppost cut in two by the blast and some incinerated Land Rover fenders scattered by the road. Next to the scene, shepherds were selling their sheep under a palm-thatch shelter, slitting the animals' throats and then skinning the carcasses before bundling them into the boots of passing cars. After sending the story, I decided on a whim to phone my father and let him know I was in the city, under British rule again after more than half a century of disastrous independence. As I was talking to him, thousands of miles away in Bristol, he told me about my grandfather, and how he himself had been to Basra in the 1950s, as a young merchant seaman. His ships sailed up the Shatt al-Arab, picking up oil from Iraqi refineries and from Abadan in Iran, just across the estuary. He recalled how the Arabs in their white robes and beards had reminded him of Sunday school drawings of the Holy Land. I told him the wooden dhows were still docked on the waterfront, their sharp prows pointing at the charred shell of the once luxurious Sheraton Hotel, which Lulu had watched being looted by desperate Iraqis when the British Army fought its way into the city a few months before.

I was startled by the coincidence that had brought three generations of Hiders to Basra, a hidden family saga reflecting the tug of imperial history. Perhaps I shouldn't have been surprised: just to the north, in the desert stretching towards the drained marshlands, the gas flares of Basra's giant oil fields danced in the heat haze, a siren's call to petrol-hungry superpowers. In places, the subterranean sea of oil oozed up through the sands, creating black scars on the land. Every Iraqi I knew thought that was why the British and Americans were here again, and it was hard to disagree, given the oil-company credentials of the entire Bush admin-istration. Not all Iraqis were upset by this, however, at least not in the immediate post-invasion flush of liberty. In a Baghdad teashop, Walid, a beaming university drama professor, joked to me that he didn't care if the allies stole 70 per cent of the country's oil wealth. 'After all,' he said, 'Saddam used to steal it all. At least we'll get some now.'

There were faded traces of the British all over the city. Saddam had moved the austere British war memorial of the 1917 Mesopotamia campaign to a strip of wasteland on the edge of town, but if you were careful you could still drive out and see the grandiose red-stone pavilion with slabs bearing testimony to the glorious and not-so-glorious dead of colonial warfare: 'Colonel John Walker and 114 soldiers of the 77th Rawalpindi Dragoons.' In the city itself, the forgotten children of that British occupation in the first half of the previous century were not quite Iraqis but not British either, despite their Anglo-Saxon surnames. These men and women kept a low profile, fearful that the growing resentment against the Christian occupiers could rub off on them.

The British stamp was not confined to Basra either: in Baghdad, a large, nondescript cemetery was the final resting place of thousands of His Majesty's soldiers who died in the disastrous campaign against the Turkish army in Kut, a town just south of the capital. A few months before my meeting with Leonard, Shiite militiamen had driven Ukrainian peacekeepers and the British governor out of the town. In the graveyard, long grass now grew among the untended tombs.

Even in Fallujah, the Sunni wellspring of anti-American violence, the lingering influence of the colonial relationship could still be felt, albeit filtered through the twisted logic of downtrodden Iraq. One day shortly after the invasion, I stood in a baying mob of furious Fallujah tribesmen, next to a blood-smeared wall where dying American soldiers had dragged themselves the night before in search of refuge following an ambush on their Humvee. As the crowd pressed in around me, eager to make their voices heard in the western press, men shouted at me, asking where I was from. I told them I was British – this was back in the days when I could still admit my nationality, when you could still make trips into Fallujah without being butchered like sheep. One of the tribesmen yelled at me, 'Why don't the British come here? We hate the Americans, but the British know us.' I pointed out that the British were also part of this occupation, and the only reason they knew the Iraqis was that they had occupied Iraq before, provoking a major uprising in the 1920s. But such logic found little resonance in the madness of that city; the men surged about me, shouting that they would fight the Americans to the death. Shortly afterwards, two US Humvees roared down the main street and screeched to a halt by the ambush scene, scattering the Iraqis, who quietly stashed away their vows of vengeance, keeping them for a more propitious moment.

After my meeting with Leonard Goodsir, I ventured out with Ali and Yassir in search of the rebels. The whole country was rapidly collapsing in a complex sectarian, tribal war that summer, and Basra was seething with anger and hostility. We headed through the city centre. Goats grazed on the rubbish in wastelands between the houses. The car would frequently sink to its axles in algae-blooming ponds of sewage.

That August, the Mahdi Army were fighting coalition

troops in the Shia holy city of Najaf far to the north. By standing up to the Americans after a year of iniquitous occupation, Moqtada al-Sadr had tapped into a powerful strand of Arab pride that turned him from a rabble-rousing, marginal thug into a hero for many of the country's poor and dispossessed Shia. The middle-class Shia, however, despised him. They distrusted his ratty militia of fanatics, who with their black clothes and tobacco-stained teeth resembled an army of Orcs. Some were mere looters, while others were angry, misguided zealots in search of a fight because they had gained nothing from the invasion, aside from the freedom to fall for the crude demagoguery of fanatics like Moqtada himself. And in Najaf, this thousands-strong force was slowly being forced back by US troops to their bolt-hole in the shrine of Imam Ali.

In this Shia centre of Basra, pre-existing class divides from Saddam's Iraq had persisted and deepened. The better-off merchants preferred British law to Moqtada's mob. When they were sure no one was listening, moderate Basrans would call his Jaysh al-Mahdi the Jaysh al-Wardi, or the Pink Army, after the pink anti-psychotic pills that its members took to supplement their religious zeal with a little pharmaceutical pzazz. I met some middle-class Basrans outside an ice-cream parlour in the city centre, where they treated their children to dripping cones. In the middle of the street was a sign warning of the dangers of firing assault rifles into the air during wedding celebrations or rare football victories – it was a crude cartoon of a boy lying dead after being hit in the head by a falling bullet, just what you want your kids to see as they suck down an ice-cream cone.

The Basrans joked that the cleric's standing among the disenfranchised Shiites had been greatly bolstered after the invasion when he had sanctioned the *hawasmeh*, the looting frenzy that reduced the country to a pre-modern state in a few short weeks. Most imams and sheikhs had ordered their congregations to return the stolen goods, arguing that the new government would need all the help it could get to restart the country. Not Moqtada – he had bought himself some easy support by telling his people all is fair in war and looting.

The Basran merchants also sniggered that the only reason Moqtada had survived the ambush that killed his revered father and brothers in 1999 was because his dad had locked him in the basement, like some shameful secret.

To stir up the lethargic Basrawi merchants to a suit-able degree of religious fervour, Moqtada's local warlord, Sheikh Saad al-Basri, had recently made a speech during which he waved a Kalashnikov in the air and urged his followers to kidnap British troops, especially female soldiers. Speeding down from Baghdad after the inflammatory diatribe, I had expected the city to be as tense and deserted as the violence-plagued capital. Instead, I was surprised to see the streets filled with the usual crowds of people out shopping, standing outside their houses watering the concrete pavement (a typical Iraqi pastime, meant to keep the dust down) and staging large wedding celebrations in open-sided tents.

That sense of civic calm made what we then encountered all the more shocking as we slowly navigated
the rush-hour traffic near Sheikh al-Basri's headquarters. On a roundabout we suddenly came across
men with heavy machine guns, rocket-propelled
grenade launchers and assault rifles. It was like bumping into a guerrilla army in Eastbourne. As ever when I
suddenly stumble on gunmen, my stomach did a brief
flip. We cautiously circled the roundabout and pulled
up outside the compound. A dozen men with AK47s
stood guard in the street outside, some of them also
holding the snub launchers of RPGs, the weapon of
choice in this hit-and-run war.

The standard but unwritten rules of engagement in
such circumstances dictate that if they've seen your
white mug in the car, and they haven't started pointing
their guns at you, then it is probably safe to exit the
vehicle with your interpreter and make contact. If, on
the other hand, they have started pointing their
weapons at you, the wisest choice is to stop the car and
freeze, and just wait for them to tell you whatever it is
they want you to do. Ali and I climbed out of the car
and walked through the crowd of gunmen to the gate,
salaam aleikum-ing, touching our hands to our chests in
respectful greeting, smiling and trying to play the role of
relaxed, neutral observers. We explained to a man at the
gate we were journalists – Australian journalists, we
lied, knowing the price on the heads of British citizens
– and were invited to sit in a concrete shack inside the
gate, while one of the militiamen went to inform his
superiors. I politely declined the traditional gift of

hospitality, a glass of highly suspicious tapwater from Basra's long-neglected pipes, leaving Ali and his cast-iron Iraqi stomach to do the honours. Instead, I pulled out a packet of cigarettes and made an equally traditional contact with the gunmen by sharing out my smokes. This also afforded me the chance to step into the yard and see the assembled regiment of militiamen.

A form of muster appeared to be under way, something between a military inspection and a lynch mob. Hundreds of men, mostly dressed in black but some clad in scraps of camouflage uniform, milled around with a motley array of military hardware: RPGs, Kalashnikovs, sub-machine guns, pistols and hunting rifles. The men at the gate were polite but distant, which was OK with me. In a surprising flash of PR savvy, the Mahdi Army had been ordered to be nice to the press, which was always a relief in a country where most militias had adopted the kidnapping and beheading of foreigners as standard operational procedure. Still, I was glad we had lied about our nationality: one of the chattier young gunmen, on being told I was Australian, laughed and said, 'So you've put your head in the lion's mouth? Lucky for you you're not British.'

'Ha ha,' I said, with as much bravura as I could summon. 'Wouldn't that be funny?'

An older man, a spokesman for the spokesman of the sheikh (all Iraqi organizations, no matter how rebellious or cobbled together, have an innate ability to instantly spawn a vast and pointless bureaucracy), came in to find out what we wanted.

'Which part of Australia are you from?' he enquired.

'Sydney.' I smiled, with only a flicker of hesitation.

'Ah,' he beamed back at me, 'I have two children living in Sydney. Which area do you live in?'

It was at points like this that I made sure never to meet Ali's eyes, just in case he was rolling them in exasperation that I was about to get us killed. In this instance I could feel him watching me with some urgency, waiting for me to utter a response which he could then translate.

'Erm, you know . . .' I began, clearing my throat, 'from around the Opera House area,' I said, naming the only landmark I knew in Sydney. 'You know, the big bridge . . .' The Sadrist nodded vaguely and was about to press on, but at that point I was saved by the arrival of the sheikh's actual spokesman, who bustled in, black turban and thick beard framing his podgy, sweating face. After the usual exchange of courtesies, during which he introduced himself as Sheikh Ali al-Mudafa, I asked him what plans he had for the mini army in the courtyard.

'If the British come down this street we will attack them!' he told me, curtly. 'As Muslims we have the right to defend ourselves against insults.' (Apparently some of his heroic warriors had been arrested by the British for looting – this was a stinging insult to the honour of the Mahdi Army.)

As he was on the point of launching into a description of why the coalition forces must release all their Iraqi prisoners and leave Basra immediately, the courtyard suddenly erupted into hubbub. I looked at Ali, who was listening to the hue and cry. He laughed rather nervously before turning to look me very purposefully in the eye.

'It seems . . . the British are coming,' he said.

In the two years I had spent in Iraq, I had never actually seen the British forces in action in the country. In this latest colonial chapter, Britain remained only a poor cousin to its superpower partner, America. While the British played up Basra's reputation as a relatively quiet backwater, most reporters spent most of their time in the decaying centre of the country, watching American troops struggle to master the role of world policeman in the new order – in addition to their roles of judge, jailor and oftentimes executioner. The difference between the armies and the distinct wars they were fighting became clear when one gauged the attitudes of the soldiers in the street. American troops, decked out in flak jackets, helmets and sunglasses, rarely walked the streets and would talk of freeing oppressed peoples from brutal dictatorship. The British squaddies, often on foot patrol without body armour or helmets, generally talked about their presence in terms of oil, orders and a break from dull tours in Northern Ireland. That was if they talked about it at all.

We went outside to see what was happening. As promised, hundreds of Mahdi fighters had surged forwards and were preparing for battle, shouting and chanting as they unslung their rifles and scuttled across the road to take up firing positions. One man stood behind a lamppost, a rocket-launcher cradled in his arms. Their leaders, however, seemed reluctant to fight, despite their bravado, and were hoarsely barking out,

'Don't shoot, don't shoot.' I briefly reflected on the irony of being killed by British troops in the rebel head-quarters. It was a nerve-tingling moment.

From the shouting, Ali could make out that a foot patrol had just appeared at the far end of the street. In the compound, a seething morass of Iraqi men whipped themselves into a frenzy to fight and die. I was glad that these were in fact British soldiers, with their famous softly-softly approach: the Americans would have prob-ably dropped a 2,000-pound bomb on the place by now and been done with it. The sheikh became very abrupt, telling us there was no way we could see al-Basri. Then he disappeared into the mob. The interview was over.

We jumped back in the car and made a swift exit from the compound, smiling politely at the taut gunmen who now regarded us with outright distrust. It was only when we reached the end of the street that we realized just how softly-softly this particular British approach was. Inching the car through knots of Iraqi fighters fanned out down the street we spotted three British soldiers crouching behind a low concrete statue in the middle of a roundabout. Just three of them. I scanned the nearby streets to see if they had any back-up, but saw none. Less than two hundred yards down the road, more than three hundred and fifty heavily armed guerrillas were shouting and readying for battle, but the British soldiers weren't even wearing helmets, just their floppy desert hats, as they observed the scene and muttered quietly into their radio headsets. It was the thinnest of thin red lines, sangfroid stepping on the toes of foolhardiness.

But in that strange Basra way, the evening rush-hour traffic kept chugging around the traffic circle between the armed antagonists, the drivers seemingly oblivious to the stand-off they were passing through. Ali and I took up a position behind the British soldiers. In the crowds moseying past the shops, the only people even vaguely interested in the scene were two policemen guarding a bank. Even they seemed to be watching only out of academic interest: local police would never intervene. For around sixty pounds a month, these poorly paid and inadequately trained cops chose not to get involved with the local militia doling out God's justice, or with foreign troops enforcing the abstract principle of western democracy. If the police were reluctantly dragged into the fray, they generally dropped their weapons and vacated their position as soon as possible. Those were the rules of the game.

I asked one of them, lounging on a plastic chair on the pavement, what he made of the scene.

'The Mahdi Army are worried the British are about to attack,' he said, 'and the British are watching out they don't spread further out of this area.'

It was true that for all their bombast, the Mahdi militia appeared to be masters only of their own street. But Iraq's guerrillas had a nasty habit of sneaking off and planting roadside bombs under piles of rubbish or inside dead animals. Some even built explosives into kerb stones they manufactured themselves, making them invisible to the soldiers. Containment was therefore all important.

We waited a while to see if either side would attack,

but the uneasy face-off continued until dark fell. We returned to the hotel. It was a tense night: through the humid air outside on the veranda I could occasionally hear, over the thrum of the hotel generator and the whine of primitive air-conditioning units, an explosion or burst of gunfire. I wondered if the sheikh had finally made good on his threat, but there was no way I was driving out in the darkness to see. It was difficult to tell in the Basra night what the gunfire signified. Even on a quiet night, you could hear the rat-tat-tat of tribal feuds being settled in time-honoured Iraqi style.

I stayed a few more days in Basra, meeting with Assad, the Christian friend who introduced me to Leonard Goodsir after I had talked to him about my family connection with his city. Assad was also a cast-off of the previous British occupation, as testified by his distinctly un-Arabic surname: Walkden. He too had a remarkable story, which he told me in his tiny workshop in Basra's teeming bazaar, where he and his brother Khalid Walkden repaired antique Singer sewing machines.

Their grandfather, Arthur James Walkden, had been a soldier in the Cheshire Regiment when the unit arrived in southern Mesopotamia as part of an expeditionary force to expel the Turks and secure the oilfields in 1917, the heyday of Lawrence of Arabia.

Arthur Walkden's career was distinctly less spectacular than Lawrence's. In 1920 the young Londoner was demobilized, but stayed in Iraq to join the new colonial police force in Amarah. Amarah is a tough, squalid town to the north of Basra full of feuding tribes. The British base there was constantly mortared, until the British were forced to hand it over to local Iraqi forces: they packaged this as a 'strategic withdrawal' to go and patrol the desert for weapons smugglers from Iran. Many of the smugglers were Marsh Arabs, who had fought Saddam's troops for years, carrying on a 5,000-year-old resistance to any invading army, be it from Sumer, Pharoah's Egypt or Churchill's Britain. Many were descendants of rebellious slaves from long-vanished empires who had found refuge in the world's largest wetlands until Saddam set about draining the marshes in the 1990s to deny them their natural cover.

In this rough, unforgiving territory, the young English policeman married a striking Arab Christian girl called Mathilda, daughter of one of the local tribes. In his shady house in Basra, where he invited me for a beer and to meet his family, Assad showed me a slightly blurred sepia picture of the two of them on their wedding day, walking into the squat Chaldean church where they had first laid eyes on each other.

'He saw my grandmother in church in Amarah. It was love at first sight. He was a handsome man, beautiful and white,' smiled Assad, a heavy-set middle-aged man with a dark complexion. After eyeing each other up in church, Arthur followed Mathilda back to her farm on his horse, and despite her lack of English and his pidgin Arabic, managed to ask her family for her hand.

Assad showed me the standard shot of them with their two sons, Arthur junior and Albert. It seemed a happy family arrangement, one that would be impossible in the current occupation, where soldiers were ticked off for becoming involved with local girls, and tribes killed any of their own women who flirted with the invaders.

But the marriage was not to last: Arthur, despite his marriage to Mathilda, fell victim to the petty-minded racism of the age. When the colonial rulers tried to sweeten the bitter pill of occupation by appointing more Iraqi officers to the police, a local man was promoted as Arthur's superior. In a fit of colonial pique, the Londoner – who in surviving photographs looked no more than a teenager in huge shorts – quit his job and tried to set himself up as a car salesman in Baghdad. The venture quickly foundered. In a desperate letter to the British High Commissioner, Mathilda begged for help in finding her husband a job, using the stilted English she had learned from her husband and his colleagues.

'Having been unsuccessful in all his attempts to find a job, your humble petitioner's husband has become very much broken hearted, and lost all interest in life, and it is feared he may desert her with the children,' said the letter dated June 24, 1926, and addressed to Sir Henry Dobbs, the High Commissioner.

'That as feared,' it continued, 'if your humble petitioner's husband deserts her, she will be thrown out into the world like one shipwrecked and no one to look for help, and the very imagination of a catastrophe like above makes her tremble and tears flow to her eyes.'

The response from the British Consul was brusque and bureaucratic. 'I am afraid I can find no work for your husband in Baghdad. The only thing I can do for him is to send him to England.' The consul would loan him twenty pounds for the passage – enough for one person. Arthur promised to find work and send for his family when he was established, then set off on a steamer out of Basra's bustling port.

That was the last they ever saw of him. He disappeared somewhere in London, while his family was ignored by the British and suffered jibes from their Iraqi neighbours. At school, his son's teacher refused to give the boy gym shoes because he was 'British'. Under the Baath Party regime, Arthur's grandson Assad and his siblings were refused higher education because of their suspicious foreign roots. Fearing more serious persecution, his uncle burned many documents in the 1970s, including Mathilda's British pension book.

There was only one more brief contact between the Basra Walkdens and their kin in London. Friends of the Iraqi family visited London in 1951, and spotted a shop called Walkden's. They went in and asked about the elusive Arthur: the shop-owners said he was their brother, heartbroken about abandoning his family. They told the visitors to come back the next day to meet him. Tragically, the foreign visitors – befuddled by the size and noise of the imperial capital – got on the Tube without noting the station or the address. They never found their way back and returned to Iraq empty-handed.

Assad had hoped the return of the British Army in 2003 might provide them with some answers about their heritage. But in the chaos that enveloped the country, no one ever found time to help the forgotten orphans of the old occupation. After a while, contact with the British became a liability in a city where Islamist gangs were blowing up Christian booze shops and the women – even Christians – were having to don headscarves to avoid the wrath of religious zealots.

Basra had once been the most liberal of Iraqi cities, with boozy casinos and plush hotels, and rich Kuwaitis nipping across the border to enjoy its fleshpots. Now, it was rapidly developing the austerity of a strict Islamic state. Buying a six-pack of Turkish Efes beer was like closing a major drug deal: I was sent to a 'dealer' in his shop near our hotel, but told to return after dark to make the illicit (albeit perfectly legal) purchase. When we returned at nine o'clock, the vendor told us to meet him in a dark alley near the hotel. We waited for twenty minutes, wondering if we were being set up for a kidnapping rather than a few brews. Eventually the flustered man darted out of the shadows and handed me a package wrapped in plastic bags. I stuffed a wad of dinars in his hand and he disappeared. I drank the beers in a stairwell of the hotel lounge and smoked my *narguilah* until the antsy manager asked me to put the alcohol away.

It was close to midnight when an Iraqi contact phoned us to tell us Steven Vincent had been kidnapped. The American freelance journalist had been grabbed off the street outside the Merbid Hotel in Basra, together with the Iraqi woman who worked as his translator. It was now summer 2005, and I had just returned to Baghdad after another visit to Basra. At such a distance, there wasn't much we could do except work the phones throughout the night, trying to let someone know Steven had vanished in a city that wanted him dead.

There was no point phoning the police. Steven had been bundled off in a white Chevrolet pick-up with the word 'Police' stencilled on the side. The men were in police uniform. When a few of the bolder people on the street approached the scuffle on the litter-strewn pavement, they were told to back off. 'Nobody intervene! We're the police, we are doing our duty,' shouted one of the gunmen struggling with the 49-year-old American. You would have to be a very brave man not to just turn away and pretend you'd seen nothing.

Steven struggled hard, and with good reason. He knew what was coming. By August 2005, the British softly-softly approach had turned into a blind eye to murder and abduction by the Iranian-backed militias, determined to park their Islamic revolution in the once cosmopolitan city. A few days earlier, Steven had written an article for the *New York Times* outlining how Basra's death squads worked: Islamist militias used off-duty policemen – around three-quarters of whom were loyal to this political faction or that, rather than to the nebulous Iraqi government, huddling under US guard in Baghdad's Green Zone – to carry out assassinations, using what locals called the 'death car'. All this, Steven said, was happening right under the noses of the British Army that had trained these same policemen to shoot straight, but not to rise above their tribal and religious loyalties. So Steven fought the men in uniform, knowing what happened once they had forced you into the death car. After the vehicle sped off – only a short distance, to a nearby warehouse where locals could hear his screams for hours afterwards – passers-by found his shoes in the rubbish of the gutter, right where he had lost them in his frantic struggle.

I had been driving around Basra with Steven just ten days before he was abducted. Making our way through the throng of evening shoppers and men heading off to smoke *narguilah* at waterside teashops on the Shatt al-Arab, we were caught in traffic close to the Corniche, the waterfront promenade. Steven, sitting in the front seat because his dark complexion and goatee beard made him look more Iraqi, rapped on the window and pointed at a white Toyota idling in the crowd of pedestrians, like a barracuda lurking in seaweed.

'Hey, that's the death car!' he barked. I told him it was perhaps not a wise idea to be pointing at the 'death car'. Lulu said that anyway word on the street was that the death squads had stopped using the Toyota Mark II and switched to another model. People weren't sure what make it was, but rumours were flying round the fearful city.

That night in early August, only a few yards from the squat compound of his hotel, Steven found out what the new death car was. It was at this hotel that I had first met him. A rangy man with an intense stare, he had seemed on edge. He rarely went out much any more, after three months of traipsing round Basra, poking his nose into the local militias' business and trying to convince trigger-happy tribesmen that American democracy and women's rights were the way ahead. As a freelance writer, working on a book about the city, he couldn't afford the security guards, the chase cars and walkie-talkies that so many media outlets had by now adopted. He knew he was taking a risk, asking questions about the Islamic militias and their crackdown on such loose public morals as singing, pop music and picnics. Hardline Shiite political parties with names like the 'Vengeance of God' or the 'Master of the Martyrs' don't take kindly to pushy foreigners asking questions about their extra-curricular activities.

Worse, Steven openly criticized them on his blog, where he detailed his often idealistic behaviour in the turbulent city where the mullahs were developing an iron grip. In one entry before he vanished, he complained that an Iraqi man had come into the hotel café where he sat with Nour, his female translator. The man was watching seductive, scantily clad Lebanese singers cavorting on screen, but when he noticed that Nour had removed her headscarf, he scowled at her.

'He's staring at us with the blank, malevolently stupid glare I've encountered so often,' Steven wrote. '"You have a problem," I snap . . . by now, I'm thinking, "What would happen if I punched this guy?"' Nour put her headscarf back on, saving him from a fist-fight. In Iraq, fist-fights rarely end as mere café scuffles. If honour is impugned, blood must be shed. Tribal feuds start for much less, and the hotel corridors were already full of malevolent gossip about the aggressive foreigner and the 31-year-old single Iraqi woman: people automatically assumed they might be having an affair. The new morality of the Islamic south was being flouted. Some western journalists I knew avoided any contact with Steven, knowing he was courting trouble.

Officially, Basra was the success story of Iraq's troubled post-war period (not counting the Kurds, who by this time were a virtual breakaway state in the north). The British had sidestepped attempts by the militias to spark an uprising, instead choosing to allow extremists to exercise their freedom of speech and their right to bear lots and lots of arms. This was less the result of an implicit faith in Iraqi homespun democracy and more because they only had 8,000 troops in the south, facing potential resistance from a Shia community who made up 60 per cent of the population. A British Army spokesman once told me at the military base at Basra airport that his troops would only use force if Moqtada al-Sadr 'comes over the hill waving an RPG'.

Steven had been a New York art critic until one day he stood on the roof of his apartment in the East Village and watched United 175 smash into the World Trade Center. In that moment he decided to stop being an art critic and immerse himself in the war that had crash-landed on his doorstep. His wife later said he would have liked to enlist, but at forty-five was too old to be a soldier (though by that summer of 2005, Vietnam veterans older than him were being pressed back into service as chopper pilots by the demands of the war). Instead, he packed his bags and became a war correspondent. Three years later, I ran into him in the lobby of the Merbid Hotel, more commonly known among correspondents as the Morbid Hotel for its dingy, coffin-like rooms. It was one of the few safe-ish hotels left in the city, by dint of its compound walls and its armed guards, who were related to the owner: anyone fighting them would find themselves in a nasty tribal spat. Steven often sat in the café writing his angry blog on his laptop. I sensed he was keen for the company of other western journalists, though wary we would encroach on his patch. He told me he had a big story he was working on, but was coy about saying too much. He was bitter at what he found in Basra, the bullying attitude of the men, the corruption and violence: the battle for democracy appeared to have been sidetracked into a victory for the Iranian revolution and corrupt tin-pot potentates. The garbage was still on the streets, he explained, because when a contract was put out to collect it, the local businessmen found it easier to pick the trash up directly from the overflowing landfills, deliver it to other waste disposal points and pick up their cash. Millions of dollars were wasted shuffling Basra's rubbish from one dump to the other, while the streets were piled ever higher with squalor.

But the most sinister development was the death squads, the enforcers of mullah morality and the will of . . . well, no one was quite sure, but everyone pointed across the Shatt al-Arab towards Iran.

I went to Basra University to ask the professors about the death squads: it seemed everyone knew about them but were too afraid to speak out, and I hoped that the professors might understand that they could trust us not to betray their confidence. We drove into the campus, the car wheels rolling across American, Israeli and British flags painted on the driveway. They looked as if they should have been put there by Saddam's regime, but were in fact a post-war addition, like the graffiti on the main street that threatened: 'British and Jewish! Mahdi army distroy you.' Campus guards – the same ones who refused to allow girls in unless their hair was appropriately covered – waved the car through, on to an estate of dilapidated departments garnished with the obligatory piles of stinking trash. This was the university campus.

A few months earlier, a crowd of students had organized a picnic in a city park, playing pop music and laughing together. A mob of Moqtada's supporters, the humourless enforcers of no fun, attacked them, firing shots in the air and beating the young people with sticks and rifle butts. The Islamists tried to rip the blouse off one girl, filming her and threatening they would tell her parents she was dancing naked with boys. When two of her friends tried to help her, they were shot. One of them later died, and the girl herself committed suicide. Another girl was beaten so badly about the head she went blind. The police who were supposed to be guarding the gathering did nothing to stop the rampage. The religious thugs were unapologetic afterwards, accusing the students of having been 'sinful': they complained that the timing of their picnic showed disrespect to the hundred Shia who had died in a particularly nasty bombing in Hilla, hundreds of miles to the north. The bomb had exploded more than a month before. When one of the students complained to the British Army, he was informed that the troops could not intervene unless asked to by the Iraqi authorities. Unfortunately, Moqtada's fanatics and their fellow-travellers now ran many of the city councils. So the students organized a protest at their own university. In response, the Mahdi Army threatened to mortar the campus. Alone and terrified, the students gave in.

Months after the notorious Basra picnic, the fear was still palpable. In the privacy of his office, I asked a hospitable, English-speaking professor about the Islamic militias. Immediately, something happened that I had never seen anywhere else before. His hands instantly started shaking. The smiled vanished from his lips and he started mopping his forehead.

'I can't talk about that. I have three kids and I love life,' he said, then laughed nervously: 'I have a very nice neck too. Very nice. I don't want to lose it.' I assured him that his identity and neck would be safe with me, and cautiously he opened up. 'The Islamic movement is very hard. Al-Qaeda is not a problem here. The Iranian revolution is the problem.'

The evidence was everywhere: the street kids selling cassettes of Arab pop music at the crossroads near the university told how 'men in black' had pulled up in a car and told them to stop their immoral behaviour immediately. They said the only reason they didn't kill them there and then was that they were children. But the kids, no more than twelve years old, had no other income and so still sold the cassettes, forever on the lookout for the enforcers.

Given the increasingly volatile climate, it wasn't a total surprise, then, when the phone call came from Basra to Baghdad, and a local journalist announced that Steven had been kidnapped. Abductions in the Shiite south were as common as those carried out in the Sunni centre, but they went underreported because there were fewer journalists covering the area. Most of them were carried out by common criminals who'd take their victim's car and money and leave them to walk home.

The call was brief and to the point: Steven had been kidnapped outside the hotel, with Nour. There were few other details. I knew it would be difficult to make contact on Iraq's notoriously unreliable phones: the southern cellphone system couldn't even connect to the one we used in Baghdad. So I used a satellite phone to call the British Army press office in Basra. I tried every number I had, time and time again. No response. My colleague Tom Bullock from National Public Radio phoned the American military in Baghdad's Green Zone. He was asked to send all the details in an email and told they'd get back to us. Whenever the US military asks for something in email form, it will be days before they respond, if they ever do. We didn't have days. In a kidnapping you have to move fast, find out who's got the hostage and establish what they want for him. Otherwise, the underground market opens for business, and the big buyer out there was al-Qaeda. They would pay up to a quarter of a million dollars for a live American or Briton.

At first, I wasn't too worried. My best guess was that this was a commercial kidnapping, or some irate member of Nour's tribe was trying to intimidate the pair. The previous year, a few days after I had left Basra, a young British journalist was abducted from the neighbouring hotel by men dressed as police. The men kicked in his door in the middle of the night, beat him up and dragged him off. He managed to briefly escape from the house where he was being held, running down the street to a cabin used by night watchmen guarding a government building. The kidnappers burst in and again dragged him off. The guards were simply too terrified to raise a hand in his defence. But he was quickly released after the intercession of Moqtada al-Sadr, prompting speculation that the young demagogue had either staged the whole thing himself as a publicity stunt or had very close links to Basra's underworld. But the journalist was released, and everyone thought kidnapping in the Shiite south was a less terminal experience than being nabbed around Baghdad.

Unable to raise anyone who might have helped, we went to bed around three a.m., after I had made that dreaded, awkward call to the editor at Steven's paper back in the States to tell him that one of his contributors had been kidnapped. The desk editor sounded nonplussed, as you might expect at receiving such news, so I suggested they contact the State Department and tell them to wake up the British military.

I had only been asleep about twenty minutes when Ali, my translator, phoned me to tell me the staff at Merbid Hotel had contacted him.

'Well, he's dead,' Ali said, in the matter-of-fact way that Iraqis have of talking about such things. 'They just found his body. He was shot in the heart.'

It was a horrible moment. I've known a number of friends killed in Iraq, but I had never had the chance to try to save them. I knew it would have made little difference even if the phones had worked: the British military considered policing an Iraqi affair, even if the Iraqi police were probably involved in the abduction. If the British had not left the policing to the unreliable Iraqi force, they risked facing a full-scale uprising. I phoned Steven's editor again to let him know. Then I went back to bed, where I couldn't help imagining the guy I had sat with in the car just a few days before, terrified as some crazy bearded fanatic pushed a pistol in his face, shouting and ranting the same furious nonsense that had so infuriated Steven in his last weeks. No doubt he had been thinking about Nour too, who had become a good friend – in fact, he had planned to marry her as a ploy to get her out of Basra. He had his wife's permission, and had been picking up the money for her dowry when they were abducted.

Nour was shot too, three times in the back, and left next to his dying body. Incredibly, when the police found them (it seems highly likely they had never actually 'lost' them), she was still breathing. She was rushed to hospital, and after a year of fighting diplomatic and bureaucratic red tape, Steven's wife managed to get her out of the country.

Steven's body wound up in the Basra morgue. His murder appeared to be a warning to others. Ironically, it was the same warning he had been trying to disseminate in his web log: southern Iraq was rapidly turning into a nasty thuggish theocracy modelled on Iran's brutal regime. This warning, in the shape of his bullet-holed corpse, reached a far wider audience. Yet still, few took any heed.

INSIDE THE SPIDER'S WEB

The Fall of Fallujah

The last time I'd heard 'Garryowen' was when I was still a kid, maybe ten years old. The Irish drinking song, picked by General George Armstrong Custer as battle hymn for his Seventh Cavalry, was the tune his pipers played as the doomed regiment rode to annihilation at the hands of the Sioux nation at the Little Bighorn. It had made its way into my parents' home in Sussex during the stifling summer of 1976, on a double vinyl album called *The Music of America*, released to commemorate the bicentenary of America's declaration of independence. By chance, 1976 was also the centenary of Custer's fatal battle in Montana.

Sandwiched between 'Dixie' and 'Shenandoah', 'Garryowen' always sent a tingle down my spine. The track started off with a ragged sputter of rifle shots and Indian war whoops, out of which slowly drifted the sound of pipes and the jaunty ballad that had captured the imagination of the ill-fated Indian hunter. I was captivated by the tune and the epic story surrounding it, which my ten-year-old mind found wonderfully exciting and adventurous. My mother was enthralled by the song too, and we'd play it time and again on our crackling record player, she carefully lifting the arm of the stylus back to the beginning as soon as it finished, and off we'd go again.

I didn't hear 'Garryowen' again until a grey afternoon in November 2004. This time, it was blaring through loudspeakers fixed to the tops of metal poles that supported row after row of white plastic tents in the vast, dusty camp on the edge of Fallujah. And this time, it was announcing to the hundreds of troopers of the Second Battalion, Seventh Cavalry, that they were, once again, about to ride into battle.

I was going with them, and the old thrill of the marching tune had been replaced by a nervous jangle in my stomach, a feeling that seemed to connect one man to another like an electric spark as they packed their bags and laughed a little too quickly and loudly at their own wisecracks.

All through the tents, troopers were packing up their portable DVD players, games consoles and laptops, smoking cigarettes and trying to fill in those last few restless hours before rolling out to the jump-off position. A company medic was watching *Rocky II* on his laptop, giving little right jabs and left hooks in time to the action on the miniature screen. A skinny kid was sitting on his bunk listening to a thrash-metal singer screaming out 'Put on your war face, show me your war face', a line culled from the Vietnam flick *Full Metal Jacket*.

Outside the tent I bumped into Sergeant Abe, whose platoon I had watched practise house clearings on an empty gravel lot near the tents, the outlines of rooms to be stormed marked on the ground with white duct tape. Sergeant Abe was the platoon's point man and crazy guy, the one who kicked in doors and walked right up to IEDs to see what made them tick. He was preparing for battle by listening to the metal-mouthed, transgender shock-rocker Marilyn Manson and eating Crystal Light, the powder that soldiers mixed with water to make flavoured drinks. He seemed in good spirits, high on adrenaline and the anticipation of the fight ahead.

'I want some,' he said, matter-of-fact. Every so often, though, he would stare at the picture of his two little kids that was taped to the inside of his helmet. His buddy and platoon sergeant Carlos Santillana, a thoughtful, good-looking man in his mid-twenties, was less gung-ho.

'I think about dying all the time,' he admitted quietly when Abe ambled off to look for more Crystal Light to chew on. Santillana, who had a baby back in the regiment's home city of Fort Hood, Texas, with his psychologist wife, was a very good soldier, his officers told me. I was surprised at how sensitive and introspective he could be at times. Maybe that was why he was good at leading men. 'All I say is, don't be afraid of dying, but don't go looking for it. When it's your time, it's your time.'

A few miles away in Fallujah, the guerrillas were preparing in a rather different manner. An Iraqi friend of mine,

Ghaith Abdul-Ahad, was the only journalist brave enough to actually take up a Mujahedin offer to report from their stronghold on the eve of the battle. He later told me that while the cavalrymen I was with were getting pumped on death-metal and Rocky, the foreign fighters were ribbing each other like suicidal frat boys, joshing about how many virgins each would receive in paradise. A Yemeni recruit, who had sold almost all his worldly possessions and left his wife and kids to get to the battle, was joking that when he and his comrades died, as he was sure they soon would, the Saudi in their volunteer unit would only get twenty-five girls, while he himself would get the full quota of seventy-two promised in the holy scripture.

In fact, the promise of scores of virgins is believed by some Islamic scholars to be a mistranslation of the ancient Aramaic word 'hur', meaning juicy white grapes, a rare delicacy in the early days of Islam when the followers of the Prophet were fighting in the deserts of the Hejaz. In Arabic, the word 'hur' means virgin. While the muddled Arab volunteer kamikazes prepared to trade in their lives for the delights of the fresh produce aisle, their Iraqi comrades were already ripping them off in the here and now: the locals jihadists often treated them simply as car-bomb fodder, charging them exorbitant prices for food and lodging and rarely bothering to give them any military training. As the first American shells fell around them, one of the Gulf Arabs was fiddling with the safety catch of his Kalashnikov. He looked at Ghaith and hopefully asked if he could show him how to use it.

Not all the men gathered in Fallujah for the battle were religiously inspired Mujahedin, however. As it happened, my translator Mohanned's cousin, who had introduced us almost a year before to the fledgling guerrilla cell of Rutba, had also turned up in Fallujah for the decisive showdown with the Crusaders. Instead of a new Salahedin's army ready to deliver Jerusalem from the infidels, many of those he came across girding themselves for battle were former Baathists, Syrian agents or local criminals on the payroll of al-Qaeda, or tribesmen simply defending their turf. Many of these were the men who had turned Fallujah into a new Taliban mini-state, beating men who failed to respect their unforgiving ideology and exporting car bombs to the capital. This was not the fight to give up his life for, he promptly decided, and sneaked out of town before the battle began. He lived on to become a car salesman in Jordan.

There were two other journalists embedded in the cavalry battalion I was with, Matt McAllester of *Newsday* and James Janega of the *Chicago Tribune*. We had been told by the battalion commander, Lieutenant Colonel Jim Rainey, that we would have to wait out the initial assault on Fallujah at the unit's field headquarters on the edge of town while he led a column of around fifty Abrams tanks and Bradley fighting vehicles straight into the heart of the Mujahedin defences, an area known as Jolan. A few hours before push-off, however, the colonel summoned the three of us to the Tactical Operations Centre, or TOC, a large canvas tent in the lee of a recently abandoned quarry some two miles from the city limits. Rainey, a tall, bluff 39-year-old with a boxer's face and a brown buzzcut, told us the regimental command had sent him copies of articles we had written about the preparations for battle and the mood of the men. Apparently, we hadn't betrayed any military secrets or maligned the US armed forces.

'You all seem like solid citizens to me,' he told us. 'You can come along with me when we go, if you want.'

For embedded journalists, compliments from the military are a double-edged sword. You live and eat with, and often suffer the same privations as, the soldiers you are in the field with, and as a normal human being you would rather they liked you than not. But you have to keep reminding yourself they are not your friends, they are the subject of the story you are covering, and you will have to write objectively about them, both the good and the bad. This often creates a friction within the journalist's mind, as indeed it should. The temptation to see them as your buddies is especially strong when the troops around you speak the same language and come from a similar culture, while the people 'out there' – the ones your armed companions are about to try and kill – are so alien in so many ways. And when your life depends on these same people, it is especially important to remember that you are there to do your job, just as they are trying to do theirs.

On this occasion, though, the three of us looked at each other and grinned. Success. We would be with the first unit into the besieged city – the 'tip of the spear', the colonel called it, and a perfect vantage point to report on the fighting. Immediately after the elation, however, there followed that shadowy, edgy feeling of dread, the knowledge that we could easily die that same night.

It was getting dark, and I sneaked out of the dusty quarrymen's hut where we were billeted to make a last call home on my satellite phone. Strictly speaking, we weren't supposed to make any contact with the outside world at that late hour, on the off-chance that the guerrillas might be able to intercept our calls. But I figured if they hadn't worked out by now exactly what the 20,000 American and Iraqi troops ringing their city were about to do, they probably weren't ever going to.

The reason I wanted to steal away was two-fold: first, the soldiers around me were strictly denied the same privilege, and I didn't want them to see me. Secondly, I figured this could be the last phone call I'd ever make, and I wanted some privacy to say goodbye to my parents.

It would have been a very Hollywood moment to tell my mum they had been playing 'Garryowen' as we left, but it just didn't occur to me. I was choked up, trying to keep my voice steady as I spoke. We all knew it would be bad – the Americans were determined to take the city at just about any cost. There were estimates that as many as 5,000 guerrillas were waiting just across the dusty flats, in the city enfolded in total darkness – Fallujah's water and electricity had been cut off days before. They were ready to fight to the death, possibly armed with cyanide gas and waiting in mined buildings that they were prepared to bring down on themselves and on the invading soldiers.

Needless to say, I didn't go into such detail with my parents. But it was a heart-wrenching conversation all the same. My father later told me he felt it was the modern equivalent of reading a letter from the trenches in the First World War as the soldiers prepared to go over the top. More painful, in a way, because it was a two-way conversation. What can anyone say in such a situation? I kept it to the obvious, then, and I told them I loved them. And I reassured them that the unit I was with was very professional, that I'd be inside a 32-ton armoured vehicle. I didn't feel I'd convinced them, and I certainly hadn't convinced myself. But then my mother pitched in with unexpected conviction.

'You'll be fine, I know it,' she told me, quite brightly. She had spent her entire career working as a nurse, and I knew she was practised in the art of delivering good news to people with terminal diseases. But her sudden change of tone gave me a lift. As I hid my phone and slipped back to the headquarters tent, I felt a certain sense of destiny wrap around me.

Then I discovered I had lost my gas mask.

There are moments in war when you have to decide exactly what is worth risking your life for. The longer the conflict goes on, the lower generally the bar becomes. You've already risked a great deal, you have the stories to tell back home and you just want to survive. Standing there, I only had a few minutes to make the decision as the soldiers were already climbing into the Bradleys, six or seven men with battle kit squeezed into a space the size of a family dining table. In the event, I only reflected for about thirty seconds on whether to risk choking to death at my colleagues' feet or miss the story of a lifetime. I consciously decided to shut down the debate inside my head and get in. As the metal ramp closed, I knew there was no going back: you couldn't knock on the vehicle commander's hatch and say you'd changed your mind and wanted to go home.

Still, I asked one of the two soldiers crammed in the back with us journalists what he thought the chances of the guerrillas having cyanide gas were.

'My sergeant says it's only about one in ten,' he said in a laconic southern drawl – the regiment was from Texas – before resting his head against the Bradley's interior wall and dozing off.

A one-in-ten chance I could be gassed to death. Statistically it was reassuring, but I still wondered if holding my fleece jacket over my nose would help. It passed through my mind to ask one of my companions if they would do buddy breathing with me if we were gassed, the way trouble-stricken scuba divers share their air supply. But I figured no one in their right mind would take off their gas mask in the middle of a cyanide attack. I rode into battle not full of the spirit of 'Garryowen', but full of self-loathing, instead.

To distract myself, I ran through all the other horrible things that could happen in the coming hours, but which would at least happen to all of us communally: there was a minefield we had to cross on the edge of town, the prospect of rocket-propelled grenade attacks or getting cut off in the guerrilla heartland. During the house-clearance training session back at the camp, I had asked Rainey what the battle plan was. Smiling slightly that a reporter would even ask such a question, he gave me a concise, cavalryman's answer.

'We'll push in there and if we get in trouble, we'll circle the wagons,' he said, spitting out a viscous quid of Red Man tobacco that was bulging under his lower lip. Rainey's manner was friendly but businesslike. He tried to act the simple soldier but was much smarter than he let on.

'Isn't that what Custer did?' I asked nervously.

He smiled again. 'I think we can do better than that,' he said and strolled off.

As we rode into the terrorist heartland of Iraq, it struck me that 'better' than a man who had led his entire regiment to be slaughtered by hostile Sioux was not setting the benchmark too high. But by that point we were already inching in a giant column of Abrams tanks, Bradleys, Humvees and armoured bulldozers towards the minefield, our way lit by the dim blue glow of chemical light sticks sprinkled on the ground like low-wattage glow worms.

There had been a tempest of Shakespearean proportions the night the Seventh Cavalry had rumbled out of Camp Fallujah to take up their attack position in the quarry outside town. Lightning flashes skittered over the huge column of metal like a terrible premonition, before darkness once again enveloped the desert, heightening the senses to the ominous growl of tanks on the move. It was unlikely anyone in Fallujah heard it, though. The thunder in the sky was matched by the din of shells falling on the city as American artillery and fighter-bombers softened up the target.

By dawn, the quarry had become a vast parking lot, quaking with lines of war machines, many of them still bearing scars from the battle of Najaf that summer. Stencilled on the barrels of the tanks were the names the crews had given them: 'Captain Chaos', 'Convicted Killer' and 'Casa de Muerte'.

Inside the quarry pit, Lieutenant Colonel Rainey had set up his khaki headquarters tent in a foot of talcum-powder dust that constantly settled on the expensive military computer gadgetry. As zero-hour approached that night, the colonel gathered his officers and NCOs and delivered a brief pep talk.

'No matter what you think about the Iraqi war or the Iraqi government, this fight is one hundred per cent about terrorists, terrorists who want to come to your home and kill you,' he said. His rather ambiguous wording made me wonder exactly how he felt about this war that was costing so much and seemed to be going nowhere. It wasn't exactly Henry V at Agincourt, but it carried the eternal message for soldiers about to go into the fight – the enemy is evil and must be annihilated. The fact that many of those men waiting for combat in Fallujah were confused, angry tribesmen who had no idea where Fort Hood might be was neither here nor there at this point.

'It's going to be tougher than Najaf,' Rainey added. 'Don't leave your honour, your values or your buddies on the battlefield.'

Outside, as dusk approached, the pounding of

Fallujah had increased to a steady rain of fire. The dark city would light up for an instant, then a rumbling detonation would roll across the plains towards us. Above the gloomy cityscape, airbursts formed giant jellyfish of white smoke, their straggling tentacles walking across the city rooftops.

I asked Rainey what caused them. He hesitated.

'Er, some kind of illumination rounds, I guess,' he said. It was only many months later that I learned that the strange, ghostly forms had been white phosphorous shells bursting over the city. Known back in Vietnam as 'Willie Pete', it is a much, much nastier version of napalm, one that can burn straight through skin and down to the bone, even under water. Strictly speaking it is a chemical weapon, but the US military has managed to re-label it as an incendiary device, and now describes it, with unwitting irony, as a smoke screen. That helped avoid the embarrassment of deploying a chemical weapon against a city, such as Saddam had done in Kurdistan. Looking back, it was hardly surprising that Rainey did not want to tell me what it was that was raining down on Fallujah that night, on a city that had hundreds, possibly thousands, of civilians still living in it.

Outside the quarryman's hut, a group of soldiers had pulled up plastic chairs and folding campstools to watch the fireworks like excited spectators, pushing away the knowledge that this show was audience participation, and in a few short hours they too would be heading into the middle of the maelstrom.

* * *

It took hours to move the couple of miles from the quarry and into the battle zone. In the dark, columns of troops crisscrossed along prearranged paths through the desert. Humvees overturned in ditches and injured marines were evacuated even before the fight started. At one point, I thought I saw an entire house shimmering its way through the dark. As it approached, I realized it was a vast armoured bulldozer slogging along like some prehistoric beetle.

A tank gunner was smoking near the vast carapace of his vehicle, watching the huge army pass by. 'I'm a Catholic, and I have to say, I feel sorry for 'em,' he said with a slightly apologetic grin.

We would inch our way forward then wait for the tail of the column to catch up, moving like a huge slinky. During the pit stops we would get out of the airless Bradley and smoke, watching the explosions flashing over the city ahead. I would silently curse myself for losing my gas mask.

The first obstacle was a minefield the guerrillas had laid on the northern edge of town, where the long-disused railway tracks ran into Fallujah station. Marine sappers blew a hole in the railway embankment and then blasted a path through the minefield using a so-called Miclic, a series of explosive charges tied together in a line and fired into the minefield. The explosives blow up the mines and clear a passage for vehicles to enter. The noise was deafening, and I was glad to see that our Bradley wasn't the first in the column of around fifty armoured vehicles to negotiate the minefield.

Emerging on the other side, we were finally in

Fallujah. Our eyes were glued to the eerie green screen in the back of the Bradley that showed both the vehicle commander's and the gunner's viewpoints. It was the ultimate in reality television – the smashed streets and explosions we saw on the luminous screen were right outside, the image about to collide with us at any moment. The Bradleys and tanks proceeded at a snail's pace, shooting mounds of earth or debris to detonate any possible booby traps. As the column fanned out into town, we could clearly see the road ahead, and gritted our teeth every time the vehicle rolled over to a mound that could have been a vast landmine.

The streets seemed deserted, but the rattle of machine-gun fire and the occasional reports from cannon reminded us that the gunners could see far more than we could.

'There were too many IEDS to count,' Rainey told me later, when we had time to catch up with him. But staring at the screen, we could make out nothing in the shifting light and dark greens. Then, around two o'clock in the morning, the column ground to a halt in a broad street lined by houses with high garden walls. There we idled for about twenty minutes, as far as I could tell waiting for the disparate elements of our expeditionary force to regroup. Even in a 32-ton fighting vehicle, we started to feel vulnerable sitting there in a city full of guerrillas intent on killing whoever dared enter their stronghold.

Then we saw a man appear in the gateway of a walled yard, a pair of binoculars held up to his face. We were at the tail end of the column, and he was scanning the armoured vehicles ahead of us. The gunner had his sights trained on him, but showed remarkable restraint in not opening fire, although the man was clearly picking a target. The Iraqi man ducked back inside the garden, only to re-emerge a few seconds later, the binoculars still in front of his face. Evidently he had not seen us in the dark, and must have thought that the next vehicle in the column, which was some way ahead of us, was the tail of the advance. Once again he disappeared back into the yard. The next time he reappeared, he had a rocket-propelled grenade on his shoulder. He pointed it at the vehicle ahead. Perhaps our anxious driver revved the engine at that moment, but the rocket man suddenly realized we were there, staring at him. Instantly, he swung the RPG round to face us. In the back of the Bradley, three journalists found themselves frozen, staring at the barrel of the rocket-launcher.

'Kill him!' someone shouted. It may have been me, I don't remember. Suddenly we were all shouting, 'Shoot!' 'Get him!' 'What the fuck . . .'

The Iraqi man wavered, perhaps overawed by the sheer surprise of finding a Bradley so close to him. He seemed about to duck back into his garden when the gunner fired the 25mm cannon. I was so transfixed by watching the Iraqi that I barely registered the noise. I just noticed the recoil of dust into the bowels of the Bradley where we sat, still staring at the screen. The man disappeared as the round exploded on the gatepost next to him. I had seen someone killed right in front of me, but all I could feel was an immense relief. So much for journalistic objectivity.

302

                              *   *   *

When morning finally came, it shed a pale grey light
over the blanched badlands that stretched north past
the captured railway station. From the interior of the
embattled city, the low chug of machine-gun fire and
occasional whump of an explosion carried across the
metallic sky. Cobra helicopters buzzed in like slivers of
shrapnel above us, unleashing Hellfire missiles into
unseen guerrilla positions. A convoy of marines,
exhausted from the night fight around the railway
depot, rolled out of the desert in a column of open-
backed Humvees and into the fray. Dehydrated and
exhausted, but excited to be alive and in a battle, I
looked at their drawn young faces, many of them
covered by blast goggles and khaki scarves against the
night chill, as they rolled past in long lines to kill or die.
As the last of the marines disappeared into the urban
battlescape, hundreds of Iraqi government troops
marched out of the desert behind them, out of step and
dressed in ill-fitting uniforms cast off by some other US
client state, like some lost army marching out of the
past. Their NCOs shouted at stragglers to keep up, and
the American soldiers I stood smoking with sniggered at
the hapless *jundis* as they ran for cover and started firing
off potshots as soon as they heard the sound of gunfire
rattling out of the city.

  Then, in a bizarre twist of war imitating the movies
imitating war, I heard the menacing refrain of 'Ride of
the Valkyries' drifting in across the dusty plains. I
scanned the gloomy wilderness and spotted a squad of
psy-ops Humvees, loudspeakers fixed to their roofs

where normally M2 machine guns would sit, bumping into town, music blaring. Either the officer in charge was a fan of *Apocalypse Now*, or he thought the guerrillas might have seen the film and associate it with impending annihilation.

The psy-ops squads, normally the US military's official taunters and mockers of their foe's fighting prowess, were this time equipped with standard surrender tapes, in which they would congratulate a holed-up enemy on his valiant fight but try to convince him the battle was over and he should take the sensible way out and concede defeat. These did not always work very well: a photographer embedded with a marines unit told me how the company he was with in a bitter fight surrounded a house with several guerrillas trapped inside, refusing to come out with their hands up. The unit called up the psy-ops guys, who played the surrender tape. That didn't work, so they started playing loud thrash metal songs, trying to wear down the fighters' psychological resistance, Noriega-style. Unlike the jihadists, the marines loved the music and started asking for requests. The siege became a juke-box jive session for battle-worn marines. Still the guerrillas refused to come out. This time the psy-ops soldiers put on the soundtrack to *Team America*, the puppet spoof that hilariously satirized the very 'war on terror' that had brought both the young marines and the jihadists to this stand-off. The marines started singing along to the chorus of 'America, Fuck Yeah!', as inside the building the guerrillas no doubt recounted the Shuhada martyr's prayer for Muslims about to face their death. Still they refused to come out, so the marines took the easy way out and called in an air strike. The last thing the holy warriors heard before the whine of an incoming rocket wiped them out of existence was the sound of puppets singing: 'So lick my butt, and suck on my balls.'

As the last of the Iraqi soldiers marched into town to take up holding positions on Jolan's main north–south street, where they were to prevent the enemy from fleeing or regrouping, I spotted Rainey standing by his Bradley on the rubble-strewn road that ran along the town's border with the desert. I strolled up to him and asked him how the battle was going. It was clear by now that the US gamble had punched a gaping hole in the Mujahedin defences: the guerrillas clearly had not expected a full-out armoured assault on their main stronghold, no doubt gambling that the winding little streets of Jolan would deter the Americans from risking their million-dollar tanks against cheap rocket-propelled grenades. Rainey was in good spirits, having led his men successfully on a highly hazardous mission and survived without a single casualty. The resistance was determined, but it was far from the apocalyptic showdown we had been led to expect.

'I think there are committed fighters out there who want to die in Fallujah,' he said, spitting a quid of tobacco on the ground. 'We are in the process of allowing them to self-actualize,' he added, allowing himself a hint of a smile at the New Age-speak in the midst of battle.

The dawn lull didn't last long. Major Tim Karcher, the

giant, shaven-headed second-in-command who looked like Superman with alopecia, told us to get back in his Bradley. The column was moving out again to a hot spot in the heart of Jolan. The 2/7 had just taken control of a schoolhouse that the Mujahedin had barricaded and probably intended to use as a field headquarters. The army's surprise thrust had forced them to abandon it, but there was still heavy fighting going on around it. We mounted up and rumbled down the central road of Jolan. After just one night of fighting, it had already been transformed from Taliban Main Street into a US military highway, clogged with massive armoured vehicles and filled with the suffocating, sickly-sweet stench of J8 fuel oil that they belched out in black clouds.

When the Bradley stopped and the rear hatch opened, we all jumped out into the middle of a major firefight. There were detonations coming from every direction and an almost constant thud of machine-gun fire. I could see no one in the street of concrete-stucco houses. Karcher led us at a doubled-up trot through a door in the wall and into the schoolhouse. The classrooms had been cleared and some of the desks piled up as barricades. We ran through a yard, then down a corridor, before emerging into a small square dominated by a high metal water tower. There was a cluster of Bradleys parked in the shade of the water tower, their cannon pointed outwards and looking for all the world like a circled wagon train. In their middle, I found Rainey and his officers discussing the situation, as their dismounted soldiers scanned the streets beyond the square. They seemed pleased with their progress and were making plans to set up their own forward base in the abandoned guerrilla position when suddenly I felt a burning sensation in my left arm.

I had a fleeting impression that someone had snuck up behind and whacked me over the arm with a red-hot poker, upon which I leapt into the middle of the commander's huddle yelping, 'Shit shit shit!' When I put my right hand up to the left bicep I felt blood squirting out, the way milk squirts from a punctured carton.

'I'm hit, I'm hit,' I shouted to no one in particular, amazed by the realization that I had actually been wounded. It didn't hurt much beyond the searing burn, but the physical shock had me shaking all over, a wave of nausea engulfing my entire body. I'd never imagined that my limbs could feel sick, but that's how it felt.

A group of soldiers, aided by my colleague Matt McAllester, sat me down on the ramp of the Bradley, and someone shouted for the medic. Luckily there was one standing right next to me, and he quickly applied a combat dressing to the bloody wound. Shaking and trying not to throw up as they stabbed an IV drip in my other forearm, I asked the medic if the shrapnel had cut the brachial artery. If so, I was in deep trouble.

'I dunno, I didn't get to look real good,' he drawled. His bedside manner didn't do much to reassure me, but then I wasn't in a bed or anywhere near a hospital. As a civilian wounded in the middle of the battle, you somehow feel that you should be able to call a time-out while you're evacuated. Unfortunately you can't. Major Karcher came over and gallantly offered to take me in his Bradley to the first-aid station back at the quarry. But I still had to run back to the vehicle. The sounds of battle echoed all around as the medic trotted next to me, holding the IV bag. It was a jog from hell: my whole body trembled; every time I stumbled on broken bricks or skidded on smashed glass, the IV needle in my arm threatened to rip itself free of my vein. The major drove me out of the city and back to the quarry, where the regiment's bored medics were glad to have a Limey reporter to practise on. They cut out the pea-sized piece of shrapnel that was poking through my upper bicep, having drilled its way clean through my arm. They put it in a ziplock bag for me to keep as a souvenir. My trousers were streaked with blood, and looked as though I had poured a pot of coffee down my leg. A friendly female medic took pity on me and gave me her spare pair of combat fatigues; she told me if I was American I'd have just won a purple heart. They joked that the unit would send me one, despite me being British.

I was patched up and taken back in a Humvee ambulance to the Combat Support Hospital, or Cash, in Camp Fallujah. An X-ray showed that the shrapnel, most likely a shard of rocket-propelled grenade, had missed the bone, arteries and elbow joint. I was very lucky: I would be left only with two very small scars, an entry and an exit wound, like permanent mosquito bites.

My wounds were fairly minimal compared to those that others sustained in the twenty-four hours I would be away from the unit. When I caught up with him again later, Matt looked quite shaky as he recalled that, just a couple of hours after I had bled all over his flak jacket in the back of the Bradley, the cavalrymen had set up a fragile base in the schoolhouse while the battle raged all around. He had been sitting down to write up a report for his paper when a rocket hit the roof of the classroom. Luckily for him, it smashed into a steel roof girder and most of the force dissipated outside the building, merely showering him in plaster. Two soldiers standing outside were hit by shrapnel. One was much less fortunate than me: the shrapnel went through his penis.

The doctor in Camp Fallujah told me I just had to keep the wound clean to make sure it did not become infected. So I sat down in the waiting tent outside the CASH and started to type out my story of the battle, one-handed. The nausea and shock had worn off, and I felt elated to have survived. As I worked, more ambulances started to come in. Most of the casualties were Iraqis. There was a government jundi who had shot himself in the foot, another who had twisted his knee while hurdling a wall. But most of the wounded were suspected guerrillas. They arrived bloodstained and handcuffed to their canvas stretchers, sometimes stacked up four to a Humvee. I watched them being carried in and felt glad I had escaped so lightly. When I had finished my piece, I hitched a ride over to the cavalry camp. A young lieutenant was sitting at a desk in the main tent, working on a computer. I told him what had happened, and asked whether he could arrange for me to return to the front. I had expected – and half-hoped – he would tell me I'd have to wait a few days, what with the confusion of battle and the pressure on supply lines. Instead, he told me I could get a lift the very next day. I hesitated, running through various reasons why I shouldn't go straight back in. But all I said was, 'OK then, I'll go back tomorrow,' and passively submitted myself, like so many men before me, to the uncaring discipline of military timetabling.

The drive into Fallujah threw us immediately back into the fray. Passing under one of the highway overpasses, we spotted an American infantryman fleeing the bridge at full pelt. Seconds later, a mortar exploded. Before I could tell what was going on, the air was a dazzling cat's cradle of red tracer fire. It took me a few panicky seconds to realize that it was the Americans on the convoy firing at a nearby rise hidden in date palms and scrubby bushes. The tracer rounds exploded in livid spark bursts as they hit rocks and trees. Apparently a guerrilla group was trying to relieve the pressure on the Mujahedin trapped in town by attacking the American perimeter. I imagined that if there was anyone in the trees they would have been torn to shreds. But late that night a rocket landed close to the camp, fired from the same position. The stakes were enormous for both sides.

Facing a twin-pronged assault from the north and the northwest, the guerrillas had regrouped to the south of the main street running through the centre of Fallujah. The next few nights became a blur of missions, baking in the bowels of a Bradley that every day came to resemble more and more a heavily armoured oven, then stumbling out the rear hatch at dawn into the cool air of the quarry to sleep on cots that barely cleared the foot-deep dust, cat-napping until the next run into Fallujah came along. The days ran into each other, with surreal snatches recalled as I pulled my sleeping bag around me and caught some sleep in the morning sun: sitting in front of a Bradley's flickering green monitor watching a garden gate blowing in the wind for almost an hour as the gunner tried to determine if there was anything to shoot at; a squad of fresh-faced soldiers riding into the guerrilla-held zone singing Brad Paisley country and western tunes and discussing the best place to eat shrimp in Fort Hood; watching a soldier swab buckets of blood out of the back of a Bradley that had been holed by an armour-piercing RPG; graffiti in a house full of sleeping soldiers that said, 'Why can't we live together in peace?' Underneath it another soldier had scrawled, 'Die ragheads die!'

One night, we stopped on a street in the rebel-held south. The ramp went down and we emerged from the relative safety of the Bradley into an ethereal mist, through which the occasional burst of gunfire screamed off in the distance like startled metal birds. It was difficult to walk for all the rubble and smashed concrete on the ground. Severed electrical wires flapped overhead like creepers, clinging at the soldiers in the pitch blackness. There were several Bradleys stopped outside a blast-scarred apartment block. I stuck close to the unit I was with, afraid I could lose them in the dark and be left behind in this alien and frightening landscape. We walked into a garage where rusting Iraqi army jeeps rigged with anti-tank recoilless rifles were hidden under tarpaulins. The soldiers jammed rocks down the barrels of the cannon and we hustled back into the Bradleys to trundle down more deserted streets. Fallujah had become a ghost town, but one where the spirits of the martyrs who had already consigned themselves to the afterlife still prowled, very much alive and armed with uranium-tipped rocket grenades and machine guns.

In the back of the battalion's headquarters tent, a small monitor bore witness to one of the terrifying peculiarities of hi-tech warfare. A cluster of curious soldiers with nothing better to do could often be seen glued to the screen. Occasionally a yelp of wrathful glee would come out of the huddle.

'Hot shrapnel in their brains!' I heard one soldier whoop.

The snuff movie they were watching was, unlike al-Qaeda's, shown in real time. It was the footage being relayed instantly from the cameras of Predator drones flying over the city, looking for guerrilla positions. Known as Unmanned Aerial Vehicles, or UAVs, and as unblinking and tireless as the Harpies of Greek mythology, they turned the last hours of the Mujahedin into a terrifying sprint from death. To pause even for a few minutes could mean instant death from an invisible enemy. Sometimes targeted fighters managed to throw off the drone, ducking into a building just as the plane jinked into a new position. But they had no way of knowing if they had dodged the spy in the sky, or whether at that very instant coordinates were being relayed to an artillery unit or circling fighter bomber. All they could do was keep moving and pray. Thanks to instant satellite communications, many of the Predators were actually operated by teams based in Las Vegas, thousands of miles from the battlefield. In theory, you could kill a gang of insurgents in Fallujah in the morning in your air-conditioned office at Nellis air force base and be at the gaming tables in time for cocktails.

One morning I watched a group of fifteen fighters, all dressed in black and carrying an array of weapons, as they fled the deadly drone. They could probably hear the lawn-mower buzz of its motor as they ran into a large house in southern Fallujah. I could hear the radio traffic and knew what was coming. Within minutes, the house they had hidden inside disappeared in a giant plume of grey smoke.

By chance, the massive explosion flushed out another group of guerrillas who had been lurking, undetected, in a house across the street. Deafened by the blast, they stumbled out into the street, formed a ragged line and started off on the marathon to postpone their deaths, the drone dogging their every step.

'The rats are trying to move about,' Major Karcher shouted across the crowded command tent as he saw the figures flitting from street to street, seeking cover close to walls. This second group was luckier: they ran long enough and hard enough for the Predator to lose sight of them, perhaps returning for refuelling.

But the unseen death from above was far from being the only way the Mujahedin could meet their end in

Fallujah's maze of death. Often as they fled from the drones, they ran into the crosshairs of American snipers whose squads had taken up strategic positions across the falling city.

I came across one such unit of cavalry dismounts huddled on the roof of a house on the front line. Iraqi rooftops are flat and almost always have parapets, as if designed for urban warfare. Cougar Company's crack shot was Sergeant Marc Veen, an undistinguished-looking, soft-spoken man in his mid-twenties with a gingery moustache.

Veen called his sniper rifle Lucille. He explained with a smile that the gun was named after the sexy woman in the film *Cool Hand Luke*, who torments Paul Newman and other members of a Georgia chain gang by splashing herself with soapy water while washing her car. Under a strap on the front of his flak jacket he had stuck the shell casing of a bullet he had hit a guerrilla with that morning. He had spotted the man, dressed in black and carrying an AK47, peering round the corner of a house some five hundred yards away from the cavalry soldiers' position. Veen shot the man in the stomach, but he got up again so he shot him again, in the shoulder. Still, the man struggled to crawl away, so the sergeant blasted him with his .50-calibre machine gun. You don't have to even hit a man with such a large calibre gun: a round passing close can be enough to rip off a limb.

'There's pretty much no feeling,' Veen told me, as many snipers had in the past. 'If I didn't get that guy, that guy would get one of my buddies some time later.'

Any guerrilla still alive at that point in the battle would find a huge change to the city they had ruled with the absolute authority of medieval caliphs. On the main streets, Iraqi government soldiers were painting over the Mujahedin graffiti declaring 'Jihad, jihad, jihad, God is great and Islam will win' with their own slogans, such as 'Long live the Iraqi army'. The countless mosques, their minarets honeycombed by tank shells and rocket blast, no longer issued calls to arms to fight the infidels. Instead, they broadcast offers by the Iraqi army of help to any of the shattered population still lingering, hungry and shell-shocked, in their homes. As the fighting died down to a few last pockets of resistance, I saw a stout middle-aged man striding resolutely down the middle of Fallujah's main street, past burned-out apartment blocks and wrecked cars. In one hand he carried a pair of white long-johns above his head as a flag of truce, while in the other he clutched a rare treasure: a packaged TV dinner called My Kind of Chicken. I stopped him and asked him why he had stayed. He seemed unexpectedly cheerful as he explained that he had never expected the battle to be so terrifically fierce, but was delighted it was now over, and could pick up some food handouts.

'The Mujahedin were very bad,' said the man, named Kemal. 'They had a prehistoric mentality.'

Which was putting it mildly: for six months, the city had been the personal fiefdom of fanatics, torturers and hardened criminals. They appeared to have vented whatever furious whim that occurred to them on the bodies of the local population, justifying it with their *takfiri* brand of Islam or the need for unrelenting resistance. Every day, marines were finding the dead and dying prisoners of the Mujahedin, like the husks of insects in an abandoned spider's web. Marines clearing Jolan unearthed a subterranean prison containing two corpses and two emaciated prisoners, close to death. Other units found piles of corpses, some with their feet cut off and bullets in the back of their heads, whom they assumed to be local men who had refused to fight with the jihadists. The choice, it seems, had not been 'Do or die' so much as 'Do and die, or just die'. A Kurdish army officer said he had heard tales of people trying to flee the city being shot dead by Mujahedin snipers as they left their homes.

In one grim cell, soldiers found a wheelchair with straps on the arm rests, a makeshift portable torture device that was presumably used for decapitations. No one knew for sure, because no reporters had been able to make it into Fallujah for almost six months, and now the inhabitants were strewn across the Sunni Triangle. Few of those still in the city wanted to talk of the horrors, either out of fear that the nightmare could return or from the simple desire not to relive such a painful past.

You could smell the rot of bodies in the ruins of Fallujah's streets. In an alley near the Euphrates, soldiers found the body of a woman, still partly clothed in a blue dress, who had been shot in the head, disembowelled and had her hands and feet cut off. As if that were not enough, her throat had been slashed too before her body was dumped on the street, wrapped in a blanket, a horrific calling card. This was not the handiwork of guerrillas or even terrorists, but of psychopathic killers giving full rein to their darkest whims.

Despite the hi-tech American operation to stamp out the Mujahedin, the battle of Fallujah did not put an end to the jihadist horrors. You can't remove an idea, even a nightmare, through surgery. Rather, it was like a seed pod smashed open with a sledgehammer, spreading its spores across the country. Most of the guerrilla leaders had fled before the Americans closed in. Already, in the north, Mosul was in flames, with insurgents taking over whole swathes of the city and the police force fleeing their bases in droves. Standing in a street reeking of decomposed bodies, in front of the wreck of a five-storey apartment block, the Kurdish army officer I had met believed that the horrors and destruction would put the people of Fallujah off supporting insurgents in the future.

'When the people of Fallujah come back and see their houses, they will kick out any terrorists. This will be an example to all Iraqi cities,' he told me, recalling that in the Middle East, brute force had been the lingua franca of government for thousands of years. Wasted cities and strong leaders earned respect, he believed. In fact, what calmed Fallujah in the end was the strict cordon the marines imposed on it after the battle, making all the residents undergo retina scans and security clearance checks before they were allowed back in. It not only tranquillized the city, but paralysed it. A colleague of mine aptly described the pacified post-war city as resembling a lobotomized psychopath.

*   *   *

As it turned out, this battle hadn't been Sergeant Santillana's time. I hadn't seen him since he and his squad had been practising house clearance just before the fighting, back at Camp Fallujah. Now, when I ran into him again, the bright young soldier of just two weeks before was grey-skinned and unable to force a smile, though he tried, out of his innate politeness. He was slumped against a concrete wall in the garden of an occupied house inside the city, where his new unit was catnapping after most of the hurly-burly was done. Santillana was the last of his eight-man platoon still in the field. In battle, the house clearances they had been practising had turned out to be a bloody affair. He told us that Sergeant Abe had been shot in the arm, severing his brachial artery and most of his nerves, while storming an insurgent-held house, while one of their buddies was on his way home in a body bag. Santillana made it through the battle with a minor bullet-shrapnel scrape, but looked like a hollow ghost of his old, easy-going self.

'That's war,' he said, staring into nowhere. 'That's all I can say.'

It's often difficult to know exactly when a battle ends, especially in a place like Fallujah, where a recalcitrant mix of furious local fighters, returning guerrillas and criminals carried on sniping at the marines for several weeks, long after it was clear they had lost. I had been sleeping out under the stars on a camp bed in a sleeping bag with a broken zip for almost two weeks, trying to keep warm in the freezing desert nights while keeping the dirt from infecting the wound in my arm. My throat was swollen and raw from the cold and the floury dust thrown up by the constant movement of men and machines. I was feeling miserable, when news came that the road from Camp Fallujah to the quarry was now safe enough to transport hot cooked meals out to the cavalry. I was overjoyed to be rid of the glutinous MREs we had all been living off in the field. When the meals-on-wheels Humvees arrived, Matt and I eagerly queued up with the soldiers to receive our dinner.

As I reached the food container, though, I peered down on what looked like a nest of deep-fried turds.

'What is that?' I asked the canteen soldier ladling out the foul lumps.

'Corn dogs,' he told me.

'What are corn dogs?' I asked. I'd never heard of such a thing, and was very suspicious of their appearance.

'Hotdogs in corn,' the soldier said. There was a muttering of impatience from the soldiers in line behind me, so I took a scoop and some Bolognese sauce and joined Matt on the stone bench outside the quarry-men's hut. With some trepidation, I bit into my first hot meal in weeks. Only it was cold by now, and tasted pretty much how it looked. I was trying to force myself to eat more when a strange smoke enveloped us.

'What's burning?' I asked a passing soldier.

He looked around and sniffed the air like a dog.

'I'd say they've emptied the latrines,' he said. 'They pour gas on it and burn it.'

Suddenly, sitting there munching on cold corn dogs

in a cloud of cesspit smoke, I knew I'd had enough.

'You know, Matt,' I said, 'I think this battle's over.'

Matt nodded. We binned our much-anticipated 'hot dinner' and strolled over to the TOC tent to arrange a ride out. The next day we were back in Camp Fallujah. It seemed like a modern city after the quarry base, with heated tents and a huge dining facility. Someone had even smuggled a bottle of whiskey into the dry base. The tents around us were full of journalists returning from their embeds, sharing stories and seeing who had come closest to dying. We stayed a few hours, before the marines put us in the back of a truck and shipped us in a convoy to the capital.

Back in Baghdad, I packed up my stuff in the hotel to take a break from Iraq. While sorting all my kit from Fallujah, I found the blood-browned scrap of metal that had punctured my arm. It was still in the ziplock baggie the doctors had presented me with. I left it on the bedside table. When I returned a month later, I found a note beside it from Anthony Loyd, the war correspondent who had rotated in for *The Times* to allow me to take a break. Anthony, who had famously written about his experiences in the Balkans wars and his heroin habit, had mistaken the shrapnel for a lump of hash and burned his fingers trying to smoke it. By my bed was a handwritten note.

'Dope here is crap. No wonder everyone here is so fucking tense.'

PANDORA'S SANDBOX

Bombs, Beheadings and Bullshit

As I walked into the compound cafeteria for dinner, I found it difficult to muster much appetite. It was summer of 2006, almost too hot to eat, and besides, the chef was a man of mediocre talents who relied heavily on a few variations of fried chicken and rice. This cook, an elderly Christian called Abu David, was standing by the buffet counter when I walked in, as though checking for any signs of revolt among our picky western palates.

I smiled at him and lifted up the metal lid of the serving dish. I froze. There before me was the Iraqi national dish, *mazgouf* – carp, split down the middle and grilled over a slow charcoal fire. It was the pride of the country, served up on any special occasion. In better times, the thriving restaurants along the Tigris sported special pools where you could select your own fish, have it clubbed to death in front of you and served fresh. When Saddam Hussein had visited François Mitterrand in the 1980s, he had flown a crateload of the bottom-feeder to the French president's kitchen and insisted on bombarding the gourmet with Iraqi native fare.

But I hated it. Carp is a greasy explosion of bones, with an aftertaste of the mud it slurps through at the bottom of silted waterways. Many was the time I had politely choked my way through the honour of a *mazgouf* supper with Iraqi friends, feigning delight as I surreptitiously hacked fishbones out of my throat.

But now it was different. Almost no one was eating *mazgouf* any more. The fish came from the rivers and lakes, and the rivers and lakes were clogged with human corpses. On Lake Thar Thar, that vast spill of turquoise out in the tawny western desert, fishermen were now out of work because no one dared eat their catches. Everyone knew that the place was a dumping ground for Sunni guerrillas disposing of the bodies of Shia men and boys they had had murdered. And in Baghdad, where fishermen used to pull fat carp out of the Tigris, all but the most diehard fans shunned the dish because the Mahdi Army dropped the bodies of murdered Sunni shopkeepers and terrorists alike in the river.

'Have some,' smiled Abu David, smiling proudly. 'It's very good.'

I looked at Tom, my American radio colleague. He shrugged.

'Er, it's just that . . . *mazgouf* comes from the river . . . and the river is full of dead people,' I said sheepishly.

Abu David frowned disapprovingly. 'This fish is from Jordan. It is OK.'

We glanced at each other, unsure whether to believe him. In any case, who wanted to eat carp shipped fifteen hours across the desert from another arid country? Hesitantly, I put the smallest piece of *mazgouf* I could find on to my plate, then loaded up on Abu David's desiccated chicken mix. Tom followed suit. We slunk off to a table and waited until Abu David had retired to his kitchen, before rushing back to the buffet counter and returning the fish whence it came. No one else touched it that evening, and Abu David, his feelings deeply wounded, never served the loathsome dish again.

The cyberpunk author William Gibson once commented that 'The future is here already; it just isn't evenly distributed.' He was reflecting on the incredible advances in technology that are transforming human existence in the more scientifically advanced parts of the world, and which may alter it even more drastically in years to come: the potential of memory-enhancing brain implants with total recall, vastly expanded life-spans, the ability to function for a week without sleep, or the use of wireless technology to create telepathy. All these things are being worked upon in labs around the planet, tomorrow's world waiting in the wings.

The past, on the other hand, appears to be mostly squeezed into a narrow belt of hot lands between the eastern shores of the Mediterranean and the mountains of the Hindu Kush, an ideological Chernobyl from which radioactive chunks occasionally spin off and impact with our cutting-edge, comfortable present, as happened on September 11, 2001.

Call it Pandora's Sandbox. Open it just a crack, to try to slip in a little democracy, siphon off some oil or launch some quixotic *mission civilizatrice*, and all sorts of nasty things come flying back out. Blood transfusions sometimes flow both ways, if the pressure is unbalanced: try to bring a little enlightenment to the Middle East, and back home, Christian fundamentalists are opening Jesus Camps in Alabama, or showing up at the funerals of soldiers killed on Iraq's battlefields, claiming the men died as divine punishment for America's tolerance of homosexuality. The craziness of Middle Eastern crackpots often seems to resonate with our own homegrown variety.

I knew full well how all those bodies ended up in the river, having watched more than my fair share of beheading videos in Baghdad. I had to watch them, in order to write about them, and I confess to the same horrified fascination that I experienced at the city morgue that long day in the crime-ridden summer of 2003. Ali Hussein, a skinny Shia translator who was working with me at that time, would always leave the room when I was getting ready to watch the latest snuff film.

'It corrodes the soul,' he'd say, scurrying out of the door.

'I don't believe in the soul,' I'd tell him. And I don't. I've come to believe in the words of Terentius, a Carthaginian slave turned playwright in second-century Rome: *Homo sum: humani nil a me alienum puto.* I am human, and nothing human is alien to me. So I sat through the horrific films, knowing that what I saw was hardly a great aberration in the sum of human history.

Some of the victims of the knife left this life with just a grunt, as though being decapitated were merely an inconvenience, like being bumped into the gutter on a busy city street. One, an American man, screamed as the ski-masked killer stabbed him in the throat: his howls turned into a pig-like squeal as the blade sawed through his windpipe, finally dying into an empty wheeze as his head was removed and his dead lungs deflated.

I felt tears of horror and rage in my eyes as I watched a camera pan along an entire platoon of captured Iraqi army recruits, hog-tied and lined up on their bellies, as a team of decapitators passed along them, slicing off their heads with muscular confidence, the shocked young men lying in their white boxer shorts and T-shirts as helpless and terrified as seal cubs on the ice floes. Their murderers would lay their hacked-off heads on the small of their backs, as though they did not want them getting mixed up for some unfathomable reason. After a while, though, the killers tired of the strenuous activity – cutting through thick neck muscle and spinal columns is hard work, after all – and sprayed the remainder with automatic rifle fire. They were the lucky ones, relatively speaking. We were all prepared to beg for the bullet if kidnapped, anything but the knife and the video camera. And if the knife, give me the man who beheaded the British engineer Ken Bigley, quickly and skilfully, not Abu Musab Zarqawi, the cack-handed al-Qaeda leader who personally cut off the head of one of Bigley's fellow American hostages, hacking away for more than a minute, like a butcher's apprentice on his first day on the job.

The film of the Iraqi soldiers being slaughtered was one too many for me. I leapt up and started ranting at Yassir and Haidar, who had been looking over my shoulder, gasping in horror.

'This place is so fucked, there's no hope for it. These people are fucking monsters,' I shouted. 'They should give Zarqawi a sex change and a burka and drop him in the streets of Kabul to beg for his living, the psychotic motherfucker.' Yassir nodded in agreement. 'They are the devil,' he said. But I knew they weren't monsters or devils, just men unhinged by their beliefs, by the conflicts swirling around them and the absurd promise of bloody justice. As the French revolutionary Saint Just said while he and his comrade Robespierre sent an endless stream of France's hapless aristocrats to the guillotine, 'There is nothing which so much resembles virtue as a great crime.' The jihadists certainly believed it. The army recruits were poor young Shia men, looking for a job in a country where the economy had long since collapsed: many of the mass kidnappings of these soldiers were made easier by the fact that the Americans refused to let the recruits carry weapons with them when they went on home leave, fearing they would sell them on the black market. They were lambs to the slaughter. Their murderers were avenging Sunnis who saw their prey as apostates for praying differently, worshipping different saints and collaborating with a government that was backed by the Americans.

Haidar lit up a cigarette on the balcony and leaned through the glass doors. 'You can see, they are Saudi,' he said as authoritatively as his strained English would allow. 'They cut right left. Iraqi, he cut other way.' Great, so there were even cultural nuances among beheaders, I thought, only half-believing Haidar, who was often full of wild stories. The problem in Iraq was that just because a story was outrageous didn't mean it wasn't true.

All across the country, people were tapping into their inner psycho. Bloodlust was the marching tune of the day. In Sadr City, the frenzied black-clad widows of Saddam's mass graves, like crows circling a dying wolf, cried for the caged dictator to be butchered and dragged through their streets after his arrest. This was far from unprecedented: Nuri Said, the last prime minister under Iraq's monarchy, was shot dead while trying to flee the 1958 military coup that deposed the country's final king (he was dressed as a woman, but his men's shoes gave him away). He was buried, but the next day his body was disinterred and dragged through the streets before being strung up, burned and mutilated. More recently, the bodies of American security contractors ambushed in Fallujah had received the same treatment, ending up dangling from the British-era girder bridge where kids on donkey carts beat their grisly remains with sticks.

Then there was the surprising note of regret I read in the pages of my own newspaper, *The Times*, the day after Saddam's arrest in December 2003. As I perused the paper's website, I came across an editorial by Simon Jenkins, the former editor, who had stayed at our Baghdad house a few months before. Simon is an urbane, sharply intelligent man, so I was all the more shocked to read him bemoaning that the American soldiers who had unearthed Saddam in his hidey-hole outside Tikrit had not simply carried out an extra-judicial murder.

'The arrest of Saddam Hussein outside Tikrit on Sunday was a mistake,' Simon wrote. 'The only good Saddam is a dead one . . . Iraq is still awash in blood. That blood would have been saved by the bucketful had a grenade been dropped into a certain foxhole at 8 pm last Saturday. It would have been the quickest way to draw a line under Iraq's wretched past.' I couldn't help but let my imagination run wild and I proceeded to conjure up the dapper ex-editor of *The Times* dressed, in a black *abbaya*, shrilly screaming with the widowed masses in Baghdad's Shia slums.

Blood was literally becoming part of the urban land-scape, the bullet-pocked walls of Baghdad buildings starting to resemble the work of some apocalyptic Jackson Pollock: the city as a palette for sickening plasma paintings, its citizens the raw materials. On Tahrir Square, across the river from the Green Zone, Lulu and I stood one day in a baying crowd of furious Iraqis trying to dig survivors out of a row of houses that had crumbled like high-tide sandcastles when a suicide bomber blew up his car outside. His target had been a convoy of white Suburbans speeding out of the Green Zone just across the Jumhariya Bridge, ferrying con-tractors to survey a plant earmarked for reconstruction – their scorched plans fluttered between the twisted wrecks that smoked and hissed on the central reservation. The Iraqis were full of rage at the foreigners who had brought this disaster on them: any foreigner would do. A man yelled in my face in Arabic and wagged a finger at me: not his finger, but a disembodied digit he'd found in the rubble, maybe belonging to a dead relative or neighbour. When I returned to the hotel and passed a mirror in my room, I noticed a streak of blood on my face from that finger, a reproach from beyond the grave.

The bloody message was writ large on the walls across the city. On the first storey of a building opposite the bomb-cracked Red Cross headquarters, I saw the rust-coloured silhouette of a torso, its upper arms and legs clearly visible, where a person had been splattered against the concrete. As often happened in massive bombings, the street was flooded because the force of the blast had punched a crater down into the tarmac and ruptured the water mains below. Power cables dangled like willow branches into the pools of blood and water: fortunately there was no electricity in them to energize the murky ponds of gore beneath. Stunned Iraqis wandered among the glass, some holding salvaged possessions from their houses, others howling in shock and grief.

That day in October 2003, six car bombs hit the city, the first squall of the gathering storm soon to engulf Baghdad. Outside the gutted Al-Khadra police station in western Baghdad, locals surged to the scene to seek relatives who had been queuing at the building for a variety of mundane bureaucratic reasons: seeking new identity cards, validating existing ones. American soldiers threw up a hasty security cordon outside and fired into the air to chase the people off, but one man refused to move away quickly enough and was shot in his side. A medic described to me, in such graphic terms that they stayed with me throughout the years, that the injured man's kidney had been flushing urine from the wound, piss and blood mixing together as he writhed on the floor, shot by the men who had come to save him and his country.

You soon get used to seeing body parts in wartime. In August 2003, when a massive car bomb killed almost a hundred people in Najaf, among them Ayatollah Mohammed Bakr al-Hakim, one of the most powerful Shiite leaders in the country, I watched a crowd scrabble through the pulverized stucco of shops opposite the shrine. A searcher pulled a dusty foot out of the ruins and held it aloft, hoarsely crying, 'Allahu akbar!' Many in the crowd took up the defiant cheer. God is great? I wondered. How do they figure that? Perhaps they just had to yell something, anything, to numb the pain. But I didn't have much time to think about it. Once again, the crowd was turning angry at the outsiders, perhaps because they blamed us for their disaster, perhaps because we were strangers witnessing such an intimate moment of agony and despair. A group of men started shouting at me and David Gutenfelder, the American photographer I was working with. His Iraqi translator, Sabah, urged us to get out of there, and quickly. We started walking away, but the snarling phalanx was tailing us, welling up around and in front of us. A man slapped David hard round the head, an apparent diversion as another grabbed the brick-like satellite phone strapped to my belt. There followed a brief ruckus, with much shouting and pointing of fingers, before Sabah somehow managed to negotiate the return of the phone. By this point, the throng around us had grown. We kept walking to a cluster of abandoned market stalls at the far end of the shrine, where our drivers had dropped us off. To our dismay, we found that they had left, no doubt scared off by the glowering crowd that was milling about. I tried phoning, but there was no answer on the notoriously unreliable sat-phone. A text message disappeared into the void. We were now facing what looked increasingly like a lynch mob, slowly closing in. We tried to present a calm face, to talk our way out of the situation if possible, although we felt like bolting. Then, just as the pack had closed to within a few feet, hurling insults, our drivers screeched up in the cars and we jumped in. The mob, unable to work itself up for immediate and bloody action, watched us speed off.

On the edge of town, outside an American army base, a makeshift morgue had been set up. Long lines of corpses were laid out, covered with colourful blankets; only the feet of the deceased visible. Some had lost their footwear in death, while others still wore a variety of sneakers, sandals and polished shoes. Seeing that parade of calloused bare feet, the occasional painted toenails, the shiny pumps or worn leather, it all felt as if we were sneaking a glimpse at some private part of a person's vanished realm, knowing they could not see you.

Ten days later I stood outside the devastated Canal Hotel in Baghdad, its blue-and-white painted facade giving way to a gaping hole in its side, like a skull opened up by shrapnel. Rescue workers dragged dead and wounded United Nations officials from the ruins of their shattered headquarters. Men and women in smart business suits coated with dust staggered out of the front door, their PowerPoint presentations on Iraq's future reconstruction cut short by a truck laden with TNT that had pulled up alongside the building's flimsy breezeblock wall.

By strange chance, at the US army cordon outside the building, I ran into a journalist who had married an old school friend of mine: we cracked a few jokes and swapped stories. I had no idea that just a few metres away lay the corpses of several people I had known well in Kosovo, back in happier days. I had last seen one of them, Jean-Selim Kanaan, a French-Egyptian who had worked for the UN in hotspots across the Balkans, at a wedding in New York just days before the 9/11 attacks. The last time I had seen him, as we walked through the East Village on the way to a restaurant, he confided in me he was having recurrent bad dreams about the horrors he had seen in Bosnia. I had not even known that he was working in Iraq. I could only hope he had died quickly and painlessly now that his nightmares had engulfed him.

These were the victims. But what of the perpetrators themselves? There are plenty of reasons to kill yourself, even without the promise of paradise. Disease, disability, despair and depression are, if not quite the four horsemen of the personal apocalypse, at least grim enough to tip the balance for many sane people. Every year, a staggering 285,000 Chinese people – the population of a medium-sized city in Europe – end their own lives, beaten down by poverty and the brutal pressures of life in a fast-changing, over-polluted, emerging capitalist society. I wonder if the sheer volume of the Chinese population somehow drowns out the sense of the individual, cut adrift in a sea of uprooted communities: once identity slips away, the prospect of release from the tribulations of life in a rapidly industrializing society may not lag far behind.

But back in the Middle East, a different psychology again presents itself before the western mind. A photographer friend of mine was once running to the scene of a suicide bombing near Jaffa Road in Jerusalem. As she ducked past the cordon of Israeli policemen trying to seal off the bombsite, she spotted something so strange that she stopped dead in her tracks, then instinctively raised her camera to snap it. On the windscreen of a parked car was a human penis, carefully wrapped up in cloth for protection.

The disembodied phallus belonged to the Palestinian suicide bomber. He had apparently subscribed very literally to the belief, common among his comrades, that the 'martyr' would be greeted in paradise by seventy-two virgins, an enticing prospect for young men from the sexually repressed refugee camps of Gaza or Nablus, where to be seen alone with a girl in public was to court potentially lethal punishment. If sex in this life carries the risk of death, then why not simply die first and have unlimited, god-sanctioned whoopee for all eternity?

The suicide bomber had presumably imagined that his member would actually be going along with him for service in the afterlife, much as the ancient Egyptians believed they would need their mummified bodies to troll through the dimensions beyond this life. Hence the cloth he had wrapped round his cock before heading off on his final mission, as carefully as someone had wrapped high explosives round his skinny teenage midriff.

Suicide bombings in the Arab world are not known as such by Muslims themselves, since suicide is a sin in Islamic tradition. Rather, they are rebranded as 'martyrdom operations', lending them a sense of serving the wider community, an elevated goal. There has been much debate over who the first suicide bombers were: the Tamils of Sri Lanka pioneered the idea of strapping explosives to oneself as a means of sowing terror, and Lebanese Shia fanatics quickly adopted the practice in Beirut during the civil war in the 1980s. But the Japanese kamikaze pilots of the Second World War had already patented the method, smashing their planes into American warships for love of the homeland and divine Emperor.

And I began to wonder: who was the first suicide bomber?

As far as I'm aware, there is no definitive contender for that dubious honour. But one afternoon, when I was out of Iraq on a break and lounging around watching afternoon television, the 1960 John Wayne movie *The Alamo* came on. I hadn't seen it in years, and for want of anything better to do, I started watching it. And there, in this all-American movie, was the suggestion of an answer. Wounded, and with Mexican soldiers over-running the Texas fort, the desperate Colonel Davy Crockett tosses his flaming torch on to a huge store-house of powder kegs and blows himself up, along with dozens of Santa Ana's troops. Coming fresh from the Middle East, I was amazed by the image. If you believe Hollywood's version, Davy Crockett, an all-American legend and early promoter of 'the Republic' – who was played by another American icon, John Wayne (who in addition to being the star, served as producer and director of the movie, and was a stalwart representative of contemporary Republican American values) – was being portrayed as the first suicide bomber! Of course, he was wounded, and it was a desperate last-ditch measure, not like the volunteer jihadists who were swarming into Iraq from around the Arab world for the honour of destroying themselves and the infidels. And to be fair, it was just a movie: there appears to be no historical evidence that the famous Tennessean frontiersman actually did away with himself in such a manner. Nonetheless, myth and popular imagination, on which Hollywood readily builds, are such a power-ful part of the suicide-bombing tradition that I was fascinated to see such overt American icons associated with it, even tangentially. If Americans could get a warm and fuzzy feeling over such heroics from their favourite cowboy (*The Alamo* was nominated six times for an

Oscar, including one for best picture), would that not shed some light on why the Muslim world was apparently so tolerant of this idealized brutality? When I started reading about the Alamo, I discovered some interesting facts the film did not allude to: principally that the brave defenders of the Alamo were actually American settlers fighting a secessionist insurgency against the Mexican government – the legal owners of the province of Texas. One of their chief objections to Mexican rule stemmed from President Santa Ana's plans to abolish that fine southern institution, black slavery. So what was director John Wayne's message behind his revision of Davy Crockett's final self-destructive moment in the Alamo: an act of self-sacrifice for a noble cause, or a rather odd choice of hero for a country so publicly dedicated to the sanctity of life and freedom?

You didn't have to go far to encounter killing in Baghdad. Paul Wolfowitz and his cronies often sneered publicly about 'hotel journalism', as if we were living it up in the Ritz. But in fact they had messed the country up so badly that you could witness a lot from your hotel window. Hell, Wolfowitz was attacked by rockets in his hotel during the one time he sneaked into Baghdad.

One morning I heard a burst of automatic fire outside the Hamra Hotel where I was staying, across the river from the Green Zone. It was a common enough occurrence, but I always went out on the balcony to see what was happening. On the broad road outside that day, between the hotel and an empty seven-storey block whose top floor was held by an Australian army sniper team guarding their nearby embassy, a Toyota had come to a dead halt in the road. An armoured Suburban was screeching off into the distance, a gun crew of western security guards poking their weapons out the rear hatch. Locals ran to the lead-spattered Toyota, extracting a screaming boy who was led away as the body of his father was removed from the vehicle. The father had apparently driven too close to one of the notorious PSDs – Private Security Details, the ex-military guns for hire who escorted contractors through the dangerous streets outside the Green Zone. Amazingly, the PSD vehicle then did a U-turn and came back to stop on the other side of the road, clearly checking out who they had just randomly killed.

An Iraqi policeman went up and tried to talk to them. Although I was much too far away to hear what they were saying, I saw the flashing of the ubiquitous DoD badges handed out by the US Department of Defense to these high-paid security contractors. The policeman, massively outgunned and aware of the immunity such badges conferred on the owner, made no attempt to take their details, and they once again sped away from the wounded boy and his dead father.

Such killings were common, and everyone kept as far away from the PSD convoys of white SUVs as they could. They carried signs in Arabic and English promising to kill you if you got closer than a hundred metres to them. Perhaps the driver of that car hadn't been able to read the sign at that distance, on a moving vehicle. But sometimes the western mercenaries would just open fire for the hell of it – one PSD posted a 'hunting trophy' video on the internet, showing them firing at random civilian drivers from the back hatch of their armoured Suburban. The bullet-riddled cars would slow down and trundle to the edge of the road, the driver slumped at the wheel. It didn't surprise me, since everything eventually ended up on the internet, that dark subconscious of humanity.

A few months later, in January of 2005, I was awoken by a massive blast and shards of my bedroom window raining down on my sheets. I waited a few moments for a second blast, but none came. Nor was there any follow-up shooting, so it seemed the hotel wasn't being stormed. I put my boots on and crunched over the broken glass to the jagged hole that was the window. On the street below, a car bomb was billowing black smoke from the bottom of the Australians' lookout building. It had been a hopelessly futile attack, since the Aussies were seven floors up in sandbagged sniper positions. In the middle of the road, a refuse collection truck had stalled from the force of the blast. On the pavement next to it, the small body of a teenage garbage collector lay stretched out on the ground. He looked like he was asleep, but he was dead. There were people already approaching the corpse. I looked at my watch. It was 7:15. The death of one boy would never make the paper, so it wasn't worth going out and reporting, and it was too early to get up. I went back to bed and fell asleep again.

I was becoming inured to the murderous pace of the city. It was bad, both as a human being and a journalist.

I needed to be outraged by the horror, but instead I slowly became acclimatized. The horizon slipped, and mass murder had become commonplace, almost humdrum.

In the spring of 2005, the slaughter moved up a gear. A distraught Shia man came to see me from the village of Mada'in, on the southwestern edges of Baghdad. A few days earlier, the police had dredged more than seventy bloated corpses, many of them headless, from the River Tigris near his village. The man who came to see me, calling himself Abu Qaddum, had brought with him a stack of photos he had collected from the local police, looking for his missing brother. He sat in my room and laid out the pictures of the mutilated bodies like a player dealing cards. I took each one and examined it. Some of the corpses had had their hands cut off, others were headless or burnt. Another was strangled, with his tongue lolling out. Abu Qaddum pointed at one of the bloated, slime-covered cadavers and said he thought this might be his brother. His poker faced cracked and he started crying.

In other times and other countries, scenes from such killing fields might have prompted calls for international intervention. But there were already more than 150,000 US and British troops in Iraq, and this was done under their noses. People like Abu Qaddum just tried to survive as best they could, watching out for themselves and their families.

Mada'in was in the Triangle of Death. As had happened in many other villages there, the police force had long since fled, outgunned by hybrid gangs of criminals and insurgents, who burned down the police station to make sure the cops never came back. There was no response from the Americans, so the guerrillas started using an abandoned Republican Guard base in the nearby village of Salman Pak as a training camp. It was an interesting choice, since this was one of the places the Americans had cited as a terrorist training base in their pre-war justification for invading Iraq. Now it really was teeming with terrorists, and they did nothing.

More guerrillas dribbled in, many affiliated to al-Qaeda, installing their usual medieval reign of terror. They started out by kidnapping government employees and members of Shia political parties. Sometimes the bodies surfaced in the palm groves, more often people just vanished without a trace, food for the Tigris carp.

When the Americans stormed Fallujah in November 2004, more displaced fighters arrived in Mada'in. During Ramadan, throngs of Sunni guerrillas mustered around a mosque, denouncing the minority Shia population in the area as traitors and spies, lambasting them for not joining the psychotic resistance. A convoy of fifteen cars filled with gunmen intercepted the car of the local Shia sheikh and blasted him to pieces in the street.

Abu Qaddum and some terrified fellow Shia travelled south to Najaf to see Grand Ayatollah Ali al-Sistani, their spiritual leader. The septuagenarian cleric, an avowed moderate, reassured them that their relatives were martyrs, and therefore in paradise, and advised them to stay their hand: the terrorists wanted the Shias to counter-attack and thereby spark a civil war, which would be even worse. Suck it up and see you in heaven, is what he effectively told his flock.

Eventually, in February 2005, a police convoy of around seventy cars nudged its way into the outskirts of Mada'in, to reclaim control of this village of the damned. But the interior ministry was hopelessly infiltrated with spies and insurgents, and the guerrillas knew they were coming. In a well-prepared ambush, they gunned down a dozen police officers, and captured two. These two men were doused in petrol and burned alive.

After that, the kidnapping and killing accelerated.

'They were taking two or three people a day, killing people in the street, going into people's houses to drag them out,' Abu Qaddum told me, the photos still spread out on the table in front of us to illustrate his tale.

The guerrillas set up checkpoints on the road to Baghdad, executing government officials when they could find them, and looting and burning lorries. People were too scared to go to market for fear of being seized. At night families stood guard in two-hour shifts. One night in March, Abu Qaddum's younger brother went to find a doctor for his sick wife and was never seen again.

But even then, things got worse. The Sunni guerrillas blew up a mosque and posted notices saying that Shias should leave town or die. The Shia political parties started a press campaign, but it was dismissed by the Interior Ministry, whose officials said that the whole affair was merely a tribal feud.

When Iraqi troops finally moved in they found no

sign of the horror. They asked through loudspeakers for witnesses to show them where the terrorists and their hostages were. The Shias were too terrified to come forward, knowing that the government forces were probably lousy with guerrilla spies, and in any case could be gone in a week. So the story of the village was dismissed as exaggeration, lies spread to stir up sectarian hatred. But then the first bodies were found. Some had broken free of concrete slabs to which they had been tied before they were thrown in the river and bobbed to the surface.

A distraught father looking for his son heard about this and hired a Baghdad diver to investigate. The diver emerged from the tea-brown waters, gasping with horror, saying that the riverbed was thick with bodies. The police divers retrieved almost sixty bodies before they too fled, terrified of ending up in the underwater mass grave themselves.

Abu Qaddum never found his brother, and the aged ayatollah's calls for restraint were soon swept away by this river of blood. Within a year, the Mahdi Army had taken to the streets in force, and by the summer of 2006, it was now Sunnis who were being kidnapped wholesale, in broad daylight by death squads dressed in army and police uniforms. And now their bodies, with their kneecaps, elbows and eye sockets gouged by electric drills, would not be hidden in rivers but left in the streets of the capital, for all to see. The civil war had started.

Just how unhealthily habituated to death I had grown became very clear to me one afternoon late in 2005, as

I was driving through Qadisiya, a leafy district of middle-class villas in southeast Baghdad. By that time, many of the streets in the city had been blocked, either by the concrete fortresses that spilled out into the road to prevent car bombers sidling up to government buildings, or simply by locals who did not want unknown cars – always bad news in Baghdad – driving down their streets. This led to epic traffic jams, which themselves became targets for bombers or kidnappers. The problem was compounded by the queues at petrol stations, which could often snake round city blocks for miles, further clogging the few arteries still open.

People tended to get edgy in such jams. Not only was there the tedium of waiting for hours, but the real threat of being killed or abducted for your troubles. So when our car ran into a massive jam in Qadisiya, I was left with an always difficult choice: wait there and risk being spotted by a passer-by, who could go and tip off local kidnappers, who would then sell you on to al-Qaeda, or try and blag our way through, flashing our US-issued press badges to the policeman who was watching the chaos. Of course, by this time there was no way of knowing if he was really a policeman or a militiaman, or a bit of both: Baghdad was a topsy-turvy place where the guerrillas were dressed as policemen and policemen looked like guerrillas, dressed in civilian clothes and ski masks. We decided to risk showing our ID cards and jumped the line: the policeman peered at our cards, not understanding the English but seeing a westerner in the back, and waved us through. A few hundred metres down the road, we found the source of the traffic jam, two bullet-riddled police cars slewed messily across a junction, their occupants slumped dead on their seats. Someone had driven past and opened fire at close range. There was not much room to get past, so Yassir squeezed our car into the narrow gap between one of the police cars and a wall. As we passed, I looked in and saw that the top of the driver's head had been blown off. The man's caved-in skull rested on the headrest, his jaw hanging slack in death.

'Why couldn't they push the bloody cars to the side of the road?' I snapped, voicing what every other driver stuck there was feeling. 'It's not as if there's going to be a crime scene investigation, for God's sake.' It was only then that I caught myself. Here I was, someone who had grown up in a middle-class market town in rural West Sussex, raised by loving parents and well educated, brought up to be polite and sensitive to the needs of others, yet I had just driven past two cars filled with murdered people and all I could see was a traffic obstacle. It was clearly time to get out.

For a while I did get out. Lulu had moved to Mexico City, and I went there and worked and travelled, from Yucatan in the south to Nuevo Laredo in the north. But Iraq was like a ghost, always hovering on the television screens and in the newspapers, impossible to escape. I loved Mexico, loved the freedom of jumping in a car and driving for hours and hours through mountains and forests, down to the sea or into remote villages to report. But I hadn't got Iraq out of my system. It was always there as a throb in the background, drawing me back like a mosquito to an artery. My friends thought I was crazy to keep going back, but a variety of factors kept luring me to return: interesting though Latin America was, it just couldn't compete with the sheer adrenaline rush of covering a war. Likewise, months of freelancing in Mexico were not nearly as remunerative as a short burst of activity in Baghdad. And my Iraqi friends were still there: Ali, Yassir, Haidar and the rest of the crew. They always greeted me with hugs at the airport checkpoint and gave me the run-down on how much worse things had got – who was dead, what area had fallen to which militia – as we sped down the airport road, dodging the convoys of US and Iraqi Humvees and the private security details in their gun cars. As we did, my pulse would quicken and I'd think: oh yeah, I'm back. And each time it was as if I'd never left.

On one of these returns, in the summer of 2006, Baghdad had become more of a level killing field. There were still Sunni suicide bombers delivering a daily dose of martyrdom to Baghdad's Shia markets, ripping innocent shoppers to pieces. But now the Mahdi Army had emerged from the shadows and set up death squads that would roam Sunni areas, kidnapping anyone they could get their hands on, bundling them in the trunk of a car and taking them off for torture and murder. One of the killers, a hefty, chain-smoking man in his forties called Abu Haidar, even told me that the men in his death squad now tailored their car purchases to the size of the trunk.

'The Toyota Super Saloon is best,' he said, with the

authoritative air of a car salesman. 'You can get up to four people in the trunk.' He described how some of the Mahdi Army executioners would take great pleasure in torturing their victims, whose drilled corpses would litter the streets of Baghdad like uncollected bin bags. 'Then when they've finished, *sikkeh*,' he smiled, making a trigger gesture and using the Arabic word for click.

Mohanned, my translator, told me one morning that he had been driving to work when the door of the car in front suddenly opened and a handcuffed, bloodied body was pushed out, while the vehicle was still moving. He had to swerve violently to avoid hitting the dead person. Despite being a doctor before working for *The Times*, he was far too afraid to stop and take a pulse.

And who would? That summer, columns of Mahdi Army death squads, accompanied by Shia policemen in uniform and using Interior Ministry vehicles, drove into the mixed area of Jihad, deep in Sunni-dominated western Baghdad, and started slaughtering people in the street, pulling them from cars and kicking in the doors of houses to shoot residents where they stood. The bodies, around fifty of them, lay in the streets for hours before the American army managed to get a large enough force together to go in and retrieve them. The Jihad massacre sent shockwaves through a city that thought itself acclimatized to genocidal violence. It seemed the killers could act as they pleased, and a wave of mass kidnappings followed: the entire Chamber of Commerce was emptied by men in army uniforms and loaded into trucks in the middle of a working day in an area hitherto considered 'safe'; other gunmen kidnapped the Iraqi Olympic Committee wholesale while it was holding a meeting. And a young Sunni computer salesman described how he narrowly escaped a mass round-up in Technology Street, in the city centre, because the trucks that his neighbours were being loaded on to for torture and murder filled up just before the gunmen arrived at his shop, where he was cowering behind the counter in terror.

To avoid such arbitrary annihilation, Sunnis started carrying fake identity cards, easily available in a country full of illegal militias and criminal gangs, to pretend to be Shia. Omars suddenly became Ammars, birthplaces switched from Ramadi to Najaf. But the Shia militiamen who had massively infiltrated the police, and who manned checkpoints across Baghdad in the name of the Mahdi Army, quickly got wise to the trick. They started quizzing suspected Sunnis on matters only a Shia would be expected to know, such as the names of the twelve Shia imams, their birthplaces and where they prayed. Stories abounded of people failing these tests and being summarily executed on the spot.

As a result, many Sunnis began the absurd task of swotting up on obscure points of Shia doctrine. Assem, a Sunni acquaintance of Ali's, took lessons every evening from his Shia wife to avoid the deadly quiz that could take place at any roadblock as he went to work in his shop.

'At first we were joking about it but when our lives started to be threatened, the joke was over,' the 43-year-old said. 'It became a serious issue.'

Assem was a former air force pilot, a group frequently

targeted by Iranian-linked Shia groups seeking revenge for the damage done by Iraqi bombers in the Iran – Iraq War almost two decades before. His wife Sausan began the lessons after hearing of a raid in Mansour, close to their home. Gunmen in Iraqi security forces uniforms had stormed a company and asked the two guards to name all twelve imams, plus their manifold titles and honorifics. One of them failed and was shot dead on the spot.

One day, when Sausan was instructing Assem on the endless names of the imams, his brother and business partner walked in. He too had served in the air force, and was at risk.

'He was laughing and boasted that he already knew the names of five of the imams,' Sausan said. 'I was surprised and asked him to name them – all five were the nicknames of the same imam. I laughed for a while, then told him to join the class.'

Fearing possible house raids, Assem had taken down the pictures of himself in his pilot's uniform and put up tapestry hangings of the revered Shiite imams Ali and Hussein in his living room. Sunnis generally frown at the display of human images as idolatry, but Assem, a middle-class Iraqi, had no strong feelings on the issue. On the other hand, he did have strong feelings about being murdered for nothing.

'I feel very grateful to my wife and am lucky to have her,' Assem said. 'I have lots of Sunni friends trying to do the same thing, but they need someone they can really trust to teach them these things.'

To that end, a Sunni group put up a website dedicated

to dissembling faith. It offered advice such as carrying a *turba*, a round prayer tablet made from clay gathered in the holy cities, or having Shia religious songs as ringtones. It also reassured devout Sunnis that it was not blasphemous to pretend to be a Shia. 'According to the clerics, both Sunni and Shia, a Muslim can lie or even say words of sin if he is threatened to be killed.'

The website also advised Sunnis to put black or green flags on their rooftops, a common Shia symbol, and to learn to curse the names of the early Sunni caliphs.

Of course, none of this helped if you were stopped by Sunni gunmen, who would kill you for being an apostate Shia. In some areas, they too were not above a little dissembling, dressing up as government soldiers and handing out leaflets offering a snitch-line to inform on Sunni guerrillas. They would trace the calls of those who offered information, then hunt down and murder the informers.

The situation was hideously complex. I dyed my own hair black to look more Iraqi. Being a pale-skinned, brown-haired Celt, I looked more like Roy Orbison's ghost than an Iraqi, but it cut down the casual glances. People seemed to take me for a very sickly Kurd whose grandmother had been raped by an English squaddie. Another colleague of mine who already had a dark complexion and could pass as an Iraqi, but who spoke no Arabic, went even further, procuring himself a fake identity badge declaring him to be mentally disabled. If his car was stopped, he would simply look vacant while his translator did the talking.

For average Iraqis, just getting to work alive

demanded a James Bond-like ability to think quickly, lie and guess who exactly was cross-examining you. The identity crisis could reach epic proportions, as I found with my own staff.

Haidar and Yassir were both Shia, but lived in a mainly Sunni area of western Baghdad. As the fight between the Mahdi Army and the Sunni Mujahedin intensified, their street became a fault line between the Shia forces raiding from the north and the Sunnis holding the district from the south. Haidar found his old street-gang friends dividing into two camps, the Shia joining the Mahdi and the Sunnis fighting with the Mujahedin guerrillas. Late one night in July 2006, he phoned me at my hotel to tell me he was in an absurd but very dangerous position: there was heavy fighting outside his house, the Sunnis defending a mosque across the street from the Mahdi Army, who wanted to blow it up. Haidar had gone out on to the roof with his gun to defend his home, should either side try to take it over as a firing position. But when he was on the parapet, one of his old Sunni friends down in the street with the guerrillas spotted him.

'Haidar,' he shouted up. 'Start shooting at the Mahdi guys!' As he was contemplating how to avoid getting dragged into the battle without appearing to sympathize with one side or the other, Haidar's mobile phone rang: it was another friend, this time fighting with the Shia.

'Haidar,' he said, 'tell us how many snipers they have and where they are!'

Haidar found himself in an impossible situation.

From the hotel, a colleague of mine phoned an American military advisor he knew who was embedded with the Iraqi army in the area. The soldier sounded grumpy that he had been woken up so late, and indifferent when we told him that a family was caught in the crossfire of a gunfight.

'There's always fighting here,' the American sighed. 'It's like chasing ghosts. There are units out there who will deal with it.'

Of course, such units rarely came in time to save the people caught up in these battles. Haidar eventually solved the situation in his own inimitable way: he told his Mahdi friend where the Sunni snipers were positioned, then to placate his Sunni friend he fired a few token bursts into the air from his rooftop. Then he and Yassir got the whole family and sheltered in the bathroom until the battle had passed. The very next day, they and their family moved into the relative safety of our hotel, refugees in their own city like hundreds of other Baghdadis.

There was another problem with Haidar and Yassir, though. As drivers for *The Times*, they earned way more money than the average Iraqi, and often had to change cars for our security purposes. If anyone knew they were working for a western newspaper, they would be kidnapped and almost certainly murdered, so they had to invent cover stories about what they did and where they made their money. At first they said they were car dealers, which presented its own problems – neighbours were constantly asking them to help them buy or sell their vehicles, which was a hassle. So Haidar opened a small mini-market to provide some cover for his work, telling his customers he was a Sunni and making up a new surname to go with his fake identity. But with the increasing tit-for-tat killings, shopkeepers had become an easy target for death squads on both sides of the sectarian divide, so he decided to close up shop. But then an objection to the closure came from an unlikely quarter – the Sunni Mujahedin, who realized they had done such a good job of terrifying everyone that they were fast running out of places to buy their cigarettes and the other basic supplies a guerrilla force depends on in the Middle East. So they told Haidar they would guard his shop, making sure no one bombed it or executed his staff. Thus we ended up with a crazy situation, where Sunni gunmen were guarding a Shia who worked for a British newspaper, making sure his fellow Shia did not try to murder him.

The very next night after Haidar phoned me from his embattled rooftop, I received a text message at about ten-thirty p.m. on my mobile phone. This time it was from Ali in Jihad, a few miles to the south of Haidar's home. It read simply: 'militias in my area'.

It was a chilling message. I immediately tried phoning Ali, but the mobile network was notoriously unreliable, with shifting black holes of coverage drifting across the city. After about ten minutes of trying, I eventually got through and cracked a joke to Ali that he couldn't be murdered that night as we had an important interview the next day. For the first time, he didn't even laugh. He was clearly scared, and that was frightening to me.

'There are cars full of gunmen in the streets, we don't know who they are, if it's the Mahdi or the Muj,' he said. His neighbours, locked in their houses, were all frantically phoning one another, trying to see if anyone had any fresh news: who were they, what were they doing, where were they headed? I could only imagine the fear as the parade of cars prowled the darkened streets of Jihad like sharks, the memories of a massacre just a few days before, when militiamen roamed the streets with impunity, pulling people out of their cars and homes and shooting them in the street, still all too vivid in everyone's minds.

But Ali had a plan, albeit a desperate one: his surname, al-Hamdani, could easily pass as Shia. Mohanned, his brother-in-law and fellow translator who was round at the house, had an unmistakably Sunni surname, al-Qubeisi. They agreed that if they could determine that the gunmen were Shia, Ali would answer the door. If they were Sunnis, Mohanned would go. Whoever didn't answer the door would hide in the kennel of Ali's ill-fated dog on the roof.

Their Plan B was simpler: to dash fifty yards to their neighbours' house – home to a dozen brothers, each one with a Kalashnikov. Together they would shoot it out with the gunmen – one of a dozen unsung Alamos being fought nightly on Iraq's blacked-out streets.

'We just have to wait and see what our fate is,' Ali told me. It was the first time in three years of bombs, battles and kidnappings that I had heard him actually scared, shorn of all bluff and nerve. Remembering the in-different response of the American military advisor from the night before, I realized there was little I could do to help. It was every man for himself out there. But I was furious with impotent rage and fear for my friends' lives. As it happened, *The Times*, like most other newspapers operating in Baghdad, retained security consultants, British, American and Australian ex-special forces soldiers who now lived in our hotels, advising journalists on how to avoid being kidnapped or blown up, and training their drivers in evasive manoeuvres and procedures. I called the number, and explained the situation to the resident advisor. He told me that, from a military point of view, it was best not to try bluffing with a superior force, and that Ali should go and take his chances with the brood of armed brothers down the street.

I reluctantly phoned Ali again with my dismal morsel of advice: run for the neighbours' house and sell your life dearly. I couldn't believe it had come to this at long last, possibly my last phone call with my friend. Of course, though, I couldn't get through. It took me around forty minutes of sweaty redialling before the phone finally connected, my mind conjuring up what might be happening right now in the aptly named Jihad. When I did get through, I was enormously relieved to hear Ali's voice, and more so to learn that the prowling militias had, apparently, moved on. Either they were sending a message to residents to flee, or they were scouting out the area for future attack. I told Ali that he too should move in with Haidar and Yassir at the hotel.

He did for a while, but eventually they all drifted back

to their homes, despite the dangers. A few months later, every Shia remaining on Haidar and Yassir's street received an envelope with a single bullet inside, and a message from al-Qaeda giving them twenty-four hours to leave. They moved the same day, to a predominantly Shia part of town, leaving all their furniture behind. It was impossible for them to find a removal man daring enough to go and pick it up, so they had to start over again. They still work for *The Times* in Baghdad.

As for Ali, he fled the country in early 2007, the dangers of Jihad having become too much for his strained nerves. I saw him the day he arrived in Damascus, and we smoked a *narguilah* together in a café behind the great Ummayad mosque, just like in the old days. He looked transformed, born again, even though he was just one more of the 1.3 million Iraqis living in another Baathist police state, something he thought he'd seen the last of four years before when the Americans invaded his city. But even though he was forbidden from working and had no prospects, at least no one was trying to kill him. And for the time being, that was enough.

CREATURES OF THE ID

Why We Fight

There's never been anything, however absurd, that myriads of people weren't prepared to believe, often so passionately that they'd fight to the death rather than abandon their illusions. To me, that's a good operational definition of insanity.

Arthur C. Clarke, 3001, *The Final Odyssey*

Something was killing Commander John J. Adams's men. It was silent, unseen and apparently unstoppable. Adams's squad had been dispatched on a special mission to locate missing nuclear scientists, only to discover upon their arrival that all but one were already dead. Investigating the killings, they soon found that their own security perimeter was being infiltrated by unseen attackers, who would rip men to pieces with terrifying sudden force.

This was not Iraq in 2004, and the killer was not an Iraqi IED team or a jihadist disguised as a soldier, walking into an American mess hall with explosives strapped to his body, although such scenarios were played out in Mosul and Baghdad. In fact, this particular story occurred on the made-up planet Altair in some unspecified future imagined by Hollywood in 1956. Commander Adams was the inimitable Leslie Nielsen, who would later gain fame in a series of spoof action movies, such as *Airplane*.

Unlikely as it may seem, with its Technicolor sci-fi effects, tight-fitting jumpsuits and the clownish Robbie the Robot, the movie *Forbidden Planet* does bear an uncanny resemblance to the Iraq conflict. So, for that matter, does the whole 'war on terror'. For the invisible monster that is killing the Americans in *Forbidden Planet* is not an alien or a rogue scientist: it is a creature of the id, a monster generated inside the head of the last remaining scientist on Altair, Dr Edward Morbius. Dr Morbius has discovered that a long-lost civilization once inhabited Altair, and has left a powerful machine that transforms the user's subconscious fears into actual physical creatures: the doctor doesn't even realize that his own worries about his attractive, scantily clad young daughter being wooed and lured away by the dashing Commander Adams from his idyllic Garden of Eden have triggered the lethal attacks on the American servicemen. The horrific creature that wreaks such mayhem and bloodshed is a figment of the imagination, made flesh by an ancient, poorly understood device.

Our world is populated by these 'creatures of the id': they are the monsters, demons and angels that propel so much warfare, the genies and supernatural deities leaping from the pages of ancient texts to play on our darkest fears, shaping our identities and destinies.

As someone who does not believe in God, it was both shocking and fascinating to travel through war-torn countries and see the absolute chaos that these make-believe gods and monsters cause. Looking at people who will blow themselves up in the name of Allah, drive others off their land to fulfil a 3,000-year-old prophecy of Yahweh, or back one side or the other in the hopes of inducing a long-awaited Armageddon, I have spent hours wondering how people can not only believe such things, but kill and die for them.

There are now countless books arguing against the existence of god or gods: many of them are compelling and gripping, but will do little to dent the faith of people who will only ever read one book in their lives, and will devour that one unquestioningly. What really has come to obsess me is how we got to this point, a world in which ideas and imagined concepts are like a pathogen that leaps from mind to mind, mutating and evolving, seizing the imagination and setting their hosts so lethally against one another.

'The only true villain in my story: the oversized human brain,' says Leon Trotsky Trout, the ghostly narrator of Kurt Vonnegut's 1985 Armaggedon novel *Galapagos*. The book tells the story of a ragtag group of holidaymakers who are shipwrecked in the islands six hundred miles off the coast of Ecuador during a luxury cruise, while financial crisis and disease wipe out humanity in the rest of the world. The book's dour narrator happens to be a decapitated shipyard worker who haunts their vessel. From his strategic, disembodied viewpoint, he observes the end of humanity while lamenting that the human brain has become far too big for its own good, an evolutionary adaptation that is as impressive, but ultimately as impeding for its owners, as the huge antlers of the extinct Irish Elk. With its capacity to develop ideas – in effect, make stuff up, and then believe its own stories – the brain has become as much of a hindrance as a help to mankind. In a wry twist, the last survivors of humanity slowly evolve back into an animal state and survive in the form of highly intelligent seals.

A decade later, Vonnegut seemed to contradict himself in his last novel, *Timequake* – the problem was now perceived by the curmudgeonly narrator as humanity not using its brains enough, instead choosing to immerse itself in banal daytime television shows and the lives of fifteen-minute wannabe celebrities, refusing to use its awesome capabilities.

Perhaps both views, though contradictory, are true: the human brain has developed some spectacularly self-destructive proclivities over the millions of years in which it has evolved the ability to build space stations and cure a multitude of diseases. But with the technical virtuosity, we have developed a feverish imagination that tends to populate the world around us with powerful spirits that drive us to seemingly insane acts. This is more than just over-zealous religious fervour or naive incredulity: when gods were shunted aside by science in the modern age, people quickly replaced religion with a ferocious series of secular ideologies – nationalism, Nazism, Communism – that led to even worse destruction. Little wonder then that the tormented human mind numbs itself with afternoon chat shows and *Judge Judy*.

How did this happen?

There has been a flurry of research in neuroscience and biology in recent years to suggest that there is an intrinsic predisposition in the human brain to believe in god. Such studies suggest that religious belief may in fact be hardwired into the architecture of our brains. God may well be, ironically, a by-product of evolution.

One theory has been put forward by Lewis Wolpert, a British developmental biologist, in his book *Six Impossible Things Before Breakfast*. The title comes from Lewis Carroll's *Through the Looking Glass*, in which the White Queen urges Alice to believe in the unreal. 'When I was your age, I always did it for half-an-hour a day. Why, sometimes I've believed as many as six impossible things before breakfast,' the White Queen boasts. It is an apt title for Wolpert's study, which traces how early hominids, forced out of their ancestral lifestyle in the African forests by climate changes, started using basic tools such as sticks for breaking shells, sharp rocks for cutting animal hides and stalks of grass for extracting succulent termites from their nest. Chimps still use such implements.

Those prehistoric ancestors with a better understanding of the use of such tools prospered over the millennia, as they could get more food and provide for the survival of their offspring. The same ability to make, use and eventually mass-produce tools ultimately led to the manufacture of weapons with which to vanquish their enemies. This evolution therefore favoured those with an understanding of cause and effect: if I want to eat this, then this is the tool I must use and this is how best I make and employ it. As that understanding of causality developed, so did the tools themselves, allowing mankind to develop the technology that would help it dominate his surroundings and rise above the traditional constraints of its natural environment. Those parts of the brain – mainly the prefrontal cortex – associated with cause and effect steadily grew towards Vonnegut's bloated villain of *Galapagos*.

Because alongside this newfound skill in tool manufacture, another, less obvious development was taking place. Functions in the brain are not ring-fenced off from each other. The toolmakers' search for cause and effect naturally spilled over into other problem-solving areas of human life. Among those were the eternal questions of why we are here, why we die, what causes volcanoes and droughts and attacks in the dark by ferocious beasts. Our precocious ancestors started to seek a cause, an agency, to explain the world around them, and solve these problems as they had solved so many technical challenges. If we were here – an obvious *effect* – there must be some *cause*, some agency that put us here. And if we were put here, there must be a reason. Thus began man's search for meaning.

With this crude but brilliant basic set of tools, an unseen twin to our early science was born: an innate predisposition to believe in beings beyond our ken that could neatly explain life's untold mysteries.

The predisposition to innately understand cause and effect has been demonstrated in human babies, who in experiments will expect a ball that is rolled up a slope to naturally roll back down. Animals mostly lack this inborn understanding, the result, biologists argue, of millions of years of our frontal lobes applying our grey matter to solving complex problems.

Some biologists argue that religion has done as much good as harm throughout our history, bringing down our stress levels, providing a key sense of community in the face of an often hostile natural environment, and even at crucial moments ensuring our survival. Belief in the great beyond gives members of the same tribe the strength to sacrifice individual members for the good of the community, allowing the greater number to survive and reproduce.

Robin Dunbar, in his book *The Human Story*, points out the surprising fact that Neanderthals actually had larger brains than our Cro-Magnon predecessors, with whom they shared the great forests of Europe until around 40,000 years ago. While the Neanderthals' advantage in brain size may have made them better hunters, their expanded cranial capacity was not in the key frontal lobes of the brain, the genie's lamp whence our spirits appear to have been conjured. Instead, Neanderthals carried their extra capacity at the back of their heads, giving them enhanced eyesight. They were probably far more adept hunters, and may well have understood their environment better. But the creatures of the id had already arrived on the scene, probably in the guise of tree and animal spirits summoned up by Cro-Magnon shamans.

It is not hard to imagine those big-brained Neanderthal hunters, at ease in their natural surroundings, lurking in the dark woods of Europe and watching the Cro-Magnons' crude spiritual rituals. Perhaps as they observed the ecstatic figures shambling around a bright fire, they frowned in curiosity or smiled at the strange and colourful beliefs of their rather inept, often brutal neighbours. If they were capable of expressing coherent thought, perhaps they would have muttered to each other: 'Look at these schmucks, they won't last long.' Yet those individualistic Neanderthal hunters were eventually driven to extinction by their neighbours. Their last remains, dating from some 24,000 years ago, were found in the caves of Gibraltar, which appears to have been their final holdout against the encroaching spiritualists. Just a few hundred miles to the north, the Cro-Magnons themselves eventually found refuge in the mountainous Basque country of northern Spain. There they weathered the explosive advance of the agriculture that another branch of their own family tree had developed in northern Iraq.

The genie was long out of the bottle by that point.

A biologist friend of mine once suggested another theory of how the spirit world might have slowly drifted into our daily lives. As early humans' brains developed the capacity to retain ordered memories, they may well have been troubled by vivid dreams they had no way of explaining. Animals would either not have such dreams, or would forget them upon waking. What must those primitive forest dwellers have made of dreams in which they appeared to see dead relatives mysteriously rising before them, perhaps even communicating with them as they had done while alive? As any child knows, dreams can sometimes seem as real as our waking experiences. How could these people, with no rational explanation of the world, incorporate such experiences into the way they understood the world? Of course, with a brain already inclined to believe in supernatural agents, they may well have had reason to believe that the dead lived on. And if people survived the experience of physical death, there were clearly other planes of existence beyond that which they saw every day while out hunting deer and gathering berries. From the dreams of cavemen would eventually arise vast Gothic cathedrals and golden-domed mosques. The same evolutionary tool that gave us the ability to travel in space gave us the ability to dream up endless permutations of the same themes, across cultures and civilizations that never even saw one another.

There is a common argument that god must exist, since such disparate human communities spread around the planet all believe in supernatural spirits. Surely a more reasonable explanation is that we all experience the world through the same awesomely imaginative lens of our brains?

And of course, belief in god and space travel are far from incompatible. Those early pioneers of astronomy, such as Galileo and Kepler, were themselves deeply religious men who half expected to glimpse the divine visage looming in their telescope lens while scouring the night skies. That spirit persists in many parts of the world today: witness these extraordinary instructions by one Dr Zainol Abidin Abdul Rashid, of the National University of Malaysia, on how Muslims in space should orient themselves in order to pray towards Mecca's holy shrine, the Kaaba, that black box recorder of a religion's yearnings.

As trips to space become commonplace, human civilization will no longer be tied to the surface of the Earth. But Muslims, wherever they are – whether on Earth or in space – are bound by duty to perform the obligations of worship.

A Muslim who wants to travel must study the techniques of determining prayer times and the direction of the Qiblah (the direction of prayer, facing Mecca) ahead of travel in order to achieve complete worship. I will elaborate the method of determining prayer times and Qiblah direction in space, primarily on the International Space Station. The ISS is more than 200 miles from the Earth's surface and orbits the earth every ninety-two minutes, or roughly sixteen times a day. Do we have to worship eighty times a day (sixteen orbits a day multiplied by five prayer times)? This seems unlikely, since it is compulsory for a Muslim to pray five times a day according to an Earth day, as determined by Allah during the creation of Heaven and Earth – no matter where in space the Muslim is located. As for the Qiblah, for Muslims there is only one, the Kaaba, located in Mecca. A Qiblah that changes in reference to a specific system is not in order! It must be remembered that Allah's creation is ordered.

A user-friendly, portable Muslims in Space calculator could determine the direction of the Qiblah and prayer times on the ISS. Its essential feature would be the use of the Projected Earth and Qiblah Pole concepts. These are based on the interpretation of the holy house of angels in the sky above Mecca. The place is always rich with angels worshipping. As many as 70,000 angels circumambulate it every day. Thus, one virtual Qiblah Pole can be taken as a universal reference to determine the direction of the Qiblah. When the Earth is projected to the height of the ISS, every point on its surface will be pro-jected also, including the Qiblah point, which can be projected upward and downward along the Qiblah Pole. This allows the direction of the Qiblah to be determined in space and in the bowels of the Earth.

Of course, this could be used as evidence of how religious people waste their time arguing over how many angels can dance on the head of a pin, or protest about stem-cell research when people are dying of potentially curable diseases. But it is also a perfect example of the immense fertility of our imaginations, one of the real and all too often overlooked driving forces of our history.

And if Dr Abidin's 'Muslims in Space calculator' sounds strange, consider the fact that the Vatican maintains an observatory in the hills above Tucson, Arizona, where it monitors outer space for signs of sentient alien life, in the hopes of converting it to Catholicism. The Mount Graham observatory was originally set up in

1930 to quash accusations that the Church was anti-scientific: environmentalists, and the San Carlos Apaches whose ancestral home it was built on, have attacked the construction as a violation of a unique eco-system, one that supports varieties of wildlife found nowhere else on the planet. But Jesuit Father George Coyne, the former Vatican Observatory director and an extremely well-informed scientist, has said that if intelligent alien life were found, the Church 'would be obliged to address the question of whether extra-terrestrials might be brought within the fold and baptized'. It was in fact a double whammy of religious doctrine: sacrificing a fragile eco-system in this life for the sake of saving the imagined souls of aliens that may or may not exist, and who almost certainly wouldn't need soul-saving.

By 2005, after two years of seeing people being slaughtered en masse for strange, invisible spirits, I was becoming obsessed by these inspirational phantoms. I had studied international relations as a post-graduate in London, and I had never come across any mention of the role played by our own delusional fantasies in all the wars, revolutions and follies of mankind. Of course, studies have revealed the often malignant role of religion in the course of history, or the madness of devout kings and generals, but there seemed to be very little in the way of how our everyday illusions shape our destinies. As a reporter, I felt compelled to hunt down this elusive culprit.

By that time, I was travelling a lot: Lulu had moved to Mexico City, and I flew over every few months to see her. On one trans-Atlantic flight I came across a report of how our perceptions of the animate and inanimate can often blur in our minds, propelled by our overactive impulse to read purpose into otherwise random events.

Paul Bloom, a Yale psychology professor, believes that evolution has made us into natural creationists. He wrote in *The Atlantic Monthly* of an experiment in 1944 in which two social psychologists, Fritz Heider and Mary-Ann Simmel, made a film in which circles, squares and triangles 'moved in certain systematic ways, designed to tell a tale. When shown this movie, people instinctively describe the figures as if they were specific types of people (bullies, victims, heroes) with goals and desires, and repeat pretty much the same story that the psychologists intended to tell. Further research has found that bounded figures aren't even necessary – one can get much the same effect in movies where the "characters" are not single objects but moving groups, such as swarms of tiny squares.'

Bloom also cites numerous examples where people see faces, characters and intent where in reality there are none, but which are superimposed by our hyperactive frontal lobes: clouds look like angry old men, rabbits and elephants. The perfect example of the interaction between supernatural agents and grim reality was September 11, 2001: after god-obsessed terrorists flew two airliners into the Twin Towers, shocked onlookers claimed they could see the face of Satan himself in the columns of smoke billowing over Manhattan. In between these two illusions, thousands of people were burned to death, suffocated or flung themselves in desperation from the top of the World Trade Center.

On a far lighter note, a bun that bore an unflattering resemblance to the wizened Mother Teresa almost became a holy relic, known as the Nun Bun, while a ten-year-old grilled cheese sandwich that appeared to have the Virgin Mary's face on it (though how anybody knows what she actually looked like is another mystery) sold for no less than 28,000 dollars.

Occasionally, while I was reading about the evolution of human beliefs, the bizarre reality would spill out of the pages of my books into real life. Riding in a crowded bus headed out of Damascus, where I had been writing about how the Iraqi refugee population in Syria had surged well past a million people, I was reading Dunbar's *The Human Story*, and its tale of triumph by 'spiritual' Cro-Magnons over godless Neanderthals. A friendly young Syrian Kurdish student, keen to improve his English, asked if he might leaf through it as we trundled north to Aleppo. The text proved too demanding for his limited grasp of English, and he asked me what it was about.

'It basically says that around five million years ago, humans and chimpanzees were the same,' I said, condensing the text to its most basic thesis. He giggled, as though I'd said something childishly silly in polite, adult company.

'I don't believe it,' he sniggered.

'It's a scientific theory,' I said, trying to be diplomatic. 'Have you heard of Charles Darwin?'

He sucked his lower lip in contemplation for a few seconds. 'In Arabic, is that Howa?'

'*Howa?*' I asked, not recognizing the name.

'Yes, Howa, the wife of Adam,' he answered. 'You say . . . Eva?'

It was my turn to smile. 'No,' I told him, 'Charles Darwin was not the wife of Adam.'

He explained then, very earnestly and carefully in case I was unaware of the true version of events, how naughty Howa was seduced by the devil into eating fruit from the tree of knowledge in heaven and how she and Adam subsequently fell to earth.

'Right,' I nodded politely. 'I think I have heard that story.' I took the book back and tucked it into the pocket on the seatback in front of me.

We appear to be born, then, with an inbuilt propensity to believe in the supernatural: everything must have been created with a purpose, by some agency beyond our ken. Children exhibit this even more forcefully than adults, studies have shown – it is not something that is drilled into us by our elders, rather something we intrinsically feel, which makes it so much more difficult to pin down. Asked why rocks are pointy, children will say it is so that animals can scratch themselves when they are feeling itchy. Why does it rain? Because we need water to drink.

Throw in our propensity for wishful thinking – after all, few people actually want to die, not even suicide bombers – and you have a heady, volatile mix. Add a few billion dollars of oil wealth and you have something terrifyingly unstable, a high-octane, awe-inspiring gelignite brewed from god and greed.

I remember as a teenager asking my father whether he believed in god. He thought a while (much later, he admitted he was a complete atheist) and said, 'I'd like to think heaven exists, yes.' At the time, I poured self-righteous teenage scorn on his superficiality and reluctance to come to grips with life's most important issues. It was only years afterwards that I realized it was actually one of the most obvious things you can say about religion. We'd all like to think heaven exists and we'll go there: so much so, that even secular psychology has borrowed one of religion's most alluring aspects. A friend of mine who was traumatized by the horrors witnessed in Iraq sought therapy to deal with the post-traumatic stress; the shrink suggested this person try to deal with stress by imagining a 'safe place'. That place can be a beach, an island, a high-walled, sumptuous castle where everything is provided for you, somewhere beautiful and relaxing, where nothing bad can get to you. Is that not simply a version of heaven for atheists, here and now?

Flying regularly into Mexico, I came across the perfect example of an entirely pointless holy war, an example of people dying in droves for gods now entirely forgotten and consigned, along with so many other once powerful pantheons, to the museums. These conflicts were known to the Aztecs as 'Flower Wars'.

These sacred, fake battles were fought by the burgeoning Aztec empire after it had conquered its neighbours in the area of what is now Mexico City and reduced them to mere vassal states. Aztec culture was rigidly hierarchical and aggressive, rather like the Assyrians who created one of the world's first empires from their base in northern Iraq. As among the ancient Assyrians, combat was seen as an act of worship to appease blood-thirsty gods, in this case Huitzilopochtli, the deity of war. Wandering around the expansive halls of Mexico City's fabulous Museum of Anthropology one day, I came across the imposing stone statue of this terrifying god, a ten-feet-tall, square-set monster with human skulls dangling from his belt. He was, apparently, a hungry god.

The Flower Wars, known in the Aztecs' native tongue as *xochiyaoyotl*, were not fought to kill enemies or win territory. In fact, they were planned combats with already subservient – and often reluctant – neighbours. The aim was for valiant warriors to take as many prisoners as possible. The captives were taken back to the islands of Tenochtitlan, an area now drained of water that covers roughly the centre of Mexico City. There, they were well fed and treated with respect. They had to be, since they were now considered as messengers to the gods. Unfortunately for them, the message they were delivering was blood sacrifice. Thousands would be lined up and marched to the top of towering pyramids where their hearts were hacked from their living bodies with razor-sharp obsidian blades. The black, volcanic glass knives were not durable enough to cut through rib cages, so priests opened up the sacrifice's stomach and reached inside to cut out their hearts. There were eighteen festivities every year that demanded human sacrifice. Conquistadors –

several of whom were snatched in mid-combat during the prolonged fighting for Tenochtitlan, and immediately dragged off to be sacrificed even as their comrades were still battling on the causeways below – said that strips of human meat were offered as gifts to the gods, but also to important dignitaries (who wisely preferred to snack on turkey). Juan Diaz, one of the original conquistadors who wrote an account of his exploits under Cortés, also described the efforts the Aztecs had made to create a real vision of hell inside the city – beneath the pyramids were enclosures filled with snakes, scorpions, wild dogs and buzzards, in honour of the underworld deities. The carcasses of the sacrificed were dumped in these pestilential halls to be devoured by these creatures that represented the spirits of the underworld.

Why did they do this? Their priests said that human sacrifice was needed to restore the blood that the sun lost in his daily battle against the darkness at sunset, and that every fifty-two years there was the possibility the world would end. Unlike the millenarian societies of Judaism, Christianity and Islam, there was no promise of redemption or divine judgment at the end of days, just the prospect of destruction that had to be plugged with human gore.

In fact, it was just the sun going down every day.

Little wonder, then, that when Hernan Cortés and his conquistadors arrived in Mexico in 1521, they found plenty of local allies willing to fight against the Aztec overlords. Cortés also famously enjoyed the advantage of having his arrival mistaken by the Aztecs for the long-prophesied return of Quetzalcoatl, the Plumed Serpent, a messiah figure in Meso-American legend. Many of the locals apparently thought his cavalrymen were four-legged Centaurs, having never seen horses before.

By contrast, in April of 2000, almost five hundred years later, a group of Japanese tourists were less fortunate. When they stepped off a bus in the main square of Todos Santos, in Guatemala, the villagers, alert to ever-present rumours of child abductions in the region, mistook the Japanese visitors for Satanists seeking to steal their babies for ritual sacrifice and attacked them, beating to death one man and the unfortunate tour guide. So it goes with our shaky belief systems: rapacious conquerors are mistaken for benign gods, friendly tourists are mistaken for devil worshippers. You never can tell what strange paradigm you might be stepping into.

There is an opinion among some unbelievers that if God doesn't exist 'out there', he must exist in our heads somewhere. If we made him up, then he resides somewhere in the scarcely mapped, tangled undergrowth of our brains. In my paper chase looking for that place where the moody, dangerous deity resides – somewhere in the gnarly amygdala at the centre of the brain, rather than on a fluffy white cloud in the sky – I came across an extraordinary theory that goes way beyond that concept, itself already too revolutionary for the vast majority of mankind.

According to Bundle Theory, we do not even exist

ourselves, never mind the gods we may have invented along the way to keep us company, like the 'invisible friends' that children talk to. We are, in fact, a figment of our own imagination, created by our ever-inventive brains. We made ourselves up as a handy trick to allow us to cope with the immensely complex interactions involved in everyday human society. This disturbing notion stems from neuroscience's failure to locate anything in our heads that might be pinpointed as a centre of consciousness. Behind our eyes, those windows to the soul, there is only meat. There are 'bundles' of instinct, ingrained behaviour, learned responses to hugely complex social and cultural procedures that allow us to exist in massive groups of highly advanced and complicated animals. When all this is put together we form what we commonly refer to as an ego. If human society was a strange new environment that slowly emerged out of our advancing brain power, we needed a guide to steer us through it, the way on-line gamers in their invented computer worlds need an 'avatar', or character, to enter the virtual environment and interact with other gamers. As Paul Broks, the neuropsychologist and author of *Into the Silent Land* put it, if the human body and brain might be compared to a computer, then the culture that a being exists in might well be described as the software that shapes and informs it. The person, he concludes, is merely the writing on the screen of the computer.

An extraordinary exhibition came to Mexico City while I was there reading *Into the Silent Land*, during one of my breaks from Baghdad. It was Gunther von Hagens' Body Worlds, and featured real human bodies, of people who had died and donated their corpses to science. The bodies were stripped down to their component parts. There were entire flayed corpses showing the interlocking layers of skin, muscle and bone, some of them set up in bizarrely normal poses, such as sitting on a chair at a table and reading a book. Preserved brains protruded from the opened skulls of chess players. The exhibition aimed to show off what an extraordinary thing the human body is, in all its meaty complexity. But having just read a scientific study arguing that we do not exist – that we are not even the ghosts in the machine, but merely writing on the screen of a computer – I found it overwhelming. As I stumbled out of the hall and into the bright midday light of Mexico City, the whole world seemed to shimmer before my eyes. The people I passed no longer looked real, just meaty engines trailing the steam of consciousness, ready to evaporate if scrutinized too closely. I felt my own self dissolve for several moments, before the simple demands of navigating Mexico City's dangerous traffic and bustling sidewalks gradually squeezed my sense of self back into place, like a dislocated joint being eased back into its socket. I was later told by a friend who had dabbled in eastern philosophy that in Buddhism such experiences are known as 'satori': moments of enlightenment where the devotee can glimpse the true nature of creation. But it didn't feel like enlightenment to me. It felt like madness.

Broks points out that Bundle Theory is in fact

nothing new. For more than 2,600 years, Buddhists have been teaching that there is no such thing as the 'self'. 'The bundle of elements is void of self. In it there is no sentient being. Just as a set of wooden parts receives the name of carriage, so do we give to elements the name of fancied beings,' says one Buddhist text.

John Gray, in his book *Straw Dogs*, states that modern discoveries in cognitive science are intriguingly similar to many of the teachings of Taoism, that life is simply a dream we can never awake from. Consciousness is a delusion, designed to allow us to believe we make conscious choices. From this sense of choice, we can construct moralities that govern our behaviour and allow societies to function. But as Gray points out, our brains are processing around fourteen billion bits of information per second. The bandwidth of our conscious selves is around eighteen bits per second. Clearly our conscious selves are a minuscule sliver of what we really are.

Bundles of instincts strung together by the thread of memory and experience, we call ourselves 'people'. Lonely and afraid, these people invented gods to look over them.

The survivors appeared only lightly injured – arms in slings, plasters on faces, limping legs supported by crutches. But what struck me as odd was that these marines who had almost been killed a couple of days before, when a car bomber rammed their truck in Fallujah, were killing time playing a simulation war game. Most of them were little more than kids, so it was hardly surprising that here, in a no-frills field hospital with little else to do, they whiled away their time with a computer game. It was a common pastime for soldiers, and I sometimes wondered if they could always tell the difference, in their monotonous, occasionally terrifying lives, between the real world and the games they played so obsessively.

The game they were playing that day was called Ghost Recon. The artificial landscape they were shooting their way through looked just like the lands outside the perimeter, where eight of their comrades had been blown to pieces next to them a few days earlier. Flat, featureless and dusty, it might have been modelled directly on Anbar: lots of games were designed to resemble current conflicts, as though that was the only way kids back home, the same age as these young soldiers, could relate to this endless war. For the wounded marines, it was as if they were getting a second chance. With each failure in the game, a new life automatically afforded another chance to go back and shoot the lurking bad guys. I had no idea whether it was therapeutic or damaging to their traumatized psyches. At least they didn't seem bored or upset, just lost in the screen in front of them.

It struck me as I watched them shooting up insurgent avatars on virtual desert roads that this was in fact where so many American soldiers and Iraqi insurgents met: both have imaginary second lives. Die in a video game and you are immediately resurrected to fight another day: die in a jihad and you automatically move up to the next level, paradise with its crystal rivers and seventy-two virgins.

You never wake from the dream.

* * *

Here's a tale to toss into that age-old struggle for possession of our unsleeping imaginations.

Millions of year ago, a group of tooled-up, super-smart apes dreamed they were human beings. Armed with that knowledge of self, they invented pantheons of moody gods and sinister devils whom they sought to appease with vast temples and vows of submission. After millennia of wars driven by avarice and phantoms, of restless explorations and scientific discoveries, their planet, that shining little dot of life in a vast, cold universe, starts to fall apart because they have been so distracted by their search for what it means to be human that they fail to recognize their true nature. They begin to realize their entire history has been based on a false assumption and they are, after all this, just a bunch of great apes whose brains, having conquered nature, become easily bored and seek something more than what they already have.

What ancient scripture, full of miracles and divine interventions, could be more fantastical than that? What Samson and Delilah, what Job or Noah, could ever compete in our febrile imaginations with a plot so strange and tragicomic?

EPILOGUE

Canaanite Karma

Tsvi Misenai was an unlikely-looking Messiah. A heavy-set man in his sixties, with mottled skin and a wispy goatee, he laughed heartily at the idea, when I put it to him, that he could be about to fulfil a central Biblical prophecy. He said he simply wanted to turn the concept of the Middle East conflict on its head.

I met Tsvi because of a flip comment I made on a bus in Israel. It was summer of 2007, and I had been sucked back into the 3,000-year-old vortex of fighting between Israel and its neighbours. I was coming back from the Gaza Strip, which had just fallen to the Islamic Resistance Movement, or Hamas, after heavy fighting with its nominally secular rivals, Fatah. The man I was chatting to on the bus was a gingery, American Jewish professor called Chaim, with a thick, tangled beard. He asked me what I thought it would take to solve the crisis. It is a question you often get asked in Israel as a foreigner, and of course there is no answer. So I cracked a joke instead.

'Since everyone is claiming they were in this land first, and therefore it's theirs, I think they should do some genetic tests and find the original Canaanites. They were here before anyone else. Then they can give it back to them.'

Chaim smiled. But in this land that has seen so much blood spilled over phantoms, no wisecrack is so farfetched that it can ever be just a joke.

'A friend of mine has been doing some research on recent genetic findings on the past population of this place. You should speak to him,' he said. We exchanged emails, and Chaim got off the bus near the Latrun Monastery, just outside Jerusalem.

So it was that a few weeks later I arrived in the neat backstreets of Rehovot, a small town on the coastal plain, wrapped in bougainvillea and tucked away behind Tel Aviv. These little lowland towns all blend into each other – Or Yehuda, Petah Tikvah, Ramle – and it took me a while to find the place. When I pulled up outside the villa in the late morning, Tsvi came out to meet me. He was bursting with enthusiasm for his idea. His friend Elon Yarden, a lawyer with a taste for historical research, was also there to greet me.

'It's a revolutionary idea,' Tsvi promised, as he sat me down in his large living room.

And so it was. He and Elon spoke for almost two hours, charging through 2,000 years of history in an attempt to rewrite the present.

In the first century after Christ, Tsvi explained, the Jews rose up against the Romans who had occupied their land. After years of fighting, in AD 70, Titus and his troops took Jerusalem and destroyed the Jewish temple. The Romans expelled much of the Jewish population that had had the temerity to stand up to their might. Those that remained struggled on in intermittent revolts, culminating in the uprising led by Simon Bar Kokhba sixty years later. They too suffered bloody defeat, with hundreds of thousands killed. Many of the surviving Jews were sold into slavery, or forced to join those already in exile across the Roman Empire. They were banned from entering the newly renamed province, Syria Palestina, on pain of death.

This much I already knew. The Jews left the land. But not all of them, Tsvi explained. He and other Jewish historians – among them David Ben Gurion, the first prime minister of Israel, and his associate Yitzhak Ben Tsvi – argue that the Roman expulsion mainly targeted the elite, the priests and the city dwellers, while leaving the peasants on their lands to raise their livestock and work the fields. After all, this was highly productive farmland, and the extremely militarized Roman Empire needed its victuals, revolt or not.

So while the cities were emptied, the remote farmers in the hills stayed on their land. They slowly adapted to the new religions that rolled in with successive waves of invaders. Some became Christians, more converted to Islam, especially under the Fatimid dynasty in the twelfth century AD. There were many incentives to do so – avoiding persecution, promotion opportunities in government service, even tax breaks like those currently extended to Jewish settlers living in the West Bank. Slowly, their past was erased, until after a thousand years their original identity as Jews had been forgotten. But they were still there.

In fact, Tsvi argued they are there yet. Only now they call themselves Palestinians.

'The story of Israel is the story of these two countries, the highland and the lowland,' pronounced Elon, his voice rising as he warmed to his theme. He was a short, neat man who had been studying the subject for years.

'There are two histories. All the invasions throughout history happened in the lowlands. In the highlands history was static, more or less. And who stands here from ancient times? The Israelites! We stayed here, we never left. In the last thousand years, after the Crusaders left, the Mamelukes destroyed all the seashore cities. If these people didn't change, the conclusion is that the Palestinians of the mountains are the Israelites. They went through a transformation. We are asking for a retransformation!'

The Jews who stayed on the land lost their identity, he said. Those who left jealously kept their sense of identity alive, but lost their land.

What made their theory more powerful than previous versions presented by Ben Gurion, half a century earlier, was the development of genetics. A recent study by a team of haematologists from Hadassah hospital in Jerusalem backed up their suspicions. Led by Dr Ariella Oppenheim, they had been looking at a rare blood disease shared by Jews and Palestinians. Their findings indicated that the Y chromosomes of the Palestinian men in the study were closer to the Ashkenazis', or Jews who lived in the European Diaspora, than to those of other Arabs. Dr Oppenheim took this as evidence that the Palestinians are, in fact, the descendants of the Jews left behind after the destruction of the Temple.

Oddly, when I told a Palestinian friend in the Old City this theory, he just shrugged and said most people suspected it.

'Especially the Palestinians in Hebron, which has always been a holy city of the Jews,' he told me.

I put this to another Palestinian a week later. He was the head man of a small village in the West Bank that was surrounded on three sides by Jewish settlements, and on the fourth by the separation barrier that cut Israel off from the West Bank. At night, the Israeli army shut the checkpoints standing on every entrance to the village from ten thirty p.m. until six a.m. The man looked suddenly hopeful.

'How long will this take? Could we become Jews by next year?' he asked.

In fact, an Israeli Arab friend of mine said that Elon's 'retransformation' was already taking place. In the Galilee, where small Arab communities lived among a dominant Jewish population, many Arabs were forgetting their native language. They mixed Hebrew and Arabic freely, and sent their kids to Jewish schools to get a better education and give them a fighting chance in a segregated society. And this was only fifty years after the reconquest of the land.

Tsvi was bubbling with enthusiasm. I put it to him that many Jewish settlers believed in the Biblical prophecies of Isaiah and Ezekiel, that peace would come to the entire world when the children of Israel were returned to their land. With a single idea, he was about to fulfil that ancient prophecy. Did he feel like the Messiah? Like a prophet? Laughing, he said that the people had to know who they really were before it could come to pass. I also felt duty-bound to remind him that the Palestinians knew that they were, at the very least, brothers, but had recently been at each other's throats down in Gaza.

I asked Tsvi if he had seen the French movie double-bill of *Jean de Florette* and *Manon des Sources*. In the films, a hunchbacked city dweller played by Gerard Depardieu returns to the farm his mother had once lived on, to escape the rat race of city life, accompanied by his wife and daughter. The neighbour, a true-bred old farmer played by Yves Montand, sneers at his attempts to breed rabbits for food. He wants him to fail because he wants the land – and its valuable water resources – for himself, so he can cultivate flowers for the market. To ensure the hunchback's failure, he blocks up the wells with concrete before the city boy can find them. Desperate to avoid his rabbits dying of thirst and his dreams collapsing, Depardieu's heroically tragic figure buys some dynamite and tries to blast his way into the water system. But in his misery he has been drinking, and wine and TNT don't mix. A chunk of rock from the blast lands on his head and he dies. Only after his death, the old farmer Montand discovers a set of letters from the hunchback's mother written forty years before. It turns out that Montand had an affair with the mother in their youth, but he had been called away on army service before he knew she was pregnant. In her despair, the mother tried to have an abortion, but failed, making her child a hunchback. The wicked old farmer has just killed his own son. In his sorrow, he takes to his bed and dies.

Tsvi had not seen the film, though his people had lived it for the past century. I shook his hand goodbye and drove out of Rehovot, across the narrow coastal plain and back up the hills into Jerusalem.

INDEX

The God Delusion

Richard Dawkins

**A timely, impassioned and brilliantly argued polemic
on atheism.**

'A very important book, especially in these times . . . a
magnificent book, lucid and wise, truly magisterial'
IAN MCEWAN

'An entertaining, wildly informative, splendidly written
polemic . . . we are elegantly cajoled, cleverly harangued into
shedding ourselves of this superstitious nonsense that has
bedevilled us since our first visit to Sunday school'
ROD LIDDLE, SUNDAY TIMES

'A spirited and exhilarating read . . . Dawkins comes roaring
forth in the full vigour of his powerful arguments'
JOAN BAKEWELL, GUARDIAN

'Passionate, clever, funny, uplifting and above all, desperately
needed'
DAILY EXPRESS

'A wonderful book . . . joyous, elegant, fair, engaging, and often
very funny . . . informed throughout by an exhilarating breadth
of reference and clarity of thought'
MICHAEL FRAYN

'Everyone should read it. Atheists will love Mr Dawkins's
incisive logic and rapier wit'
ECONOMIST

'Richard Dawkins's The God Delusion should be read by
everyone from atheist to monk. If its merciless rationalism
doesn't enrage you at some point, you probably aren't alive'
JULIAN BARNES

'There is not a dull page in Richard Dawkins's The God Delusion,
a book that makes me want to cheer its clarity,
intelligence and truth-telling'
CLAIRE TOMALIN

9780552773317

The Lemon Tree

Sandy Tolan

'Moving and painstakingly researched'
MARINA LEWYCKA, author of *A Short History of Tractors in Ukranian*

IN THE SUMMER of 1967, Bashir – a young Palestinian man knocks on the door of his childhood home in the town of Ramla in Israel, a home from which his family was driven some twenty years earlier. The door is opened by a young Jewish woman, Dalia, whose family were settled in the house after fleeing persecution in Bulgaria at the end of the Second World War.

Thus begins an unlikely and difficult friendship, which bridges religious divides and lasts more than four decades. *The Lemon Tree* tells the story of this extraordinary friendship and offers a much needed human perspective on the Israeli-Palestinian conflict.

'Reads like a novel . . . an informed take for anyone interested in the human stories behind a conflict'
NEW STATESMAN

'A fascinating and highly absorbing account full of warmth, compassion and hope'
BELFAST TELEGRAPH

'Extraordinary . . . a highly readable and evocative history'
WASHINGTON POST

'Affecting . . . sensitively told. Humane and literate – and rather daring in suggesting that the future of the Middle East need not be violent'
KIRKUS REVIEWS

9780552155144